Transnational Environmental Crime

This book provides a comprehensive introduction to and overview of eco-global criminology. Eco-global criminology refers to a criminological approach that is informed by *ecological* considerations and by a critical analysis that is *global* in scale and perspective. Based upon eco-justice conceptions of harm, it focuses on transgressions against environments, non-human species and humans.

At the centre of eco-global criminology is analysis of transnational environmental crime. This includes crimes related to pollution (of air, water and land) and crimes against wildlife (including illegal trade in ivory as well as live animals). It also includes those harms that pose threats to the environment more generally (such as global warming). In addressing these issues, the book deals with topics such as the conceptualisation of environmental crime or harm, the researching of transnational environmental harm, climate change and social conflict, threats to biodiversity, toxic waste and the transference of harm, prosecution and sentencing of environmental crimes, and environmental victimisation and transnational activism.

This book argues that analysis of transnational environmental crime needs to incorporate different notions of harm, and that the overarching perspective of eco-global criminology provides the framework for this.

Transnational Environmental Crime will be an essential resource for students, academics, policy-makers, environmental managers, police, magistrates and others with a general interest in environmental issues.

Rob White is Professor of Criminology in the School of Sociology and Social Work at the University of Tasmania, Australia. He is also the editor of *Controversies in Environmental Sociology* (Cambridge University Press), as well as author of *Crimes Against Nature: Environmental Criminology and Ecological Justice* and editor of both *Environmental Crime: A Reader* and *Global Environmental Harm: Criminological Perspectives* (all Willan Publishing).

Transnational Environmental Crime
Toward an eco-global criminology

Rob White

Routledge
Taylor & Francis Group

LONDON AND NEW YORK

First published 2011
by Routledge
2 Park Square, Milton Park, Abingdon, Oxon, OX14 4RN

Simultaneously published in the USA and Canada
by Routledge
711 Third Avenue, New York, NY 10017

Routledge is an imprint of the Taylor & Francis Group, an informa business

British Library Cataloguing in Publication Data
A catalogue record for this book is available from the British Library

Library of Congress Cataloging-in-Publication Data
White, R. D. (Robert Douglas), 1956-
Transnational environmental crime: toward an eco-global criminology/Rob White.
p. cm.
Includes index.
ISBN 978-1-84392-803-4 (hardback) -- ISBN 978-1-84392-802-7 (pbk.) --
ISBN 978-1-84392-804-1 (ebk.) 1. Offenses against the environment.
2. Environmental justice. I. Title.
HV6401.W455 2011
364.1'8--dc22
2010049278

ISBN 978-1-84392-803-4 (hbk)
ISBN 978-1-84392-802-7 (pbk)
ISBN 978-1-84392-804-1 (ebk)

Typeset in Times New Roman
by GCS, Leighton Buzzard, Bedfordshire

MIX
Paper from
responsible sources
FSC
www.fsc.org
FSC® C004839

Printed and bound in Great Britain by
CPI Antony Rowe, Chippenham, Wiltshire

Contents

List of boxes, figures and tables   *vii*
Acknowledgements   *ix*

1   Transnational environmental crime   **1**
Introduction   1
What is transnational environmental crime?   3
Types of transnational environmental crime   7
Contextualising transnational environmental crime   10
Studying transnational environmental crime   15
Conclusion   18

2   Eco-global criminology   **19**
Introduction   19
Conceptualising environmental crime   20
What is the eco in eco-global criminology?   24
Researching the global in eco-global criminology   28
Conclusion   33

3   Climate change   **36**
Introduction   36
Climate change   37
What does climate change have to do with criminology?   38
Paradoxical harms   45
Conclusion   51

4   Biodiversity   **52**
Introduction   52
Biodiversity   53
Biodiversity and plants   56
Biodiversity and animals   63
Conclusion   69

5 Waste and pollution   **71**
Introduction   71
Waste and pollution   72
Waste removal and externalising harm   76
Waste production and climate change   79
Waste and the legal–illegal nexus   82
Conclusion   85

6 Perpetrators   **88**
Introduction   88
Systemic perspectives on responsibility   89
Studying perpetrators   95
State–corporate collusion   101
Conclusion   103

7 Environmental victims   **105**
Introduction   105
The other victims   106
Environmental victimology   108
The politics of knowing and knowledge   117
Conclusion   122

8 Criminal justice responses   **123**
Introduction   123
Environmental law enforcement   123
Penalties and remedies   128
Measuring the value of environmental harm   132
Conclusion   137

9 Transnational activism   **140**
Introduction   140
Internationalism as a practical tool of activism   142
A moral framework for transnational environmental activism   145
Environmental activism, crime and criminalisation   149
Conclusion   156

References   *158*
Index   *172*

Boxes, figures and tables

Boxes

6.1 A chronology of events associated with toxic dumping
    in the Ivory Coast   97
9.1 Letter to Gunns from Nippon Paper   146

Figures

1.1 Map of the world, by political divisions   11
8.1 Normalised graphs of responses by three British
    Columbia forest sector industries to environmental
    law enforcement programmes   129
8.2 World production of chlorofluorocarbons, 1950–97   130

Tables

1.1 Examples of transborder pollution incidents in Europe   13
2.1 Ecological and social dimensions of transnational
    environmental crime   28
2.2 The conceptual framework for environmental horizon
    scanning   34
3.1 Select transnational agreements relating to climate
    change   38
3.2 Climate change and social conflict   41
3.3 The changing pattern of world grain trade 1950–98   42
3.4 Transnational environmental crime and climate change   44
4.1 Selected international agreements protecting species   54
4.2 Animal categories   65
4.3 Survival status of species   66
4.4 Harm and species decline   68
4.5 Transnational environmental crime and biodiversity   70
5.1 Selected international agreements pertaining to waste
    and pollution   74

5.2	Transnational environmental crime and pollution/waste	86
6.1	The world's major water and waste corporations	94
6.2	Focus for market reduction approach to wildlife crime	96
7.1	Environmental victimisation	109
7.2	Erikson's classification of disasters	114
7.3	Key dimensions of environmental victim activism	118
7.4	Matrix of discourse diversity	119
8.1	Agencies at different tiers dealing with environmental law enforcement: Australia	126
8.2	Criteria to determine seriousness of environmental offences	133
9.1	Continuum of activist engagement	142
9.2	From environmental justice to ecological citizenship	147

Acknowledgements

First and foremost I wish to acknowledge the systematic and critical feedback on this manuscript provided by my colleague Diane Heckenberg. Without Di's strong sense of conceptual rigour and her insistence upon theoretical clarity this book would not have come together the way it has. I am especially grateful for Di's close reading and insightful comments on various drafts, and for keeping me on the right track.

Many others have contributed to the book in their own unique ways, including Hannah Graham and John Cianchi, Andrea Michaelson, Lynnette Devereaux and Denise Jones. Thanks are due to Jules Willan and the rest of the crew at Routledge for their assistance in the production phases of the project.

Finally, I wish to dedicate this book to Brian Willan. As a publisher Brian was instrumental in setting me on the pathway towards 'green criminology' in general and 'eco-global criminology' in particular. Brian's ongoing support for projects of this kind has been nothing short of inspirational, and I thank him for all he has done for me over the years.

1 Transnational environmental crime

Introduction

This book provides a comprehensive introduction to and overview of eco-global criminology. At the centre of eco-global criminology is analysis of transnational environmental crime. The book extends work that is ongoing in the area of environmental crimes and harms, much of which has been designed to promote discussion and debate within and beyond the field of criminology about key global environmental issues (White 2008a, 2010a). For this book, the underlying premise is that *transnational environmental harm is a crime*. Consistent with this view is the argument that any analysis of transnational environmental crime needs to incorporate different notions of harm, and that the overarching perspective of eco-global criminology provides a useful framework to do this.

One of the characteristics of the contemporary world is the interconnectedness of people, systems and networks, a concept that is captured in the notion of the 'butterfly effect'. What happens in one part of the world, no matter how small or seemingly trivial, will have an impact – and sometimes a very large impact – in another part of the world. Thus, so the story goes, the fluttering of butterfly wings in the southern hemisphere can translate into hurricane force winds in the northern. We are all interconnected, in complex ways, for better and for worse. The local is indeed global in this worldwide system of networks and flows.

This book reflects these concerns with interconnection and causal forces. The focus of the book is on transnational environmental crime and the many dimensions pertaining to this kind of social and ecological harm. My intention is to provide a theoretically informed, yet empirically based, account of transnational environmental crime. The primary purpose of the book is in fact to develop the conceptual universe within which such phenomena can best be understood, rather than provide substantive and extensive documentation of these crimes as such (for this, see White 2009a, 2010a). In order to do this, further development of eco-global criminology is essential.

Eco-global criminology provides a 'framework of analysis' that directs our attention to particular problems and particular ways of seeing and analysing the world around us. It is based upon three intertwined conceptual categories: the ecological, the transnational, and the criminal/harmful. Eco-global criminology is not a 'theory' as such, since it does not purport to offer an overarching causal explanation for transnational environmental crime. It does not seek to answer the question of why things happen or occur; rather, it is concerned with matters of how things are as they are. Answers to the 'why' question are instead devolved to lower levels of abstraction (i.e. concrete cases relating to prosecution of offenders) and are specific to the topic at hand (e.g. explanations for the low penalties assigned to environmental offenders). Nevertheless, the book as a whole is oriented towards the theoretical rather than the descriptive, towards exposition of concepts rather than reporting of empirical studies.

As a theoretical text, the book is intended to deal with a series of basic questions pertaining to transnational environmental crime. These initially pertain to definitions of transnational environmental crime (and its varied dimensions), and the development of a criminological framework whereby we can interpret such crimes (eco-global criminology). The centrality of ecological considerations is also given weight by the inclusion of chapters that specifically frame environmental crimes through an ecological lens. Chapters on climate change, biodiversity and pollution demonstrate the profound ways in which 'nature' is being transformed, used and abused across several different dimensions. These chapters also illustrate the urgency and immediacy of environmental issues in relation to the health and well-being of all living creatures and ecosystems on the planet.

The book then returns to more conventional criminological approaches to the study of crime. We want to know who the main perpetrators of the crimes are, and how and why they do what they do. We want to expose the different types of victimisation associated with environmental crime, including non-human animals and specific local environments. We want to examine how environmental criminals and vandals are being dealt with by the institutions of criminal justice and its relevant agencies such as environmental law enforcement officials and courts. The limits and contradictions of formal criminal justice responses are explored through the advent and impact of transnational activists into the environmental crime arena. In each of these chapters, key concepts will be identified as well as current trends and issues.

This book is one in a rapidly emerging list of green criminology texts. Its specific contribution lies in its attempt to consider the main issues pertaining to transnational environmental crime in explicitly theoretical terms. My interest is in asking and responding to two core questions of social analysis: What (or who) is x, and how do we study x? This entails both conceptualisation of what it is, and the development of methodological strategies to study it. As a theoretical text, what follows is both exploratory and never-ending. It is and must always be a work in progress. As we illuminate the past and the present, the future opens up new doors and new ways of looking at the world. Yet, as the chapter on climate change especially highlights, our future is fragile. Theory must be tied to action if it is to have meaning. This, too, is a major underlying theme of the present work.

This chapter begins the exploration by considering the main features of transnational environmental crime. This involves consideration of borders and geographical spaces, of specific transgressions labelled as environmental, and of harms that are deemed serious enough to be crimes.

What is transnational environmental crime?

To speak of *environmental crime* or *eco-crime* is to acknowledge some kind of specificity in the act or omission that makes it distinctly relevant to environmental considerations. Yet, as with crime generally, there is much dispute over what gets defined as environmentally harmful and what ends up with the legal status as 'crime' per se.

Transnational environmental crime, as defined in conventional legal terms, refers to:

- unauthorised acts or omissions that are *against the law* and therefore subject to criminal prosecution and criminal sanctions;
- crimes that involve some kind of *cross-border transference* and an international or *global dimension*; and
- crimes related to *pollution* (of air, water and land) and *crimes against wildlife* (including illegal trade in ivory as well as live animals).

These are the key focus of national and international laws relating to environmental matters, and are the main task areas of agencies such as Interpol.

In its more expansive definition, as used by green criminologists, for example, transnational environmental crime also extends to *harms*. It therefore includes:

- transgressions that are *harmful to humans, environments and non-human animals*, regardless of legality per se; and
- environmental-related harms that are facilitated by *the state*, as well as *corporations and other powerful actors*, insofar as these institutions have the capacity to shape official definitions of environmental crime in ways that allow or condone environmentally harmful practices.

The definition of transnational environmental crime is, therefore, contentious and ambiguous. Much depends upon who is defining the harm, and what criteria are used in assessing the nature of the activities so described (for example, legal versus ecological, criminal justice versus environmental justice) (see Situ and Emmons 2000; Beirne and South 2007; White 2008a). These issues are discussed in further depth in Chapter 2.

The post-Second World War period has seen major growth in the internationalisation of treaties, agreements, protocols and conventions in relation to environmental protection and with respect to the securing of environmental resources. Nation states have in recent years been more interested in taking governmental action on environmental matters, since much of this pertains to national economic interests. Moreover, the transboundary nature of environmental harm is evident in a variety of international protocols and conventions that deal with such matters as the illegal trade in ozone-depleting substances, the dumping and illegal transport of hazardous waste, illegal trade in chemicals such as persistent organic pollutants, and illegal dumping of oil and other wastes in oceans (Hayman and Brack 2002). A major concern today is the proliferation of 'e'-waste generated by the disposal of tens of thousands of computers and other equipment.

Some of the major international initiatives that formally specify certain activities as offences include (Forni 2010):

- Convention for Prevention of Maritime Pollution by Dumping Wastes and Other Matters;
- Convention on International Trade of Endangered Species of Wildlife Fauna and Flora (CITES);
- International Tropical Timber Agreement;
- Vienna Convention for the Protection of the Ozone Layer;
- Montreal Protocol on Substances that Deplete the Ozone Layer;
- Basel Convention on the Control of Transboundary Movements of Hazardous Wastes and their Disposal;
- United Nations Framework Convention on Climate Change;
- Kyoto Protocol.

Specific international agreements are also identified and spelled out in the subsequent substantive chapters on climate change, biodiversity and pollution/waste.

Examination of transnational environmental harm also needs to take into account geographical locations of varying environmentally harmful practices. This might include analysis of production (toxic materials), transit points (illegal trade – at sea, on land, in particular regions) and end points (waste dumping). A global mapping of harmful practices can serve to provide useful insights into how harm is transferred around the planet, and ultimately who or what is responsible for which kinds of harm. Simultaneously, the combined effects of human transformations of nature are having repercussions well beyond the local and regional. This is especially the case when it comes to global warming, as discussed in Chapter 3.

Environmental crime

A basic argument of this book is that environmental harm is a crime. The question then becomes what criteria can be used to substantiate specific claims that something is harmful, and whether it is harmful to the extent that warrants application of the label 'criminal'.

Typically the definition of 'crime' is usually bound up with the state. Crime is thus ordinarily defined as being an act committed or an omission of duty, injurious to the public welfare, for which punishment is prescribed by law, imposed in a judicial proceeding usually brought in the name of the state. This approach to defining crime sees the state as occupying the central place in defining what is criminal and what is not, and crime is always defined in relation to the law.

Crime is also defined in terms of seriousness of harm. That is, the criminal law identifies certain wrongful behaviour which society regards as deserving of punishment. People breaching the criminal law are labelled as criminals and are penalised by the state. Given these severe consequences, the criminal law is normally reserved for limited kinds of wrongdoing. The question then becomes one of deciding which types of activity constitute a 'real crime' and which warrant lesser kinds of response since they are perceived to be less serious in nature.

Even within this formal legal framework, major questions exist regarding how to define a crime and according to what criteria. The overall aim of criminal law is to prevent certain kinds of behaviour regarded as harmful or potentially harmful. But the purposes of criminal law vary, and involve a constant weighing up of concerns having to do with moral wrongness, individual autonomy, and community welfare (Findlay *et al.* 1994). What falls within the ambit of criminal law (and what does not) is a social process that is ongoing and inherently political, since it embodies basic principles and visions of the kind of society one prefers to live in.

In technical legal terms, transnational environmental crime has been defined as follows:

> ... transnational environmental crime involves the trading and smuggling of plants, animals, resources and pollutants in violation of prohibition or regulation regimes established by multilateral environmental agreements and/or in contravention of domestic law.
>
> (Forni 2010: 34)

This definition embodies huge complexities of scale, scope and content. For example, the legal framework governing environmental matters in international law is defined by over 270 Multilateral Environmental Agreements and related instruments (Forni 2010: 34). The laws and rules guiding action on environmental crime vary greatly at the local, regional and national levels, and there are overarching conventions and laws that likewise have different legal purchase depending upon how they are translated into action in each specific local jurisdiction. In part, differences in law-in-practice and conceptions of what is an environmental crime stem from the shifting nature of what is deemed harmful or not.

A primary task of criminal law is to stipulate the degree of seriousness of criminal conduct. This involves assessing such factors as the physical impact of the conduct on the victim, psychological trauma, the monetary value of property crimes and so on. Those who study crime from a social scientific perspective argue that 'harm' is what needs to be measured and assessed, but in doing so the study of crime has to go beyond existing legal definitions and criteria. This is so for several reasons.

First, wrongdoing is perpetrated by states themselves, yet it is the nation state that defines what is criminal, corrupt or unjust. There is a need for the development of criteria and definitions of crime that are not restricted to specific states' laws but that are more universal in nature (for example, appeal to 'human rights' or 'ecological justice'). Second, harms perpetrated by powerful groups and organisations, such as transnational corporations, are frequently dealt with by the state as civil rather than criminal matters. This reflects the capacity of the powerful to shape laws in ways that do not criminalise their activities, even when they are ecologically disastrous. Third, there are extralegal concepts and factors that need to be studied if we are to fully appreciate the nature of environmental harm, and this requires a different way of framing the issues. An ecology-based analysis of activity may well provide quite a different picture of 'harm' than an economic-based analysis. What is defined as criminal harm, and the measure of the seriousness of that harm, is contingent upon the social interests bound up with the definitional process.

What the history of crime and punishment shows is that the definitions, purposes and applications of the law change over time. The nature of what is 'a criminal act' and how the 'criminal' is socially and legally portrayed shifts according to particular socio-economic circumstances (White and Perrone 2010). What is deemed to be a serious social problem, and who is deemed to be the proper target for state intervention, thus is contingent upon the material conditions that shape the formation of identifiable groups (e.g. corporations, environmental activists) and the resources available to particular groups. 'Crime' is thus a product of society – at the level of definition, causal factors, types of offences, and the objects of state intervention. To appreciate and understand fully the nature of crime and criminal law, therefore, it is essential to examine the nature of one's society. The degree to which environmental crime is considered harmful has a major bearing on how and why perpetrators do what they do, and on how criminal justice institutions respond to such harms (see Chapter 8).

Transnational crime

The notion of 'transnational' is, like crime generally, also contentious from the point of view of definition and analytical focus. Mainstream concerns of criminal justice, as reflected in police agencies such as Interpol and the new international academic criminology, tend to view transnational crime in fairly conventional legal definitional terms (Madsen 2009; Van Dijk 2008). Specifically, the concern is with those activities that have been officially criminalised and thus that are against the law.

Typically, transnational crime includes such activities as:

- drugs trafficking;

- money laundering and the black or underground economy;
- terrorism;
- organised crime;
- corruption and business activity;
- Internet-based criminal activity;
- human trafficking.

Those writing within a critical criminology tradition tend to raise issues that challenge both the conventional notion of crime (preferring often to use terms such as 'harm' or 'human rights' or 'ecological citizenship' as the appropriate yardstick) and the scope of analysis (which tends to go beyond conventional criminal categories or the standard criminological literature per se).

For instance, Aas (2007) situates analysis within the context of globalisation, and sees matters pertaining to crime as inherently contestable. Harm is defined broadly and what is deemed to be 'criminal' is not bounded within the usual legal constraints. For instance, issues which are of concern include many of those identified in conventional criminology, but they also include:

- exploitation of workers and barriers to global movements of people;
- global cities as sites for social exclusion and widespread social inequality;
- migration and the emphasis on cultural essentialism as manifest in things such as nationalism, xenophobia, racism and fundamentalism;
- the transformation from the more inclusive welfare-oriented state to the contemporary security state, featuring high levels of incarceration;
- the need for a global frame that might benefit the rights of globally marginalised populations.

Questions of how best to define environmental crime per se are discussed in further detail in Chapter 2. For now, it is sufficient to note that basic definitions are disputed and flexible depending upon the perspective of the writer.

Types of transnational environmental crime

Differing conceptions of harm give rise to different understandings and interpretations of the nature and dynamics of transnational environmental crime. One result of this is that contemporary discussions of transnational environmental crime engage with a wide range of issues (White 2008a; Elliot 2007; Hayman and Brack 2002). Among the many topics under scrutiny are phenomena such as:

- illegal transport and dumping of toxic waste;
- transportation of hazardous materials such as ozone-depleting substances;
- the illegal traffic in real or purported radioactive or nuclear substances;
- proliferation of 'e'-waste generated by the disposal of tens of thousands of computers and other equipment;

- the safe disposal of old ships and aeroplanes;
- local and transborder pollution, that is either systematic (via location of factories) or related to accidents (e.g. chemical plant spills);
- biopiracy in which Western companies are usurping ownership and control over plants developed using 'traditional' methods and often involving indigenous peoples in the third world;
- illegal trade in flora and fauna;
- illegal fishing and logging.

Rather than simply listing the myriad examples of transnational environmental crime it is useful to think about how we might group different kinds of crime. This can be done in several different ways. This section considers transnational environmental crime from the point of view of different thematic groupings.

Theme 1: general crimes related to transformations of nature

From a global political economy perspective, transnational environmental crime can be viewed from the perspective of four intertwined social processes that are affecting the nature of world ecology (White 2010b; United Nations Environment Programme (UNEP) 2007; Mgbeoji 2006). These relate to varied forms of extraction and exploitation of nature, generally for purposes of private profit. They include:

Resource depletion – extraction of non-renewable minerals and energy without development of proper alternatives, overharvesting of renewable resources such as fish and forest timbers.

Disposal problems – waste generated in production, distribution and consumption processes, pollution associated with transformations of nature, burning of fossil fuels and using up of consumables.

Corporate colonisation of nature – genetic changes in food crops, use of plantation forestry that diminishes biodiversity, preference for large-scale, technology-dependent and high-yield agricultural and aquaculture methods that degrade land and oceans and affect species' development and well-being, biopiracy of Indigenous knowledge, lands and techniques.

Species decline – destruction of habitats, privileging of certain species of grains and vegetables over others for market purposes, superexploitation of specific plants and animals, due to presumed consumer taste and mass markets.

Some of these issues will be examined in greater depth in Chapter 4 in a discussion of the threats to biodiversity in relation to specific types of environmental crime.

Theme 2: specific crimes related to disposal of waste

More specific study drills down to particular kinds of problems and the peculiarities of these. For example, the waste management area presents numerous opportunities for crime (Van Daele *et al.* 2007). This is acknowledged in relation to the illegitimate international trade and transportation of hazardous wastes, the role of organised criminal syndicates in waste management, and the illegal dumping of waste by legitimate corporations (Dorn *et al.* 2007; Pellow 2007).

What is meant by the term 'hazardous waste' is itself subject to much ambiguity and debate. It is notable in this regard that in November 2008 the European Union enacted a new Waste Framework Directive, with several articles and an appendix dealing specifically with hazardous waste, and the properties of waste that render it hazardous (European Union 2008). The definition of hazardous waste, and the link of disposal of hazardous waste to specifically criminal activity, warrants close scrutiny. Certainly from a criminological perspective, in many countries there is little knowledge of the scale of the problem, the types of criminality involved, or the precise nature of the disposal (e.g. illegal dumping, combining illegal with legal waste, illegal export). These issues will be explored further in Chapter 5 when the nature and dynamics of waste production and disposal is investigated.

Theme 3: global crimes related to worldwide processes

One consequence of global trends related to climate change is an expected upsurge in social conflict (White 2009b; Smith and Vivekananda 2007). The conflicts include those pertaining to diminished environmental resources, to the impacts of global warming, to differential access and use of nature, and to friction stemming from the cross-border transference of harm. To take one example, Inuit populations in the eastern Canadian Arctic and Greenland have among the highest exposures to persistent organic pollutants and mercury from traditional diets of populations anywhere in the world. They have had no choice in the matter, since the problem actually originates outside of their territory.

> Scientific assessments have detected persistent organic pollutants (POPs) and heavy metals in all components of the Arctic ecosystem, including in people. The majority of these substances are present in the ecosystems and diets of Arctic peoples as a result of choices (such as using the insecticide toxaphene on cotton fields) by industrial societies elsewhere. Contaminants reach the Arctic from all over the world through wind, air and water currents …, entering the food chain.
>
> (UNEP 2007: 20)

Specific practices that are deemed to be good and productive for the global political economy have dire consequences for environments, humans and non-human animals throughout the world. These issues will be considered once again in Chapter 3 as part of the discussion on climate change.

Theme 4: specific crimes related to particular geographical regions

While there are broad similarities in the types of environmental crimes that traverse borders – such as pollution, the international transfer of hazardous wastes, and the illegal trade in wildlife – it is still necessary to examine such crimes in the context of their immediate geographical and criminal specificity. The export of 'e'-waste to South East Asia and to Africa, for example, has the same general drivers as, but quite different specific dynamics from, the export of hazards, especially related to agriculture and mining, to Latin America (Elliot 2007; Cifuentes and Frumkin 2007). Illegal fishing varies greatly depending upon location, and particular types of illegal fishing, such as abalone (Australia), lobster (Canada) and toothfish (Southern Ocean), show great variation in motives, techniques, local cultures and scale of operation (Tailby and Gant 2002; McMullan and Perrier 2002; Lugten 2005). Elephant poaching in Africa is very different from bioprospecting in South America, while the taking of 'bush meat' is a distinctive African phenomenon very different in character from illegal fishing by Indonesian fishers off the coast of Australia (Lemieux and Clarke 2009; UNEP 2007; White 2008a).

The point is that different regions of the world share overlapping problems – such as those related to climate change and those involving international transfers of harmful products. But at the same time it is vital that criminologists be aware of distinct local and regional variations in the kinds of harms that are evident, and in the specific forces at play in each region. This is discussed in greater depth below. Indeed, the question of scale of analysis, one that ranges from the local through to the global, is at the heart of contemporary efforts to study transnational environmental crime.

Contextualising transnational environmental crime

To appreciate fully the nature of global environmental crime it is useful to consider the physical location of harm within particular geographical contexts (see Figure 1.1). On a world map, it is possible to plot out a myriad different types of harms, some of which are common across the surface, others of which are specific to particular locales, regions and countries. Layer after layer of harm, present and potential, can be determined by, on the one hand, investigating ecological trends that involve degradation and destruction of environments (such as clear-felling of forests) and, on the other, by considering existing documentation of specific types of environmental crime (such as illegal international trade in flora and fauna). The harms so described are interconnected and intertwined in various ways: the 'butterfly effect' is real in more ways than one. As has been pointed

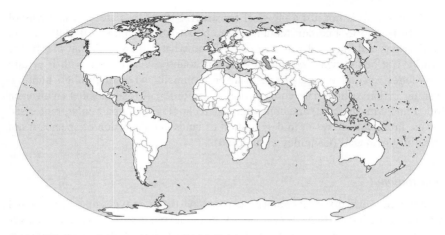

Figure 1.1 Map of the world, by political divisions

Source: Johomaps.com http://johomaps.com/world/worldblank_bw.html

out, what happens at the local level has consequences for those on the other side of the planet. What happens in any one place is thus intrinsically important to what happens worldwide.

The local

The local basically refers to where we live, work and often play. It is what we are most familiar with, and yet at times least knowledgeable or questioning about. In Tasmania, for example, some communities have to boil their water before drinking it. The problem is local, and many of the locals do not think twice about doing something they have grown up doing. There is no 'environmental issue' as such, in that people have not framed the activity (yet) in this manner. Off the coast of Nova Scotia, many local people partake in the catching of lobsters for personal use. Lobster poaching – that is, the illegal taking of lobster – is ingrained in long-standing popular culture, and for many there is no problem as such (McMullan and Perrier 2002). In both cases the activity and the response stems from how local people over time create their own spaces, their own routines and their own sense of what is right and wrong, of the normal and the unusual. The cause and the consequence of each activity, however, may be far-reaching, both in terms of future viability (of humans, of lobster) and in ultimately leading to a widening of the search for clean, fresh water and more abundant crustaceans.

The idea of 'local' can have particularly important connotations for Indigenous people who reside in particular geographical areas. Ontological being can be intertwined with specific locations. In Australia, for example, the idea of 'country' has specific territorial and special meaning for many Indigenous people (Connell 2007). It is, literally, a different way of looking at the world and being in the world. It is not just a physical construct, but encapsulates a whole way of life. To belong to a certain 'country' is to be an intrinsic part of it, with certain obligations and knowledge that are specific to what it is to be in that part of the world. But being identified in and through 'country' also carries with it certain privileges relating to use of the local environment, whether through hunting, fishing or harvesting. The combination of 'traditional' relationships (with each other and with the land) and contemporary technologies (in particular, motorised boats, firearms) can result in degradation of lands and depletion of species if not carefully managed (Caughley *et al.* 1996).

The national

Around the world different countries tend to have different types of environmental problems and issues. In New Zealand, for example, big questions have arisen over the use of pesticides and overuse of land for agriculture and pastoral purposes. Land and water are being contaminated through existing systems of production. By contrast, pressing issues of concern in Canada relate to the ecological impact of the huge oil tar sands projects in Alberta, and to the impact of insect blights on the pine trees of British Columbia. In Palestine, Israel, Syria and Jordan, issues of water, for drinking and for agriculture, are at the top of the environmental agenda. Water is vital to life; perceived national interests dictate that its scarcity is in part generated by efforts to control it for some population groups over and above use by others. National context is important in both the objective nature of the problems at hand (e.g. pollution, deforestation, lack of adequate water) and in regards to subjective processes relating to the politicisation of issues (e.g. the role of social movements in shaping public consciousness and state action on specific issues).

The national context is vital for investigation and analysis of environmental crime because the nation state, as such, is still the key political unit when it comes to environmental protection and law enforcement. The nation state thus remains an essential platform for concerted action to deal with the causes of environmental harm, as well as mitigating the worst outcomes of such harm. It is also a major facilitator of harm in its own right, either on its own or in conjunction with specific sectional interests (such as particular transnational corporations). Moreover, the collapse of the nation state, through civil war and unrest, has major repercussions for specific types of environmental crimes such as the illegal poaching of bush meat and of elephant tusks in the Republic of the Congo or illegal dumping of toxic pollutants in Somalia.

The regional

Most countries of the world have borders with another country. Rivers flow, mountains soar, air currents weave their way through the atmosphere, and plants and animals cross artificial boundaries that, for them, do not exist. There are issues that are specific to particular regions of the world. Huge tropical forests are found in the Amazon, an area that encompasses several different countries such as Brazil and Peru. Such forests also cover parts of South East Asia, spanning Indonesia, Malaysia, Thailand and Burma, among other countries. Africa is home to elephants, reptiles, giraffe and other creatures that are unique to particular parts of that continent, and not the preserve of any one country. Desertification and drought are phenomena associated with the dry lands of Northern Africa and the island continent of Australia. Meanwhile, cross-border pollution in Europe, and between China and Russia, are matters that demand a regional rather than simply national response. Acid rain traverses provincial and state demarcations and can affect environments, animals and humans many kilometres away. A nuclear accident in the Ukraine makes its presence felt in Britain, as well as the immediate vicinity of Chernobyl.

Even within regions, however, the types of environmental crimes will vary according to which countries border on which, and the opportunities for the commission of crime in each place. Table 1.1 provides an example of different kinds of crimes pertaining to different countries within the European context.

The opportunities for certain types of crime are influenced by very specific local and regional factors. For example, the penetration and dominance of the Mafia in the waste disposal industry in Italy provides a unique but devastating illustration of national difference (compared with countries where organised crime is not involved in this industry) that has an international impact (through dumping of toxic waste in international waters).

The global

Changing weather conditions appear to be the harbinger of much greater changes to come. Climate change is something that affects us all, regardless of where we live, regardless of skin colour, income, ethnicity, religion and gender. How it does so is mediated by the power of some to ameliorate the worst effects of global warming, for themselves, often at the expense of others. Rising seas and diminished glaciers, turbulent winds and extreme heat, fundamental alterations in local weather – all of these will have major implications for the well-being of humans, animals and local ecologies. Climate change has direct implications

Table 1.1 Examples of transborder pollution incidents in Europe

Country	Description of transborder pollution incident
Austria	Water pollution case with Slovenia
Belgium	Illegal transport of waste
Denmark	Illegal transborder shipment of waste and oil spills
Finland	River pollution from Finland to Russia
Germany	Waste disposal, water pollution, import of nuclear materials
Italy	Sinking of 80 ships with radioactive waste
The Netherlands	Import of household waste with export to third world countries

Source: drawing from Faure and Heine 2000.

for biodiversity; responses to climate change likewise have implications for disposal of waste. The scale and scope of global warming are of international proportions.

There are also other environmental issues that are intrinsically global in scope. Our oceans are filled with rubbish, and huge gyres spin round and round collecting plastic from all over the planet, and killing marine life in the process. Satellites proliferate in the upper reaches of the atmosphere and a new junk yard is fast being created above our heads. Subterranean spaces are repositories for radioactive waste, and potentially for carbon emissions (as if these spaces are not alive too). Genetically modified organisms are distributed worldwide, with major potential to further diminish biodiversity through concentration of production into smaller numbers of species and products. Environmental harm comes in many different forms, and is sold to us in many different guises including that of economic development.

The transnational

The production of global environmental harm is partly determined through complex processes of transference (Heckenberg 2010). Harm can move from one place to another. Harm can be externalised from producers and consumers in ways that make it disappear from their sight and oversight. The global trade in toxic waste (often under the cover of recycling), the illegal dumping of radioactive waste, carbon emission trading and the shifting of dirty industries to developing countries constitute some of the worst aspects of the 'not in my backyard' syndrome. The result is a massive movement of environmentally harmful products, processes and wastes to the most vulnerable places and most exploited peoples of the world.

Tracking the movement of harm is as important as establishing its more fixed manifestations at the local, national and regional levels. In this vein, environmental degradation is not only about what is being done to local environments because of 'brown' issues such as pollution, it is also about the transfer of flora and fauna across borders and into new ecological habitats. Similarly, the Southern Ocean becomes the slaughterhouse that satisfies the palate of the Japanese for whale meat. If the harm cannot be done in the national waters of particular nation states due to legal prohibitions, then transnational space is where the whaling will occur.

The transnational also provides the context for the emergence of specific types of criminal activity. For instance, the decline of fisheries off the coast of Somalia, due to overfishing by many different nations and groups of fishers, has robbed the local people of their main traditional livelihood. One consequence of this has been the move into another line of work – the most notorious being piracy on the high seas. Environmental harm, whether legal or not, can generate its own spin-off crimes.

Studying transnational environmental crime

Within criminology in recent years there has been renewed interest in the idea of global or international criminology (see Pickering and McCulloch 2007; Larsen and Smandych 2008). For students of transnational environmental crime, there are several different ways in which to approach the issues, which will be explored shortly (see also Chapters 2 and 3).

There are certainly interesting complexities in undertaking the study of international or transnational crime. Consider, for example, Madsen's (2009: 8–9) discussion of transnational organised crime. These three distinct areas of concern – transnational crime, international law, and organised crime – overlap in varying ways. There are crimes that are *transnational* and a *violation of international law*, yet not part of organised crime. An example of this is parental dispute over custody of a child, when one parent takes a child from one country to another without consent of the other parent. There are crimes that are *organised* and a violation of international law but which do not cross borders. An example of this is slave trading within a country, which involves organised syndicates. There are crimes that are organised and transnational, but not violations of international law. An example of this is the smuggling of genuine but non-taxed tobacco product from one country to another. Then there are crimes that are transnational, organised, and a violation of international law. An example of this would be international drug trafficking.

The notion of transnational crime evokes at least two different conceptual concerns. First, the crime must involve the movement of people, objects or decisions *across borders*. Second, the harm must be *recognised internationally* as a crime. There are limitations with each of these considerations. For example, genocide is universally acknowledged as an evil (even if there are disputes in practice as to whether or not genocide is in fact occurring; witness the debates over Sudan and how to interpret the tremendous loss of life in its southern regions due to systematic military interventions by various parties), but it may occur within a particular country's borders. Furthermore, transnational harms may happen (such as disposal and congregation of plastic waste in the ocean, or the migration of toxic substances from producer countries to formerly pristine wilderness areas, thereby affecting humans and animals in the latter even though they have no connection whatsoever with the former), but these may not be considered 'crimes' in international law. In other words, the study of transnational harm or crime always involves contested definitions (restrictive or expansive, depending upon the place of formal legality in the definition) and complexities related to scale (since it may manifest in specific local or regional contexts, as well as across regions).

The study of transnational crime involves different approaches that have various names. These include *comparative* criminology (the nature of the crime problem in countries around the world); *transnational* criminology (cross-border forms of crime such as drug trafficking, arms trafficking, human trafficking and money laundering); *international* criminology (crime that is specifically recognised widely across nations as crimes against humanity, such as genocide); *global* criminology (how globalisation and its consequences cause harm, such as structural adjustment policies of the World Bank); and *supranational* criminology (an encompassing study of international crimes, that includes terrorism, war crimes, state crime and violations of human rights) (see Friedrichs 2007). As will be seen below, these categorisations are also indicative of at least some of the concerns of those who study transnational environmental crime.

Bearing in mind the varieties of criminology described above, a distinction can be made between a *global perspective on crime* and the notion of a *transnational crime*. To illustrate this difference we can consider recent work that examines youth gangs. Hagedorn (2007), for instance, argues that a global analysis of gangs can demonstrate certain common features among groups regardless of locality, and indeed the sharing of ideas and images across borders becomes part of this process But the local gang is not the same as a transnational gang, which operates in more than one country and whose activities transcend borders (see White 2011).

What recent global study has demonstrated is that methodologically it is essential to have both a sense of history and a sense of place in the study of the phenomenon at hand. Specific historical and material conditions shape how particular activities come to predominate in particular places around the world. It is through global, comparative and historical analyses that the differences not only in environmental crime, but also in the study of, and state and civil society responses to, environmental harm are best understood.

As demonstrated in this chapter, consideration of scale and focus are implicit in the framing of research into transnational environmental crime. There are at least three different ways in which transnational research can be approached (White 2009a).

- *Global* – refers to transnational crimes, processes and agencies (universal effects, processes, agencies across the globe);
- *Comparative* – refers to differences between nation states, including 'failed states' (particular differences between nation states and regions);
- *Historical* – refers to epochal differences in modes of production and global trends (systemic differences over time, within and between different types of social formation).

The first approach focuses on globalisation as a far-reaching process in which crime can be traced in its movements across the world and its presence documented in many different locales (Smandych and Larsen 2008). For example, the idea of globalisation incorporates consideration of transnational harms, processes and agencies that span the globe. It implies that there are universal effects (such as climate change) that require united responses worldwide.

The second approach has a comparative focus, with a concern to study particular countries and regions, including failed states, in relation to each other

(Gros 2008). The nature of similarities and differences is fundamental to this kind of study. Thus, the differences between nation states and regions must be acknowledged and explained in their own right. For example, some countries and regions are more liable to be polluted than others.

The third approach is based upon historical appreciation of social change and social differences (Wright Mills 1959; Cornforth 1976). It views trends and issues in terms of major epochs, such as the transitions from feudalism to capitalism, or the shift from competitive capitalism to global monopoly capitalism. There are differences in modes of production and global trends (e.g. peasant-based feudal agriculture versus capitalist agribusiness), and it is important to track systemic changes over time, within and between different types of social formation.

The researching of transnational environmental crime provides a useful illustration of how these approaches might be utilised and combined. After all, environmental harm crosses borders to incorporate all nation states on planet Earth (as evident in ozone depletion and global warming). Comparative analysis shows us where some of the 'weak links' are (especially failed states, states at war, civil unrest) and thus hot spots for particularly worrisome environmental problems (such as dumping of toxic waste). Historical studies can alert us to the ways in which 'growth states' churn up natural resources, but also how ecological consciousness can grow out of affluence and a growing middle class. And a global awareness of environmental harm may direct our concern to not only particular nation states and regional issues, but also non-state environments, such as the open seas of our oceans, that require our attention as well.

We also need to be aware of the problems generated by the so-called growth states, such as China and India, where pollution and environmental issues have gone hand-in-hand with accelerated industrial development. Even in these nation states, however, environmental reform is increasingly on the political agenda. This is due to several reasons. In some cases, specific environmental problems are now simply too dire to ignore (e.g. tree felling and land use, lack of clean drinking water). In other instances, if the problem crosses international borders (e.g. air pollution as a result of fires), and can no longer be ignored by authorities in neighbouring countries, then action may be foisted upon the originating country. In another example, where there is growth in an affluent middle class due to economic growth and development, there is also, usually and eventually, a call to limit environmental destruction. Ecological consciousness is often a sign of affluence rather than necessity.

The study of transnational environmental crime has to incorporate investigation of the different types of crime that occur under this umbrella label and the different scales or levels at which crimes may occur. With respect to the latter, it is important not to focus solely on one level. Problems such as climate change, for example, are not just a global problem but a multilevel problem that has harmful (and criminal) impacts across the local, regional, national, international and transnational spheres (Bulkeley and Newell 2010).

Conclusion

A concern with environmental crime inevitably leads the analytical gaze to acknowledge the fusion of the local and the global, and to ponder the ways in which such harms transcend the normal boundaries of jurisdiction, geography and social divide. This observation is important because so much environmental harm is intrinsically transnational in nature. Contemporary discussions of environmental crime, for example, deal with issues such as the illegal transport and dumping of toxic waste, the illegal traffic in radioactive or nuclear substances, the proliferation of 'e'-waste generated by the disposal of tens of thousands of computers and other equipment, transborder pollution that is either systematic (via location of factories) or related to accidents (e.g. chemical plant spills), the illegal trade in flora and fauna, and illegal fishing and logging. This list goes on, but the point is that environmental harm, whether conceptualised in conventional legal terms or based upon more encompassing ecologically based conceptions of harm, is by nature mobile and easily subject to transference.

Moreover, the systemic causal chains that underpin much environmental harm are located at the level of the global political economy – within which the transnational corporation stands as the central social force – and this, too, is reflected in the pressing together of the local–global at a practical level. International systems of production, distribution and consumption generate, reinforce and reward diverse environmental harms and those who perpetrate them (White 2002, 2008a). These range from unsafe toys to reliance upon genetically modified grains, the destruction of out-of-date ships and planes through to the transportation and dumping of hazardous wastes. A basic premise of green or environmental criminology is that we need to take environmental harm seriously, and that in order to do this we need conceptualisations of harm that go beyond conventional understandings of crime (Beirne and South 2007). However, the doing of green criminology also requires a sense of scale, and of the essential interconnectedness of issues, events, people and places.

This chapter has provided an introduction to transnational environmental crime by exploring its varied dimensions. Of crucial importance is the bringing together of certain key concepts – the notion of movement or transference across borders, the idea that the harm is related specifically to environmental concerns (including, for example, those of wildlife as well as pollution) and the recognition that such crimes occur within specific geographical and social contexts. As indicated throughout this chapter, there are nevertheless ambiguities and controversies associated with defining transnational environmental crime. These primarily stem from diverse views of what criteria ought to be drawn upon in determining what is deemed to be a criminal or non-criminal activity. This is the subject matter of Chapter 2.

2 Eco-global criminology

Introduction

The specific interest of this chapter is to introduce and map out an analytical framework that combines an orientation towards ecology and justice (eco-justice) with global studies. This is what I call eco-global criminology.

The study of transnational environmental crime can be approached from several different angles. For example, it is a focus of international law and international relations. It is of interest to development and peace studies. There are burgeoning literatures in each of these areas on topics relevant to investigations of environmental crime. For the purposes of this book, however, the key concern is with criminological analysis and interpretation – of a very specific kind.

Eco-global criminology finds its political and conceptual home within the broad area of green criminology, an evolving field that is primarily concerned with the study of environmental harm, environmental laws and environmental regulation by criminologists (White 2008a; Beirne and South 2007). What we have learned from green criminology is that dealing with specific environmental issues demands that we think critically about the social and natural world and, indeed, reconceptualise the relationship between humans and nature in ways that accord greater weight to the non-human when it comes to assessing issues such as environmental harm. And, of course, many of the key features pertaining to environmental harm are inherently international in scope and substance.

The chapter begins by once again considering the distinction between 'crime' and 'harm'. This is a perennial issue within criminology and continues to be of nagging concern when it comes to understanding and analysis of transnational environmental crime. The first section of the chapter raises yet again the issue that much of what is harmful is in fact legally allowed to occur. Questions of power and social interests can never be too far from such an observation. The chapter then considers three broad conceptualisations of harm that have been employed in the study of environmental issues: conventional criminological, ecological, and green criminological. For study of transnational environmental crime, it is argued that all three approaches make a contribution, but it is most essential that an ecological perspective come to the fore. The chapter then provides a discussion of how to engage in the doing of such an eco-global criminology.

Conceptualising environmental harm

An eco-global criminology refers to a criminological approach that is informed by ecological considerations and by a critical analysis that is worldwide in its scale and perspective. It is based upon eco-justice conceptions of harm that include consideration of transgressions against environments, non-human species and humans (White 2008a). For this kind of criminology the first question to ask is, 'What harm is there in a particular activity?', rather than whether the activity is legal or not. Some associated questions might include, for example:

Is the activity

legal	illegal
sustainable	not sustainable
for subsistence	for market
for livelihood	for profit
small-scale	large-scale?

The argument here is that if ecological (and social and economic) welfare is to be maximised, then we need to expand our notions of what actually constitutes an environmental crime. Harm, as conceived by critical green criminologists, for example, demands more encompassing definitions than that offered by conventional law and mainstream criminology. This is because some of the most ecologically destructive activities, such as clear-felling of old-growth forests, are quite legal; while more benign practices, such as growing of hemp (an extremely strong fibre), are criminalised. When criminalisation does occur, it often reflects very limited anthropocentric (human-centred) notions of what is best (e.g. protection of legal fisheries and legal timber coups) that treat 'nature' and 'wildlife' simply and mainly as resources for human exploitation. It is about private property and business interests and monopolies and sustainable development. The intrinsic value of specific ecological areas and species tends to be downplayed or ignored.

Nevertheless, recent years have seen greater legislative and judicial attention being given to the rights of the environment per se, and to the rights of certain species of non-human animal to live free from human abuse, torture and degradation. This reflects both the efforts of eco-rights activists (e.g. conservationists) and animal rights activists (e.g. animal liberation movements) in changing perceptions, and laws, in regards to the natural environment and non-human species. It also reflects the growing recognition that centuries of industrialisation and global exploitation of resources are transforming the very basis of world ecology – global warming threatens us all, regardless of where we live or our specific socio-economic situation. The transnational nature and consequences of pollution, resource depletion and threats to biodiversity have likewise over the past few decades called forth a variety of international legal responses, some of which were identified in Chapter 1.

The study of transnational environmental crime must include the study of the legal–illegal divide, as well as pose questions regarding legal and non-legal definitions of 'crime'. This is because when it comes to environmental crime, profit-making is frequently made possible and/or enhanced through the overlapping relationship between licit and illicit markets, and the close connection between legal and illegal practices (see for example the discussion of waste disposal in Chapter 5). Crime is not only socially constructed into specific legal categories, it is also made possible by entrenched activities that ostensibly present as legal and by attitudes and practices that deny 'harm' as such.

The close relationship between the legal and the illegal, especially when it comes to environmental harm (White 2008a), also means that eco-global criminology frequently has to confront issues of power and powerful social interests. This has several implications in regards to gaining access to data and information, and for carrying out research in various parts of the world. The link between vested private interests, state interests and environmental harm is also of concern.

A basic premise of green criminology is that we need to take environmental harm seriously, and that in order to do this we need a conceptualisation of harm that goes beyond conventional understandings of crime (Beirne and South 2007). Green criminology occupies that space between the old, traditional concerns of criminology (with its fixation on working-class criminality and conventional street crime) and the vision of an egalitarian, ecologically sustainable future (where the concern is with ecological citizenship, precautionary social practices and intergenerational and intragenerational equity). For eco-global criminology, the main substantive focus is on transnational environmental crime. But, like green criminology generally, a relevant and innovative perspective on transnational environmental crime demands new ways of seeing, judging and acting in the world around us.

Environmental harm can be conceptualised in relation to legal, ecological and justice criteria. Its definition is in fact associated with quite diverse approaches to environmental issues, stemming from different conceptual starting points.

Conventional criminological conceptions

Over the past four decades, issues of pollution and illegal disposal of toxic waste, among others, have generated various legal and law enforcement responses, including the development of environmental protection agencies. Local and national interest in environmental issues, including specific incidents and harms, have further led researchers to undertake specifically criminological investigations of such harms (Situ and Emmons 2000). As discussed in Chapter 1, recent years have also seen a major growth in international agreements of various kinds relating to environmental issues. In accordance with these developments, conventional criminological conceptions of environmental harm tend to be based upon legal conceptions of harm as informed by such laws, rules and international conventions. The key issue is one of *legality*, and the division of activities into legal and illegal categories. Typically, from this perspective, environmental crimes include such matters as:

- *illegal taking of flora and fauna*, including such activities as illegal, unregulated, and unreported fishing, illegal logging and trade in timber, and illegal trade in wildlife;
- *Pollution offences*, which relate to issues such as fly-tipping (illegal dumping), through to air, water and land pollution associated with industry;
- *Transportation of banned substances*, which refers to illegal transport of radioactive materials and the illegal transfer of hazardous waste.

Many such offences are acknowledged in both domestic legislation and via international agreements. What makes these activities problematic is that they are deemed illegal. It is breaking the law that is at the centre of conventional criminological concern.

Ecological conceptions of harm

By contrast, we can explore a different kind of approach to environmental harm. In this instance, the main focus and interpretative lens is that of *ecology*. The United Nations Environment Programme provides a classic illustration of this approach (UNEP 2007). In this framework, harm is conceived in terms of ecological well-being and holistic understandings of interrelationships between species and environments. The key issue is that of sustainability, and the division of social practices into benign and destructive, from the point of view of ecological sustainability.

The past four decades or so have seen much greater international cooperation and sharing of knowledge among scientists from many different areas of scientific endeavour. One result of these efforts at collaboration and synthesis is a better sense of global ecological health. This is well documented, and baseline data are now available with which to measure the impact of human activity on all types of life on the planet. Basically, the message is that the human ecological footprint is too big to sustain us, and everything else, for much longer into the foreseeable future.

In succinct terms, an ecological perspective, as demonstrated by the UN Environment Programme, sees the world in terms of three areas of harm, risk or threat. These are:

- *the problem of climate change*, in which the concern is to investigate activities that contribute to global warming, such as the replacement of forests with cropland;
- *the problem of biodiversity*, in which the concern is to stem the tide of species extinction and the overall reduction in species through application of certain forms of human production, including use of genetically modified organisms;

• *the problem of waste and pollution*, in which the concern is with activities that defile the environment, leading to such phenomena as the diminishment of clean water.

As with the earlier criminological approach, ecological understandings of harm view these matters in essentially transboundary terms: there is worldwide transference of harms. The bottom line is that, regardless of legal status, action must be taken now to prevent harms associated with global warming, threats to biodiversity and further pollution and waste generation. The imperative is ecological, not legal, and the goal is human survival.

Green criminological conceptions

The advent of green criminology was signalled by work undertaken in the early 1990s that highlighted environmental issues as being of significance to criminology (Lynch 1990). A growing band of criminologists have formed an increasingly coherent international network of researchers, scholars and activists whose brief is to think critically about environmentally related issues (see, for example, White 2010a).

From this perspective, environmental harm is best seen in terms of *justice*, based upon notions of human, ecological and animal rights, and egalitarian concerns. The key issue is weighing up of different kinds of harm and violation of rights within a broad eco-justice framework, and stretching the boundaries of conventional criminology to include other kinds of harm than those already deemed illegal.

Within green criminology, three broad approaches to justice have been identified, each with its specific conceptions of what is harmful (White 2008a). They are:

• *environment rights and environmental justice*, in which environmental rights are seen as an extension of human, or social, rights, so as to enhance the quality of human life, now and into the future;
• *ecological citizenship and ecological justice*, in which ecological citizenship acknowledges that human beings are merely one component of complex ecosystems that should be preserved for their own sake via the notion of the rights of the environment;
• *animal rights and species justice*, in which environmental harm is constructed in relation to the place of non-human animals within environments and with their intrinsic right to not suffer abuse, whether this be one-on-one harm, institutionalised harm, or harm arising from human actions that affect climates and environments on a global scale.

For the green criminologist, the biggest threat to environmental rights, ecological justice and non-human animal well-being are system-level structures and pressures that commodify all aspects of social existence, that are based upon the exploitation of humans, non-human animals and natural resources, and that privilege the powerful minority over the interests of the vast majority. Those who determine and shape the law are very often those whose activities need to be criminalised for the sake of planetary well-being. Environmental harm is thus intrinsically contestable, both at the level of definition, and in terms of visions of what is required for desired social and ecological change.

There are important areas of overlap and synergy between the three approaches to environmental issues. Activity such as illegal fishing, for example, is of concern to the conventional criminologist as it would be to the marine scientist and the green criminologist. But, for the latter two perspectives, so too would be the harms associated with fish farms, such as spread of infections and use of carcinogenic substances to ward off fungi among penned fish populations. Indeed, the distinction between sustainable and non-sustainable is increasingly important in terms of how harm is being framed and conceived. Yet, as green criminology in its various strands indicates, the notions of legal/illegal and sustainable/non-sustainable themselves need to be interrogated from the point of view of eco-justice. This takes us into the realm of eco-philosophy and the value of living and non-living entities, as much as into the practical determination of how best to conceptualise harm (see White 2008a).

What is the eco in eco-global criminology?

What makes eco-global criminology distinctive is the attention given to specifically ecological considerations of harm, as well as its concern with a global perspective on issues and events. Accordingly, this section briefly elaborates on some key ecological harms in order to illustrate the major threats to planetary well-being posed by climate change, diminished biodiversity and pollution. These will be elaborated on in subsequent chapters as well, from the point of view of specifically criminological dimensions.

The problem of climate change

A key problem identified by the United Nations Environment Programme (2007) is that of climate change. According to UNEP there are several interrelated dimensions to the problem. These include ozone depletion, climate change linked to various kinds of emissions, and the impact on global warming of air pollution.

Stratospheric ozone depletion can result from:

- industrial production (e.g. ozone-depleting substances [ODS]);
- agricultural production (e.g. methyl bromide);
- transport;
- population.

Climate change can be the result of:

- population (discharges of carbon dioxide);
- agricultural production (e.g. methane emissions);
- deforestation;
- electricity production;
- transport;
- consumption of luxury goods.

Air pollution can also have many causes, such as:

- population, especially with increasing urbanisation;
- agricultural production (ammonia and pesticide emissions);
- increasing frequency of forest fires;
- industrial production;
- electricity production;
- transport;
- large emissions from traditional biomass (i.e. rural areas).

In large measure, the problem of climate change is directly related to how humans across the globe produce and consume, distribute and exchange the fruits of their labour. Again, this is a systemic issue inseparable from global political economy and the institutions and ideologies that drive the (capitalist) world system. Some efforts have been made to prevent or criminalise the worst aspects of environmental damage associated with this system. Thus, for example, international systems of environmental regulation, as well as a proliferation of laws against pollution, have emerged over the past few decades. The adequacy of these, however, is best measured in actual impact, rather than simply by reference to legislative statute or international convention (see Collins 2010).

One thing is certain, and that is that climate change generally is bound to affect everyone on the planet. While, to date, the impact of climate change has been felt disproportionately in the developing countries, recent estimates indicate that the more affluent countries of the West are now beginning to experience climate-related disasters (see UNEP 2007). Coping with climate change means dealing with the unexpected. This poses a major challenge for planners, policy-makers, regulators and others tasked with the job of minimising the potential threats, while considering possible solutions. Criminologists, likewise, have a role in these processes.

The problem of biodiversity

Genetic manipulation and species regulation have long been a concern of humans. Indeed, throughout our history, humans have engaged in many different kinds of animal husbandry and plant usages that, over time, have shaped the contemporary living planet. A wide range of issues have emerged in recent times that are radically, and quickly, altering the type and extent of species worldwide.

Many contemporary environmental harms are related not only to questions of ownership and control (see, for example, Mgbeoji 2006 on biopiracy) but also to how the basic means of life of humans are being reconstituted and reorganised through global systems of production. For example, the 'globalisation of food production and manufacture and the use of new technologies and chemicals in farming and food processing have created a variety of risks to humans, non-human animals, the environment and health' (Croall 2007: 206). In many cases we still do not know the longer-term effects of new developments in the food area.

What is happening to food generally is symptomatic of how commodification is taking place in regards to all aspects of human life, and in all parts of the globe. The global political economy of genetically modified organisms (GMOs) provides a case in point, insofar as the promotion of GMOs by large transnational corporations has continued apace, regardless of serious reservations being raised about significant potential risks to human health and safety, antibiotic immunity and contamination of the environment (Walters 2004, 2005).

These kinds of developments ultimately lead to reliance upon fewer species (of plant and of animal).That is, the transformation of genetic material via science and biotechnology also tends towards homogenisation of species composition – it is more profitable to reduce variety at the same time as increase quantitative productivity with the 'winners'. The overall result is an attitude of 'fewer species is better' (and more profitable), especially if control over these is vested in private hands.

Illegal trade in plants and wildlife represents its own kind of threat, as well. The threat here is both to biodiversity in relation to endangered species, and to the economic viability of industries such as agriculture, forestry and fisheries. Whether contaminants enter into the food production system through illegal importation of banned organic substances or the legal use of patented materials, the result will be the same – devastation to the basic requirements of life.

The problem of waste

A third major area of environmental concern has to do with the problems associated with waste and pollution (White 2008a, 2009c). Some of the more pressing issues include the following:

- the proliferation of 'e'-waste generated by the disposal of tens of thousands of computers and other equipment;
- the safe disposal of old ships and aeroplanes, which likewise contain metals, chemicals and other contaminants;
- the illegal shipping and dumping of hazardous waste materials to countries made vulnerable by weak regulatory or enforcement systems;
- pollution of air, land and water.

Much of the transfer of waste has been from advanced industrialised countries to developing countries (Clapp 2001). So, too, the most polluted places on earth tend likewise to be developing countries. Meanwhile, hazardous residues and contaminated sludge are most likely to find a foreign home in a Third World country.

When it comes to the disposal of waste, the distinction between legal and illegal is increasingly irrelevant from the point of view of human well-being and health, much less the impact on local environments. For example, according to the United Nations, about 20–50 million tons of e-waste is generated worldwide annually (United Nations Environment Programme 2006). The waste contains toxins such as lead and mercury or other chemicals that can poison waterways if buried, or release toxins into the air if burned. As mentioned, much of this waste ends up as transfers from rich countries to poor. Old computers and mobile phones, for instance, are often not declared as waste, but shipped abroad as material for repair or recycling, according to bills of lading. Much of it ends up in Nigeria, where it is burned in huge rubbish dumps (Lambrecht 2006).

We can add to the list of transborder problems the threats to health posed by smog, and more generally indoor and outdoor pollutants. These have been shown to have a major impact on human health and well-being, and the negative health consequences are apparent in both developing and the more developed countries (UNEP 2007: 55). Air pollution also adversely affects agriculture, among other things.

In combination, present trends relating to climate change, biodiversity and waste reinforce one another and constitute massive threats to the world as we know it today. Recognising the existing harms, being sensitive to potential harms and documenting the forces behind them are essential if they are to be adequately addressed. A global perspective is of course vital in understanding the magnitude and shaping forces behind developments across these domains.

These trends also have major implications for the nature of crime, the dynamics of criminality and the operations of criminal justice systems. From an eco-global perspective the goal is to expose sources of social conflict and likely areas of criminal behaviour arising from the massive ecological changes currently under way. An indication of the ecological and social dimensions of transnational environmental crime is shown in Table 2.1. This provides examples of specific types of environmental offences related to particular areas of ecological concern, as well as the more conventional offences arising from the ecological impacts associated with climate change, biodiversity loss and pollution. Future chapters will elaborate on the environmental offences and the associated criminal offences pertaining to each of these areas.

Specific and detailed investigation of each of these areas of concern is beyond the scope of the present book (and, as pointed out in subsequent chapters, is already subject to criminological analysis by various researchers and scholars). Rather, the main concern is to identify key issues and to begin the process of mapping out a theoretical framework and methodological strategy for examining such issues.

Table 2.1 Ecological and social dimensions of transnational environmental crime

Ecological concern	Subject of offence	Nature of offence
Climate change		
	Examples of environmental offences	
	Industrial pollution	Unlicensed pollution
	Illegal land clearance	Destruction of habitat and forests
	Examples of associated offences	
	Public order offences	Food riots
	Trafficking	Migration and people smuggling
Biodiversity		
	Examples of environmental offences	
	Forestry	Illegal felling of trees
	Wildlife crime	Trade in endangered species
	Examples of associated offences	
	Corruption	Bribing of government officials
	Money laundering	Illegal financial transactions
Pollution/waste		
	Examples of environmental offences	
	Contaminated land	Failure to comply with remediation notice
	Waste management	Illegal waste disposal
	Examples of associated offences	
	Threats of harm	Protection rackets, stand-over tactics
	Public order offences	Conflicts over local land use

Researching the global in eco-global criminology

Undertaking study of transnational harm is not only a matter of choosing one's focus (e.g. global, comparative or historical) or substantive subject (e.g. pollution, illegal fishing). There are also epistemological issues at stake. Consider for example the recent work by Connell on 'southern theory' (2007). Connell queries whose knowledge, whose perspectives and whose ideas come to dominate our understandings of the social world. To some extent, this can be appraised by asking a series of key questions:

- Where does the claim of universality (e.g. about globalisation) actually stem from? How is universality linked to metropole/periphery relations?
- Whose literature is actually read and acknowledged? Whose voices are heard?
- Whose ideas are excluded from discussions of social theory? Whose perspectives are not addressed?
- What is erased in metropolitan accounts of the global – what space is presumed to be cleared or empty (e.g. especially those of Indigenous

peoples)? What happened to colonisation and imperialism in the globalisation narrative?

Similar questions have been asked in regards to mainstream criminology. That is, commentators have tried to understand and explain why the knowledge which is most valued in global criminological circles is that which is primarily produced in and by the metropole of the United States, the United Kingdom and Europe (Marshall 2008; Aas 2007).

The hegemony of the centre influences the criminological project, whether this is in regards to terrorism or to environmental harm. For example, there are hegemonic accounts of how 'globalisation' is conceived and great selectivity in which authors are perceived to be authorities on the processes and effects of such. As Connell (2007) points out, rarely are authors, writers and researchers from the South (that is, developing countries, Indigenous peoples, Islamic scholars and so on) consulted, read or acknowledged in the academic studies and research of the centre. This occurs even when the topic is their own country, and when the issues are of most pertinence and direct relevance to themselves and their people.

Thus, from what vantage point are we going to assess global environmental issues? Those who study are themselves physically grounded in the world – they live and work and play in specific places. They are embedded within particular intellectual fields and cultural contexts. To speak of the transnational, therefore, demands an appreciation that the 'transnational' is very often conceptually located within familiar scholarly universes. The development of a truly global criminology will require breaking the chains of parochialism, elitism and (implicitly) a colonialist mentality.

Engaging in research into transnational environmental harm involves a number of practical, scientific and political challenges (see for examples, Bayley 1999). The kinds of problems and difficulties discussed below are not unlike those encountered in pursuing cross-cultural crime and justice studies more generally. Thus, for example, issues of parochialism and paternalism (see Aas 2007), and matters pertaining to the quality and limitations of comparative crime statistics (see Van Dijk 2008), are familiar to those engaged in the new global criminology, as well as to those interested specifically in analysis of transnational environmental crime.

Moving beyond one's own national borders to work with people in other locales and from other cultures is easier said than done. Gaining access to countries, regions and specific sites may be an issue, as is the expense associated with transnational study. Language differences and the subtleties of culture may intrude into the research process by causing delays, and lead to misunderstandings about substantive issues.

The expertise required to undertake research is a perennial issue: outside 'experts' are the bane of many a developing country's existence insofar as local knowledge and capacity building is ignored in favour of relying on 'trained' personnel from the metropole (for a critique of this kind of process, see Stanley

2008). On the other hand, the political realities within some nation states suggest that it may be best that an 'outsider' carry out the research if issues of safety, security and independent knowledge production are at stake. Insider/outsider relationships are contingent, therefore, upon local resources, staff availability and political contexts, and thus require 'sensitivity to situation' on the part of researchers.

Such sensitivity in turn points to the importance of collaboration as a guiding concept of transnational research. This necessarily includes cross-disciplinary and cross-cultural considerations. How can one be sensitive to situation if one is not actually talking and engaging with local people (including local intellectuals, broadly defined)? The notion of outsider/insider is a real and meaningful distinction that is forged in the crucible of local experiences, long-standing cultural traditions, relationship to imperial power and positioning in the wider global political economy. Bridging the gap requires dialogue (not monologue), listening (not lecturing) and give-and-take interchange (not just giving, or just taking). Informed expertise is built upon processes that expand the horizons of knowledge and that, as part of this, incorporate the insights of many people from many different backgrounds. This requires openness to the interplay between class, race, ethnicity, gender and other social attributes in positioning people (individually and collectively) differently in regards to social location and situated knowledge. It also demands adoption of multiple methods of study and a wide variety of ways in which to engage in dialogic social relationships (see, for example, Banerjee and Bell 2007).

By contrast, exploitation occurs where knowledge is organised in and through processes that privatise, commodify and extract – a tendency frequently associated with, for example, Western corporations (and, dare we add, intellectuals) in relation to non-Western regions. The phenomenon of biopiracy provides a case in point. Biopiracy is linked to exploitation of Third World resources and Third World peoples and knowledge, and refers to 'the unauthorized commercial use of biological resources and/or associated traditional knowledge, or the patenting of spurious inventions based on such knowledge, without compensation'(Mgbeoji 2006: 13). Under the banner of free trade and the global (competitive) commons, the race to patent features among the activities of many transnational companies. Effectively this represents the private appropriation of knowledge and techniques that have been developed by collectivities over many years of agricultural practice. This is knowledge mining, not collaborative research.

There are ways to ensure that researchers are not simply 'taking', that they are not exploiting the vulnerable, and that they are not misleading in their re-presentations of situated knowledge. For instance, Dodson *et al.* (2007) describe the dilemmas and opportunities associated with research about the lives and perspectives of marginalised people living in a variety of social settings. Interestingly, and usefully, they speak of a methodological practice called 'interpretive focus groups'. On the one hand, research is oriented towards involving a wide range of participants in the research practice (i.e. hearing the voices from below, including those groups which historically have been disregarded or excluded from such research conversations). On the other hand, people from the same localities and social backgrounds are then asked to be part of panels to discuss and interpret the findings (i.e., assessing the meaning of what has been said in the first phase of the research). This acknowledges that marginalised populations will, on occasion, be silent or hide certain things due to fears or suspicions related to what might be revealed about themselves and their lives that could make them vulnerable vis-à-vis authority figures and mainstream institutions.

The experience and expertise of local residents helps us to understand why and how respondents speak as they do, and is thus privileged over that of the 'academic' per se, which, without this interpretive lens, may lead to misinterpretation of what people are actually saying. The process of utilising interpretive focus groups enables researchers to collaboratively approach data analysis, and thus to capture more accurately, and ethically, the 'truths' of those with whom they are interacting (for more discussion of this see also Chapter 7).

When it comes to more traditional academic research the availability of data is complicated by many things, some of which are inherently political. For example, if logging is a prime source of government revenue in some regions or countries, then investigation that potentially threatens certain logging practices or that links environmental harm to the logging industry may cause it to be stymied. Resistance to data collection may go hand in hand with denial of harm on the part of the powerful. Research may also be seen as 'dangerous' to vested interests if corruption of officials is widespread. Research into environmental harm may well provoke negative reactions on the part of powerful interest groups. In some cases, as with the outspoken critic of the Nigerian government and the oil exploring companies in his country, Ken Saro-Wiwa, the penalty for mobilising against these interests was arrest and execution (see Saro-Wiwa 1995).

Less authoritarian methods are also used to silence critics, to dampen resistance and to minimise public outcry. This can take the form of governments banning the publication of criminal statistics that threaten to tarnish the reputation of a country (see Van Dijk 2008). It is also apparent in the efforts of private companies to protect their interests through the use of strategic lawsuits against public participation (commonly referred to as SLAPPs), one effect of which is to curtail the free flow of information (see White 2005). The violation of the human rights of environmental victims and environmental activists is an issue of grave and growing concern (see Chapter 7 and Chapter 9).

Even where data is collected on environmental harm (as conventionally defined – such as pollution offences, illegal trade in flora and fauna, illegal disposal of waste), problems are apparent. In most jurisdictions worldwide, for example, there has been little sustained effort to bring together official and alternative sources of information, much less data between different government departments and criminal justice agencies (such as police files, data collected by non-government organisations and activist groups, animal welfare service providers, journalist accounts and so on). Who is collecting what, for whom, and why, are essential questions when it comes to data on environmental crime.

In regards to record keeping and data collection, agencies such as the United Nations Environment Programme (UNEP) have acknowledged the limitations in what is provided to them. It has been observed, for example, that some governments

> ... were too vague in their purposes, other entities did not have the background or training to undertake serious monitoring efforts, and data, once collected, were often not usefully aggregated (or even comparable). Even now, data collected for other purposes by individual states or researchers are often either not comparable or not representative.
>
> (DeSombre 2006: 15)

By comparison, we can consider data collected as part of specific report-back purposes. For instance, the GEO-4 report on the state of the world's environment produced by the United Nations Environment Programme (2007) involved about 400 individual scientists and policy-makers and more than 50 GEO Collaborating Centres, and a comprehensive peer review process of 1,000 invited experts. The result is a document that involves lots of data from many different sources that, collectively, adds up to a reasonable picture of who is doing what, where, and how. It also provides a series of benchmarks and models that allow for comparison between regions, countries and over time in relation to matters such as biodiversity, pollution levels, illegal trade in bush meat (i.e. wildlife, that can include apes and other primates, rodents and birds), and production of waste.

Horizon scanning

Another useful methodological approach to the study of transnational environmental crime is that of horizon scanning. This provides one means by which to examine issues associated with climate change, for example, as well as other issues of transnational environmental significance.

The use and need for horizon scanning as an intellectual exercise and planning tool is related to the idea that many threats and opportunities are at present poorly recognised. Accordingly, a more systematic approach to identification and solution to issues is required rather than reliance upon *ad hoc* or reactive approaches. For example, Sutherland *et al.* (2009: 1) point out that 'the need for horizon scanning of environmental issues is illustrated by the recent failure to foresee both the widespread adoption of the range of biofuels currently in use, and the environmental consequences of biofuels production' (see also Chapter 4). Horizon scanning can provide insight into risks (potential problems) and harms (actual problems). It provides a mechanism to discern where emerging threats (and positive opportunities) may arise and potential ways to mitigate or adapt to these.

In analysis of horizon issues a variety of concepts might be deployed. Certainly matters of time, space and scale are relevant. For example, risks and harms may be direct or indirect, and their consequences may be felt in the immediate or in the long term. Harm may be specific to local areas (such as threats to certain species, like coral in the Great Barrier Reef) yet manifest as part of a general global pattern (such as being an effect of wide-scale temperature changes affecting coral everywhere). Harm is central, but this may be non-intentional (in the sense of being a by-product of some other agenda) or premeditated (insofar as the negative outcome, for some, is foreseen). The demise of the polar bear due to the impact of global warming in the Arctic is an example of the former. The displacement of local inhabitants from their land due to carbon sequestration schemes is an example of the latter.

There are several other concepts that are particularly relevant to horizon scanning. Three of these address matters of justice, past, present and future: environmental justice, ecological justice and species justice. Three of these look to the future: intergenerational equity, the precautionary principle, and transference over time. Collectively these concepts provide a values framework for assessing and analysing risks and harms as part of the exercise of looking over the horizon (see also Leiss and Hrudey 2005; White 2008a). Table 2.2 provides a summary of these key ideas.

The challenge for eco-global criminology is to marshal ideas and evidence from many different sources and disciplines in order to identify where harms and risks are emerging as matters of possible social and political importance, and to develop pre-emptive strategies to begin to address potential problems before they create further harms and risks pertaining to humans, environments and animals.

In practice, the doing of horizon scanning is premised upon three interrelated tasks. These include attempts to theorise causal forces in regards to any specific issue; to employ multidisciplinary methods; and to deliberate on potential policy responses. Theory, in this instance, is based upon the notion of anthropogenic causes – that is, the interest is in human responsibility for harm and thus issues pertaining to identification of specific perpetrators and degrees of culpability. Methodologically, the concern is to use a wide variety of methods and insights in an eclectic fashion in order to expose broad patterns of action (and omission) and causal chains of harm. Policy basically refers to matters relating to regulation and enforcement strategies, as well as issues of remediation and compensation. Any analysis based upon horizon scanning will most likely involve creative lateral thinking and plans of intervention that may occasionally sit uncomfortably with the existing institutional status quo.

Conclusion

From the point of view of eco-global criminology, analysis of transnational environmental crime needs to incorporate different, albeit interrelated notions of harm. These include *legal conceptions* of harm that are informed by laws,

Table 2.2 The conceptual basis of environmental horizon scanning

---

Substantive orientation

Risk – a prediction or expectation that includes the perspectives of those affected about what is important to them, concerning a hazard or danger in which there is uncertainty over occurrence but which may involve adverse consequences as the possible outcome within a certain time period.

Harm – an actual danger or adverse effect, stemming from direct and indirect social processes, that negatively impinges upon the health and well-being and ecological integrity of humans, specific biospheres and non-human animals.

Cause – analysis of causal chains that may involve many interrelated variables but which ultimately are linked to specific practices and human responsibility for environmental harm.

Justice orientation

Environment justice – in which environmental rights are seen as an extension of human or social rights so as to enhance the quality of human life, now and into the future.

Ecological justice – in which it is acknowledged that human beings are merely one component of complex ecosystems that should be preserved for their own sake via the notion of the rights of the environment.

Species justice – in which harm is constructed in relation to the place of non-human animals within environments and their intrinsic right to not suffer abuse, whether this be one-on-one harm, institutionalised harm or harm arising from human actions that affect climates and environments on a global scale.

Futures orientation

Intergenerational equity – refers to the principle of ensuring that the generations to follow have at least the same or preferably better environments in which to live than those of the present generation.

Precautionary principle – when an activity raises threats of harm to human health, non-human animals or the environment, precautionary measures should be taken even if some cause-and-effect relationships are not fully established scientifically.

Transference over time – in this context refers to the transfer of harm involving both cumulative impacts and compounding effects.

---

rules and international conventions, and that pertain to things such as illegal fishing and the transportation of banned substances. They include consideration of *ecological well-being* and holistic understandings of harm that are informed by the interrelationship between species and environments, and that see the key issue of ecological sustainability in the light of global warming and species extinction. They include *justice conceptions* of harm that are informed by notions of human, ecological and animal rights and egalitarian concerns, and that are concerned with preserving complex ecosystems for their own sake and preventing animal abuse.

The complexity of the issues relating to these kinds of harm demands an investigatory approach that includes a wide number of sources, and that provides both quantitative and qualitative data. That is, we want data that consists of counting things (i.e. numbers) as well as how people interpret the world around them (i.e. meanings). Rather than being restricted by the limitations of the legal/illegal divide, we need to assert the prior importance of and urgency associated with *ecological sustainability*. This means assessing 'harm' in many different contexts and guises, regardless of legal status and existing institutional legitimations.

Also important to bear in mind is that research ought to take place at different levels of scale (local through to global), and draw upon different methodologies. Specific issues such as illegal logging or trade in endangered species demand specific types of research, and the development of responses that are specific to the nature of the problem. A case study approach may be appropriate for some types of investigation; others will require statistical comparisons and analyses. Whatever the specific methodology, it is important to be conscious of the diversity of social situations and situated knowledge – related to class, race, ethnicity, gender and age – that will have a bearing on knowledge about the environment. A socially inclusive research programme is one that acknowledges this, as well as the intersections of class exploitation, colonial oppression, racial injustice, gender inequality, age-based discrimination and environmental degradation.

Eco-global criminology provides a distinctive type of analytical lens for the study of transnational environmental crime. As a perspective, it requires one to be highly conscious of the specifically ecological basis of environmental crime or harm, and to incorporate this into the core concerns of its criminological analysis. As an approach, it demands that one be highly sensitive to the intricacies of doing research on a global scale (even if localised to specific regions), and to develop methodologies that are socially and culturally inclusive while maintaining a strong critical edge.

The question of how to define the problem is an intractable and necessary part of the development of eco-global criminology. Many areas of harm to humans, environments and non-human animals are at present not criminalised. This includes such destructive, degrading and dehumanising practices as clear-felling of old-growth forests, reliance upon battery hen forms of egg and poultry production, and use of depleted uranium in weapons. From an analytical point of view, conceptualisation of harm ought not to rely upon the legal–illegal distinction per se, especially since some of the world's most environmentally disastrous practices are in fact still legal. Eco-global criminology may well entail the exposure of negative, degrading and hazardous practices as a prelude to the banning and close control of such practices. New concepts of harm, as informed by ecological sciences and environmental values, will inevitably be developed as part of this process.

3   Climate change

Introduction

Climate change is arguably the most important issue, problem and trend in the world today and is a key area of interest to eco-global criminology. The purpose of this chapter is to explore some of the ways in which this is so by discussing issues such as the social conflicts that are emerging as a consequence of climate change.

The starting point for eco-global criminology is the overarching ecological issue (for example, climate change or loss of biodiversity) rather than the legal issues as such (for example, fraud related to carbon emission schemes or wildlife trafficking). Eco-global criminology asks the questions 'What harm is there associated with climate change, and what can we do about it?' As part of this it also explores the conventional environmental and non-environmental crimes that are linked with this particular ecological issue.

Fundamentally life on planet Earth is ever more rapidly being transformed in ways that are profound and for many of us unimaginable. This is due to global warming. Until very recently (see White 2009b; Stretesky and Lynch 2009; Lynch and Stretesky 2010) few criminologists have participated in analysis of climate change, criminology and criminal justice. This is starting to change and undoubtedly more work will be undertaken in this area in the coming years.

In many ways, and from the vantage point of future generations, present action and lack of action around climate change will most likely constitute the gravest of transnational environmental crimes. The harms grow more evident every day, but the main protagonists continue to support policies and practices that contribute to the overall problem. With foreknowledge and scientific proof in hand, powerful interests continue to dominate the climate change agenda to the advantage of their own sectional interests – and it is the poorest of the poor who currently experience the harbingers of things to come for the rest of us. The failure to act, now, is criminal. Yet, things continue much as they have, the status quo is maintained, and the harms mount up.

Climate change

Public debate on climate change has generally focused on two separate issues:

* Is climate change actually occurring?
* Is climate change caused by human activity or is it simply part of a natural process of change?

While there are still a handful of climate change sceptics around, the weight of scientific evidence (see, for example UNEP 2007 and more recent United Nations reports) and popular experience (of, for example, unusual climate events such as unprecedented summer heatwaves in Russia and incessant summer rains in Saskatchewan, Canada at the same time in 2010) have convinced the vast majority of the world that climate change is indeed a real threat. Most governments thus acknowledge that there is a problem and that it must in some way be addressed.

There continues to be disagreement, both scientific and political, when it comes to the causes of climate change. This is because how this question is answered has important social and economic consequences. If climate change is 'natural', then what governments can do is to try to adapt to changed circumstances as best they can, since change is inevitable (and blameless). In this scenario existing institutions are not perceived to be the cause of the problem, although they will nonetheless be implicated in the changes that must occur into the future (such as caps being put on carbon emissions).

If human activity is found to be at the genesis of climate change, then this implies that substantial change is needed to the dominant mode of production characteristic of much world activity. Global production and consumption patterns, for example, feature an insatiable energy appetite (which, in turn, justifies use of destructive energy sources such as coal-fired power stations) and are founded upon a growth model (that feeds polluting and waste industries). The attribution of global warming to human activity also assigns a certain responsibility to the most polluting and damaging industries and countries to make right the wrongs to which they have contributed through their actions. Mitigation and adaptation in this scenario demand redress as well as a major alteration in existing ways of doing things.

Our understandings and responses to the heating up of the planet carry with them important expectations about potential courses of action. Global warming describes the raising of the earth's temperature over a relatively short time span. Climate change describes the interrelated effects of this rise in temperature: from changing sea levels and changing ocean currents, through to the impacts of temperature change on local environments that affect the endemic flora and fauna in varying ways (for instance, the death of coral due to temperature rises in sea water or the changed migration patterns of birds).

In recent years a number of international instruments have emerged that deal with some aspects of climate change and global warming (see Table 3.1). The fields of international relations and legal studies have been saturated with copious commentaries and prescriptions regarding how best to legally and diplomatically tackle such important issues. Effective and systemic responses, however, have been less than forthcoming. Indeed, the abject failure of the 2010 Copenhagen talks to actually do something about carbon emissions and to address climate change issues in a substantive fashion is a striking example of the difficulties in gaining concerted international action on such issues.

For eco-global criminology, climate change is of profound concern and is a major ecological issue, especially since the future of the world is literally tied up with the progression and impacts related to global warming. The purpose of this chapter is to explore some of the ways in which eco-criminology can shed light on certain aspects of the issue. Climate change frames much of what is to come in the next two chapters as well, since it is having huge impacts on both biodiversity and how pollution is being reconfigured at this point in time.

What does climate change have to do with criminology?

Climate change and global warming pose a number of important questions for criminology. Not the least of these are problems relating to personal and national security, and the management of social conflict. Moreover, as governments and communities search for solutions to the underlying issues of climate change, and adopt measures to mitigate and adapt to the consequences of global warming, other problems will also inevitably emerge. Indeed, the aim of this chapter is to indicate how certain responses to climate-related issues generate their own sort of negative feedback loop, resulting in further degradation of environments

Table 3.1 Select transnational agreements relating to climate change

The United Nations Framework Convention on Climate Change, 1992 (UNFCCC) aims to achieve stabilisation of greenhouse gas concentrations in the atmosphere at a low enough level to prevent dangerous anthropogenic interference with the climate system.

The United Nations Convention to Combat Desertification In Those Countries Experiencing Serious Drought and/or Desertification, Particularly in Africa, 1994 (UNCCD) combats desertification and mitigates the effects of drought through national action programmes that incorporate long-term strategies supported by international cooperation and partnership arrangements.

The Kyoto Protocol to the United Nations Framework Convention on Climate Change (1998) aims to further reduce greenhouse gas emissions by enhancing the national programmes of developed countries aimed at this goal and by establishing percentage reduction targets for developed countries.

The International Tropical Timber Agreement (ITTA 1994) aims to promote the conservation and sustainable management, use and trade of tropical forest resources through the creation of the International Tropical Timber Organisation (ITTO).

and further threats to basic human rights. The pressures associated with these emergent harms (stemming from climate change responses) will in their own way add to the social conflicts already associated with climate change.

Social conflicts

One consequence of global trends is an expected upsurge in social conflict. From the point of view of nation states, borders certainly do count when it comes to responding to transborder harms and to incidents that bring with them the transference of harm from one country to another. Social conflicts are essentially conflicts between different sets of people, and between different nation states. In either case, there is clearly a need for regulation, resolution and, in some instances, restitution.

For present purposes, our concern is with four areas in which climate change and associated environmental transformations are giving rise to significant social conflict. The areas of concern include: conflicts over environmental resources (e.g. water); conflicts linked to global warming (e.g. climate-induced migration); conflicts over the differential exploitation of resources (e.g. biopiracy); and conflicts over the transference of harm (e.g. cross-border pollution).

As indicated in Chapter 1, borders do not mean much in the case of many instances of environmental harm, especially those pertaining to contamination, pollution and the movement of materials/particles through water and air (see, for examples, White 2008a; Schmidt 2004; United Nations Environment Programme 2006). Nor do borders have much material relevance when it comes to environmental harm associated with global warming. Climate change affects us all, regardless of where we live, regardless of social characteristics.

However, the effects of climate change, while felt by everyone, are not the same for everyone. Claims to a universal victimisation in fact belie crucial differences in how different groups and classes of people are placed quite differently in relation to key risk and protective factors (see also Chapter 7). Social conflict linked to climate change is, as much as anything, a reflection of social inequality, and not simply determined by changes in environmental conditions.

It has been observed that those most vulnerable to the 'consequences of consequences' of climate change are people living in poverty, in underdeveloped and unstable states, under poor governance (Smith and Vivekananda 2007). Indeed, it has been estimated that over half the world's population is potentially at risk.

There is a real risk that climate change will compound the propensity for violent conflict, which in turn will leave communities poorer, less resilient and less able to cope with the consequences of climate change. There are 46 countries – home to 2.7 billion people – in which the effects of climate change interacting with economic, social and political problems will create a high risk of violent conflict.

There is a second group of 56 countries where the institutions of government will have great difficulty taking the strain of climate change on top of all their current challenges. In these countries, though the risk of armed conflict may not be so immediate, the interaction of climate change and other factors creates a high risk of political instability, with potential violent conflict a distinct risk in the longer term. These 56 countries are home to 1.2 billion people.

(Smith and Vivekananda 2007: 3)

The consequences of global warming will thus impact most heavily on those least able to cope with climate-related changes.

The global ecological situation is unlikely to improve very much, if at all, in the near future. Indeed, there is every chance that things will get much worse before too long, particularly as the Arctic heats up. The damage will be felt in the form of extreme weather events, increased competition for dwindling natural resources, outbreaks of disease and viral infections, further extinctions of species, continued pressure to trade off food for fuel, and the list goes on. These issues will be explored in greater depth in this and subsequent chapters.

Table 3.2 provides a survey of likely areas of conflict in the foreseeable future. The conflicts include those pertaining to diminished environmental resources, to the impacts of global warming, to differential access and use of nature, and to friction stemming from the cross-border transference of harm. The table also indicates some of the countries already implicated in some of these forms of conflict.

The urgency of and need for progressive criminological intervention is illustrated by this kind of charting up of emergent social issues related to climate change. Managing social conflict, much less dealing with the grossest incidences of environmental harm, will demand great resolve, sharpened analytical tools and high-level strategic thinking. It also demands that we interrogate the causes of specific conflicts, the general deterioration of global environmental systems and the distributions of power, energy and wealth on a world scale. Eco-global criminology in general can contribute to this analysis, as can the specific insights offered by horizon scanning that is informed by eco-global concerns and concepts.

The transnational corporation stands at the apex of global social and economic power, and so analysis must at some point take their role in ecological matters into consideration (see, especially, Chapter 6). Confronting the present realities of the North–South divide, and the legacies of imperialism and colonialism, constitutes yet another dimension to the social conflicts mapped out above. Indeed, underpinning many of the conflicts occurring 'elsewhere' (i.e. in the non-Western world) are processes and decisions made in the metropole – the United States and the European Union.

Grain for biofuel rather than food is one example of how conflict over food in some countries has its origins in changes in commodity production in another (see Chapter 4). As demonstrated below, who sets the overall ecological agenda

Table 3.2 Climate change and social conflict

Conflicts over environmental resources

e.g. water – anti-privatisation protests and diminished clean drinking water resources (Bolivia, South Africa, Israel, Palestine)

e.g. food – food riots, particularly in relation to grain prices associated with tension between crops for food and crops for biofuel (Mexico, Haiti, Indonesia, Cameroon)

e.g. fish – competition between local fishers and commercial and industrial fishers, leading to 'war' over specific fisheries (Canada, Spain)

Conflicts linked to global warming

e.g. climate-induced migration of peoples – 'environmental refugees' (South Pacific Islands)

e.g. demographics – population size and profile (such as structural ageing) linked to distribution, availability and carrying capacity of land (China)

e.g. loss of territory and border disputes – receding coastlines and desertification (Egypt, Greenland, Canada, Russia, USA)

Conflicts over differential exploitation of resources

e.g. indigenous people and biopiracy – theft of plants and indigenous knowledge and techniques under guise of legal patent processes (Brazil, Peru)

e.g. subsistence versus industrial production – uses of biotechnology such as GMOs and other forms of technology to increase yields beyond the norm and beyond precaution, for profit purposes (Zambia)

e.g. conflicts over energy supply – related to the concentration of the world's hydrocarbon reserves in specific regions (Iraq, Iran, Venezuela)

Conflicts over transference of harm

e.g. cross-border pollution – movement of pollutants through fluid medium such as water, or via air currents (China, Russia, Germany, Hungary)

e.g. transborder movement of toxic waste – corruption of companies and organised crime in redistributing waste to countries of least resistance, or the oceans and deserts of the world (Somalia, Ivory Coast, Nigeria)

e.g. circulation of pollution and waste – such as concentration of plastics in specific geographical locations and planetary sinks (ocean gyres, Antarctic ozone hole)

Source: White 2009b

is fundamental to the conflicts occurring now and into the future. Transnational corporations, in conjunction with hegemonic nation states and local political elites, are implicated in many of the present changes occurring in global food production and consumption.

Struggles over food

The exploitation of the world's natural resources by the major transnational corporations occurs through the direct appropriation of lands, plants and animals as 'property' (including intellectual property as in the case of patents). It also occurs through the displacement of existing systems of production and consumption by those that require insertion into the cash buyer nexus; in other words, the purchase of goods and services as commodities. This has happened in the area of food production as it has in other spheres of human life.

Table 3.3 provides a snapshot of world grain trade over four decades from 1950. What the table demonstrates is a major shift in the status of developing countries from exporters of food to importers of food. Africa, according to this table, was virtually self-sufficient in grain production in 1950; by 1998 it was heavily reliant upon outside producers. Western Europe, by contrast, has gone from net importer to major exporter of grains. North America, and Australia and New Zealand, have systematically increased their share of world grain production over the same period of time.

This shift in world grain trade has been facilitated by neo-liberal economic restructuring, which has transformed countries such as the Philippines from a net food exporter to a net food importer. The process has involved structural adjustment practices, under the auspices of the World Bank and the International Monetary Fund. This has consisted of the simultaneous phenomena of state divestment from agricultural production (e.g. lifting of price controls on fertiliser), and trade liberalisation that has allowed heavily subsidised US and EU meat and grain producers to flood host markets with cheaper commodities. For example:

> From $367 billion in 1995, the total amount of agricultural subsidies provided by developed-country governments rose to $388 billion in 2004. Since the late 1990s subsidies have accounted for 40 percent of the value of agricultural production in the European Union and 25 percent in the United States.

> (Bello 2008)

The result has been the collapse of local producer capacities and markets; and the transformation from self-sufficiency amongst peasant producers to national dependency upon corporate supplied food (Bello 2008).

Table 3.3 The changing pattern of world grain trade, 1950–98[1]

Region	1950	1960	1970	1980	1990	1998
North America	+23	+39	+56	+125	+101	+86
Western Europe	−22	−25	−28	−7	+27	+19
Eastern Europe and former Soviet Union	0	+3	0	−45	−29	+3
Latin America	+1	0	+6	+8	−1	−5
Africa	0	−1	−4	−16	−27	−38
Asia and Middle East	−6	−17	−33	−63	−71	−81
Australia and New Zealand	+3	+8	+12	+12	+15	+21

[1]Plus sign indicates net exports; minus sign, net imports. Imports and exports do not balance out due to differences in export and import data and lags in shipment times

Source: French 2000: 52

What is happening to food generally is symptomatic of how commodification is taking place vis-à-vis all aspects of human life and in all parts of the globe. Patent protection ensures that the big agribusiness companies are able to control markets and production processes (see White 2008a; Mgbeoji 2006). This is based upon patents of existing organic materials (that is, through biopiracy) and technological developments (that is, through genetic modification of organisms). The point is to make direct producers – the farmers – reliant upon commercially bought seeds (and related products such as fertiliser and pesticides). This is explored more fully in Chapter 4.

This kind of analysis – one that examines specific events such as food riots from the point of view of global processes – offers insights into the causes and consequences of particular trends. Importantly, eco-global criminology provides a framework for explaining social disorder within specific regional and national contexts. It also provides an eco-justice framework that can illuminate the close interconnections between exploitation of environments, non-human animals and humans via dominant systems of production and consumption.

Climate-induced migration

When subsistence fishing, farming and hunting wither due to overexploitation and climate change, then great shifts in human populations and in resource use will take place. The forced migration of the environmental refugee poses a whole new set of questions for criminology (see, for example, Refugee Studies Centre 2008). Indeed, the relationship between environmental change, climate-induced displacement and human migration is already generating much angst within some Western government circles and is reinforcing the development of a fortress mentality within particular jurisdictions (whether this is the joined-up countries such as the European Union or discrete nation states such as Australia).

While the phrase 'environmental refugee' is contentious (see Castles 2002), displacement of people due to environmental-related causes has major legal, human rights and national security concerns (McAdam and Saul 2008; Refugee Studies Centre 2008). This is not a new problem; such migrations have been experienced in Southern Africa (Singh 1996) and are currently at the top of the agenda for many Islanders living in the South Pacific.

From the point of view of national interests and international security, the mass movement of peoples is generally presented as a significant problem (Solana and Ferrero-Waldner 2008). In particular, there is a popular inclination to view Third-world ecological ruin as first and foremost a threat to First-world stability and existing wealth. For eco-global criminology, the challenge is to critique and respond to images and social constructions of the climate-induced migrant as someone who should be subjected to criminalisation and law enforcement rather than on the basis of humanitarian issues (Pickering 2005). The reaches of state security are expanding beyond state borders through varying forms of pre-emptive action in order to restrict the migration process. The so-called 'Pacific Solution' in Australia, for example, had meant the detainment of asylum seekers offshore in neighbouring island states, rather than allowing them entry into Australian territory proper. As environmental conditions deteriorate due to global warming, the size and extent of migration will be shaped by geography, global power relations and defence of human rights.

Various crimes tied to climate-related events such as food riots and climate-induced migration will become more prevalent. Some of these, for example, include looting and blackmarketeering in relation to foodstuffs, illegal fishing and killing of birds and land animals, trafficking in humans and in valued commodities such as water and food, and carbon emission trading fraud. A bifurcation of crime will occur. The rich and powerful will use their resources to dump toxic and radioactive waste on the lands of the less powerful, and to build up their carbon credits by exploiting the financial hardships of others. Crimes of the less powerful will be crimes of desperation generated by falls in rainfall, failure of crops and subsistence concerns. Child soldiers and armed gangs will flourish in conditions of welfare collapse or non-existent government support. People will flee and be criminalised for seeking asylum; others will stay, to fight for dwindling resources in their part of the world. Communities will be pitted against one another, and industries against communities. Law and order will be increasingly difficult to maintain, much less enforce in other than repressive ways.

Understanding the complexities of environmental issues is an important step in forging a transnational value system protective of specific biospheres, non-human animals and human interests. A number of specific environmental offences are linked to the phenomenon of global warming. As the consequences of global warming manifest in significant climate changes, there will be various associated offences, some of which will be seriously criminal in nature. Examples of each of these are presented in Table 3.4.

Table 3.4 Transnational environmental crime and climate change

Environmental offences

Subject of offence	Nature of offence
Forestry	Illegal felling of trees
Air pollution	Emissions of dark smoke
Industrial pollution	Unlicensed pollution
Illegal land clearance	Destruction of habitat and forests
Clearing native vegetation	Reducing biotic mass

Associated offences

Subject of offence	Nature of offence
Public order offences	Food riots
Eco-terrorism	Arson, tree spiking
Trafficking	Migration and people smuggling
Violent offences	Homicide, gang warfare
Carbon trading	Fraud

Public policy and governmental action on climate change ultimately need to address the causal foundations of global warming rather than attempting to just deal with managing the symptoms (Lynch and Stretesky 2010). If the latter course of action is taken, then the tendency will be towards controlling people and repression of conflict, rather than empowering people and getting to the nub of the underlying problem.

The ambiguous nature of public policy and different responses to climate change are revealed in other ways as well. Even though not necessarily explicitly concerned with either crime or ecology, various policy responses to climate change may well exacerbate environmental problems and generate further forms of social deviance.

Paradoxical harms

For instance, solutions to the problems associated with climate change are generating new forms of social and environmental harm. I refer to this group of harms as *paradoxical harm*. This is harm that arises out of an apparent contradiction (for instance, we have to pollute certain parts of the planet in order to save it from other types of pollution). Specific examples of paradoxical harm include the adoption of compact fluorescent light globes to save energy (but which contain toxic mercury), promotion of nuclear energy (but which involves disposal of nuclear waste), and carbon emission storage (that penetrates and despoils the subterranean depths of land and sea). Such harm is paradoxical precisely because the harm stems from the pursuit of sectional social interests that inevitably fashion responses to, rather than resolution of, the key contradictions of the present age (namely, preservation of the capitalist growth economy versus transformation towards sustainable ecology).

Paradoxical harm is not the same as unintended consequences. In many instances the harms are known, and the acts leading to the generation of the harms are intentional. The harm is paradoxical in the sense that while seemingly contradictory (we generate harms as a means to forestall other harms), it is perfectly logical from the point of view of the imperatives of the system as a whole. Economic and social interventions that sustain the status quo (in favour of hegemonic nation states and the leading transnational corporations, and that include maintaining the viability of 'dirty' industries) are favoured over those that might tackle the key drivers of climate change and that could diminish the burgeoning threats to ecological sustainability worldwide. Universal human interests are thus superseded by pursuit of specific sectional interests, to the detriment of all (White 2007). While this happens by design, there is no grand plan. It is an outcome of a global system of production and consumption that is fundamentally premised upon private profit and narrow self-interest. The triumph of neo-liberalism is simultaneously the death knell of collective well-being. This, too, is the lynchpin of contemporary class struggles occurring around the globe.

The problem of global warming is complex and entails many different factors and elements. It involves stratospheric ozone depletion, and deforestation, through to air pollution associated with urban life and certain forms of agricultural production (United Nations Environment Programme 2007). So, too, responding to climate change and global warming entails many different types of intervention – that have the potential to create paradoxical harms.

Greenhouse gas emissions and food production

Changes in climatic conditions are putting new and additional pressures on existing global food stocks. One response by governments and agribusiness has been to foster ever greater reliance upon large-scale agricultural techniques and methods, and on new technologies such as the use of genetically modified organisms (GMOs). This has involved converting land to industrial forms of agricultural production, and the application of practical restrictions on what is being grown and how. These, in turn, have implications for both climate change and human well-being.

The reduction of biodiversity associated with contemporary agricultural practices (see Chapter 4) itself feeds into the larger pattern of climate change (see United Nations Environment Programme 2007). One way in which this happens is through adoption of types of food production that, in turn, lead to increases in carbon emissions.

Consider for example food production in New Zealand, which is heavily dependent on international trade, with exports contributing 29 per cent of gross domestic product and natural resource-based exports (from agriculture, forestry, fishing and aquaculture) accounting for a large share (Organisation for Economic Cooperation and Development (OECD) 2007: 1). Indeed, the relatively recent history of New Zealand (the past 200 years) is a history of remarkable transformations in land use. While 80 per cent of Aotearoa New Zealand was once forested, only about 20 per cent of indigenous forest cover now remains – that is, only 22 per cent of the land surface of the indigenous habitat remains in more or less primary condition (Conservation International 2007). Moreover, 'Land use analysis shows a net loss of nearly 175 km² of indigenous habitat between 1996 and 2002' (OECD 2007: 5). In many cases this land clearance has occurred without proper permits and resource consents (i.e. it has occurred through commission of an environmental offence rather than through formal channels).

Transformations in land use are directly linked to export earnings. The emphasis and reliance upon certain types of export earnings have a number of consequences. For instance, pollution and degradation are directly linked to the economically productive use of land. Such issues are particularly central to discussion of environmental harm in the New Zealand context. They are also associated with both past practices and contemporary realities. For example, just over 39 per cent of New Zealand's total land cover is pasture, and it is from within the pastoral industry that we see the main environmental problems surfacing.

The New Zealand Ministry for the Environment has observed that:

Recent trends in land use in New Zealand include an increase in intensive pastoral land use (for example, higher stocking rates, increased use of fertilisers and agricultural chemicals, and increases in irrigation use). ... by 2006, dairy cow and deer numbers had increased to just over 5.2 million and 1.5 million respectively. Between 1996 and 2006, the national dairy herd grew by 24 per cent.

(New Zealand Ministry for the Environment 2007: 40)

The amount of nitrogen fertiliser used in New Zealand has increased about ten-fold since 1985 and had doubled since the mid-1990s. Nitrogen from livestock manure, which contributes around five times the amount of nitrogen to the land as nitrogenous fertilisers, also steadily increased. These changes coincide with the trend towards more intensive forms of farming; particularly dairy farming, with its high density of grazing stock. Dairy cows excrete almost seven times the amount of nitrogen and phosphorus in their faeces and urine as breeding ewes, and around three-and-a-half times that of breeding hinds (deer).

(New Zealand Ministry for the Environment 2007: 42)

The combination of the sheer number of animals and the use of nitrogen fertilisers is having a major negative impact on the surrounding environments. Indeed, dairy farming has been identified as the single largest cause of environmental decline in New Zealand, due to fertiliser and animal waste run-off from farms, and the use of water itself (Scoop Independent News 2008). This is placing severe demands on New Zealand's natural resources, some of which are being used unsustainably. Irrigation in arid regions, cow dung and urine that affect nitrates in groundwater, and sewage discharge into freshwater lakes are all issues of concern, as noted in an OECD report on environmental performance:

Water quality in rivers and lakes has declined in regions dominated by pastoral farming, where high nutrient inputs and microbiological contamination destabilise natural ecosystems and pose risks to human health. In lowland areas, surface waters regularly exceed national water quality guidelines, and consequent damage to aquatic ecosystems is widespread, mainly due to run-off and leaching from pastoral farming and rural septic tanks.

(OECD 2007: 3)

The same report notes that:

In contrast to many OECD countries, GHG [greenhouse gas] emissions from agriculture (e.g., methane and nitrous oxide) account for some 50% of the national total, and are rising. Changes in agricultural production have led to increased intensity of inputs, including fertiliser and irrigation water, with consequent increases in environmental pressures.

(OECD 2007: 7)

Things are hardly likely to get better vis-à-vis good environmental practices and outcomes in the near future. This is so for several reasons. First, there is a huge export market for agricultural and pastoral commodities. The global situation in regards to grain, for example, and more generally the scarcities associated with certain foods, means that profit is to be made and farmers (and their political fellow travellers) will be keen to secure as much return as possible in such circumstances. Intensification of production, that also includes the extensive use of fertilisers, is one by-product of the global pressures on food production. As the worldwide competition over resources intensifies, so too will forms of food production that most readily contribute to global warming.

Moreover, there is the related issue of how to maintain resilient ecosystems in the face of pressures associated with climate change and inappropriate land uses by humans. 'Biodiversity brings resilience to ecosystems by spreading risk and making ecosystems more able to reorganise and adapt after change and disturbance. Ecosystems are particularly resilient if there are many species contributing to the same service' (Victoria Government 2009). Responding to climate change thus involves efforts to protect and maintain biodiversity. Feeding the world through forms of production that reduce biodiversity is, ultimately, counterproductive and a generator of social and environmental harm (as further demonstrated in Chapter 4).

Carbon emissions and energy demands

Paradoxical harms stemming from climate-related energy issues can be analysed in terms of the use of alternative energy sources (see Chapter 5), and efforts aimed at dealing with carbon emissions. In each case the answer to the energy crisis involves measures that in some way contribute to other types of environmental harm. The consequences for humans, local environments and non-human species are in some cases unknown, and certainly demand consideration of the precautionary principle.

Measures to deal with climate change through development of new energy sources and restriction or regulation of carbon emissions are best understood in the context of unequal trading relations between countries. From a world systems perspective, there is an energy rift between regions resulting from unequal energy flows between the producers and users of resources. Such analysis is based upon significant social, economic and military differences between metropole (e.g. US, Japan, Germany, UK, France), semi-periphery (e.g. Russia, Brazil, Mexico, China) and periphery (e.g. Bolivia, Haiti, Zimbabwe, India) countries (see Baer and Singer 2009).

For example, in the period 1860 to the Second World War, research has found that both developed and less developed countries were almost self-sufficient in energy – this changes in the 1950s as the less developed countries began exporting energy to the developed core countries that were beginning to consume more than they produced (Lawrence 2009). Not surprisingly, less developed countries (dependent upon foreign investment in manufacturing) have been found to emit higher levels of per capita noxious gases, and the total carbon dioxide emissions and emissions per unit of production are higher than in the core countries. Nonetheless, the core's usages remain far disproportionate to its population. 'In 2005, its percentage of total world energy use was 61.2 percent and in 2004 CO_2 emissions were 60.4 percent, yet its population was only 21.5 percent of the world total' (Lawrence 2009: 348).

Stretesky and Lynch (2009) argue that on the basis of analysis of carbon emissions and consumer imports to the United States, it is US consumer demand that is fuelling harmful production practices in other importing countries.

> ... the effort of core nations to shift costs and product toward nations where labor costs are lower and raw material and energy resources are less expensive and less well regulated creates the appearance that peripheral nations contribute to escalating levels of carbon pollution. Behind this appearance lays a more complex function where CO_2 pollution increases are fuelled by the consumption practices and economic interests of core nations. Moreover, among all nations, the U.S. stands out for its impact on the expansion of the level of CO_2 pollution among peripheral and rapidly industrializing nations.
>
> (Stretesky and Lynch 2009: 246)

The authors examined the relationship between per capita carbon dioxide emissions and exports for 169 countries. The data suggest that consumption practices in the United States are partially responsible for elevated per capita carbon dioxide emissions in other nations, and that carbon dioxide trends in other nations are in part driven by US demands for goods. US consumers, however, are unaware of how their consumption fuels rising global carbon emissions, because of the disconnection or dissociation between the two phenomena.

Much public debate has occurred over the regulation and reduction of carbon emissions. At the heart of the matter is the fact that carbon emissions are directly contributing to global warming, and that without adequate mitigation and adaptation strategies the problems associated with climate change will get worse before they get better. The urgency surrounding the reining in of carbon emissions has been matched by the audacity of businesses in lobbying to defend their specific economic interests.

Insofar as one of the key proposed solutions to global warming is carbon emission trading, and the sequestration of carbon emissions (in the form of carbon emission storage, as well as through protection of the world's tropical and other old-growth forests), the introduction of a wide range of regulatory sanctions is inevitable. One issue of concern is the tendency for many businesses to either publicly pronounce their green credentials with little evidence, or to exaggerate the potential threats to their industry or business as a result of specific government policies (such as carbon reduction schemes). In either case, there is an element of green washing and basic dishonesty. Such corporate misconduct may be misleading, and may constitute a form of fraud. Responding to climate change in this instance revolves basically around the sentiment and public atmosphere created by businesses which unscrupulously portray their interests in ways that, one way or another, undermine a stronger regulatory environment vis-à-vis carbon emissions.

Given the vested interests involved in protecting and maintaining existing interstate inequalities, as well as those associated with particular industries (such as oil and coal), the critiques of carbon emissions trading schemes, in practice, are predictable. As much as anything carbon emission trading favours the polluter and the practice of polluting (Shiva 2008). For example, the European Union's Emission Trading Scheme has been criticised because it sets lax national emission targets, encourages and grants the right to pollute, and encourages the export of the problem from rich to poor countries. The cap on carbon dioxide emissions was so lenient that the price on carbon dioxide drastically decreased, thus eliminating the incentive to reduce emissions (see Baer and Singer 2009).

Critiques of carbon offsetting make similar points and ask similar questions. For instance, it is hard to calculate how much carbon dioxide is being absorbed in tree planting projects and how quickly it will be absorbed from the atmosphere (Baer and Singer 2009). More generally, it is hard to know what is actually being planted if the offset is halfway around the world in a poor country. In the end, carbon offsetting has also been criticised for not encouraging a change in consumption practices since it implies that the problem is being offset by the measure. It is also associated with various forms of carbon colonisation which involve displacing local peoples off their lands as part of carbon credit schemes (see Chapter 7).

Given the rationale behind carbon emission trading schemes, it is legitimate to consider alternative policy options to these (such as prohibition and restriction strategies) as broad responses to climate change. If, however, governments persist with baseline and credit schemes, and cap and trade schemes, then analysis needs to identify and consider the specific kinds of fraud associated with emissions trading schemes and associated activities.

Description of developments relating to food production and energy production reveal a series of paradoxical harms that are generated in the context of strategic decisions regarding how production (and consumption) are to take place. When it comes to food the key issues are shortages, unequal distribution globally and emerging social conflict. In responding to these, however, measures involving further industrialisation of agricultural and pastoral production and the adoption of biotechnologies are contributing to greenhouse gases, pollution, and loss of habitat and biodiversity. When it comes to energy, again there are problems relating to shortages (relating especially to peak oil), global unequal distribution and expanding demand. However, poor regulation of carbon emissions, and reliance upon biofuels and other new technologies, is likewise contributing to global warming, as well as transferring problems to the poorer countries and adding additional forms of toxic pollution into the equation.

Conclusion

The pressing issue today is that of climate change. As will be seen in the next couple of chapters, it is a feature that touches all aspects of contemporary social life. The future of humanity is inextricably linked to climate change and global warming. The future of many other species and particular ecosystems is likewise bound up with climate change. To speak of the future of criminology, of eco-global criminology and of academia itself is to imply that that there is a liveable future that lies ahead of us. This may not be so.

Climate change is a problem that is global in nature, yet has localised impacts as well. Environmental effects will be both universal, affecting everyone on the planet, and particular, affecting vulnerable population groups more than others. The divides between North and South, geographically and metaphorically, will deepen as crises related to food production and distribution, energy sources and pollution, and changing climates reorder the old world order. Social inequality and environmental injustice will be the source of continuous conflict for many years to come, as the most dispossessed and marginalised of the world's population suffer the brunt of food shortages, undrinkable water, climate-induced migration and general hardship in day-to-day living. Women will suffer more than men, people of colour more than the non-Indigenous and the non-migrant, and the young and the elderly more than the adult.

Eco-global criminology can provide a sounding board for critical reflection on the dynamics of social change associated with climate change. This is also where, in particular, the use of horizon scanning may be especially useful and important. The world is changing so rapidly and events are occurring so quickly that strategic thinking is required more than ever. We need to anticipate the expected and to be prepared for the unknown. We need to put progressive values to the fore before (and as) panic and repression gain sway. To do otherwise is to risk civilisation as we know it, and moral decency as it should be expressed.

The recent floods in Pakistan provide a terrible vision of what the future holds for many around the world today as temperatures rise and climates do, indeed, alter local landscapes and people's lives in a radical way. The challenges are there, whether we like it or not, and the relevance of criminology in general very much depends upon how criminologists respond to these challenges. For eco-global criminology, the present marks only the start of a long period of ecological, social, economic and political turbulence for which we are only now beginning to prepare.

4 Biodiversity

Introduction

The loss of biodiversity in all three of its main components – genes, species and ecosystems – continues at a rapid pace today and the five principal pressures directly driving biodiversity loss (habitat change, overexploitation, pollution, invasive alien species and climate change) are either constant or increasing in intensity (Secretariat of the Convention on Biological Diversity 2010). This chapter explores the links between threats to biodiversity and the perpetration of a variety of transnational environmental crimes and harms. The overall situation is not good. One task of eco-global criminology is to explore the reasons why this is the case.

Biodiversity is generally defined as the variety of all species on earth. It refers to the different plants, animals and micro-organisms, and their genes, that together make up life on the planet. It also includes reference to the terrestrial (land), marine (ocean) and freshwater (inland water systems) ecosystems of which they are a part.

In recent years criminologists have begun to give concerted and detailed attention to questions relating to animal and plant life. This work has been motivated by either a concern with species justice or an interest in conventional environmental crimes such as illegal fishing. For instance, work over the past decade has been carried out in respect to:

- genetically modified organisms (GMO) and the abrogation of human rights and United Nations agreements in attempts to impose GMO crops on reluctant nation states (Walters 2004, 2005);
- deforestation and the devastation to plant, animal and human welfare and rights that has accompanied this process (Boekhout van Solinge 2008a, 2008b, 2010; Halsey 2005; Green *et al.* 2007);
- the illegal theft and trade in reptiles in South Africa (Herbig 2010);
- fishing-related crimes, including the poaching of abalone and of lobster (Tailby and Gant 2002; McMullan and Perrier 2002);
- animal abuse that involves both systemic uses of animals, such as factory farming, and one-on-one abuses of animals (Beirne 2009; Sollund 2008);

- crime prevention and the illicit trade in endangered species involving many different kinds of animals (Wellsmith 2010; Schneider 2008);
- the illegal wildlife market in Africa (Warchol *et al.* 2003), and in particular the trade in elephant ivory (Lemieux and Clarke 2009).

This particular interest in environmental crime has generally involved engagement with activities and circumstances that span many parts of the globe. In part this is because the producers and consumers, the markets and the institutions of world trade (both legal and illegal) are linked together in complex chains of transference that can involve quite sophisticated relationships. The transnational nature of environmental crime is well established in and through such studies. For much of this burgeoning literature the key or central category of analysis is that of legality rather than harm. If the latter, then 'harm' itself is generally constructed in relation to the specific species or the human community at hand.

In addition to conventional and green criminology definitions of (transnational) environmental crime, another way in which eco-global criminology attempts to interpret issues is through the employment of ecological concepts. For the purposes of this chapter, this involves consideration of biodiversity as the main frame of reference rather than, for example, wildlife theft.

Biodiversity

With biodiversity, the key ecological message appears to be 'the more the merrier' – the greater the number of species the greater the resilience of the system as a whole to potential catastrophe, whether this is fire, drought or climate change. Any particular ecosystem is made up of both abiotic components (air, water, soils, atoms and molecules) and biotic components (plants, animals, bacteria and fungi). Changes to an ecosystem through human intervention may occur through manipulation, contamination or destruction of these components (for example, through mining or land clearance or use of pesticides), although it is not only human intervention that can lead to change (for example, the spread of invasive species can transform local ecologies).

There are many international instruments that speak to matters pertaining to the protection of biodiversity (see Table 4.1).

The protection, maintenance and extension of biodiversity are important in ecological terms. Such concerns are also reflected within criminological circles in the form of research and law enforcement (especially Interpol) efforts relating to trade in endangered species. As one of the key international instruments of relevance to criminology, the Convention on International Trade in Endangered Species of Wild Fauna and Flora (CITES) has the aim of ensuring that international trade in specimens of wild animals and plants does not threaten their survival. CITES works by subjecting international trade in specimens of listed species to certain controls, based upon where the roughly 5,000 species of animals and 28,000 species of plants are situated in the three Appendices to the

Table 4.1 Selected international agreements protecting species

---

International Convention for the Protection of Birds (1950) protects birds in their wild state, considering that in the interests of science, the protection of nature and the economy of each nation, all birds should as a matter of principle be protected.

International Convention for the Protection of New Varieties of Plants (1961) recognises and protects the rights of breeders of new varieties of plants and their successors in title, and to do so in a harmonised way.

Convention on Wetlands of International Importance Especially as Waterfowl Habitat (1971), also known as the Ramsar Convention, brings together the protection of birds and the preservation of wetlands. States party to the agreement must designate at least one wetland within their territory that they agree to safeguard from human encroachment.

Convention on International Trade in Endangered Species of Wild Fauna and Flora (CITES) (1973) focuses on protecting endangered species through limiting trade, since it is often demand in one part of the world that impacts on conservation status in another part of the world.

Agreement of the Conservation of Polar Bears (1973) achieves protection of the polar bear as a significant resource of the Arctic region through further conservation and management measures.

Convention on the Conservation of Migratory Species (1979) (also known as CMS or the Bonn Convention) aims to conserve terrestrial, marine and avian migratory species throughout their range. CMS is differentiated from CITES by its focus on naturally migrating species rather than species moved internationally by human trade.

Convention on the Conservation of Antarctic Marine Living Resources (CCAMLR) (1980) has as its goal to ensure that the marine resources of the Antarctic are used sustainably so that they can continue to be harvested indefinitely.

Convention on Biological Diversity (CBD) (1992) focuses on the whole of biodiversity conservation, the idea that it is the diversity of species and genetic material that must be protected rather than specific species or locations.

The Cartagena Protocol on Biosafety (2000) focuses on avoidance of possible harms from genetic modification of organisms and the export of living modified organisms.

The Convention on Fishing and Conservation of Living Resources of the High Seas (short title Marine Life Conservation) (1958) encourages international cooperation to solve the problems involved in the conservation of living resources of the high seas, considering that because of the development of modern technology some of these resources are in danger of being overexploited.

The International Convention for the Regulation of Whaling (1946) aims to protect all species of whales from overhunting; to establish a system of international regulation for the whale fisheries to ensure proper conservation and development of whale stocks; and to safeguard for future generations the great natural resources represented by whale stocks.

Convention that reflect the extent of the threat to it, and the controls that apply to the trade.

Appendix I

This contains about 800 species that are deemed to be threatened with extinction and are or may be affected by trade. Trade in wild-caught specimens of these species is illegal (permitted only in exceptional licensed circumstances) (e.g. the red panda, gorilla, tigers, Asian elephant).

Appendix II

This contains about 32,500 species that are deemed not necessarily threatened with extinction, but may become so unless trade in specimens of such species is subject to strict regulation in order to avoid utilisation incompatible with their survival. International trade in these specimens may be authorised by the granting of an export permit or re-export certificate (e.g. American black bear, African grey parrot, bigleaf mahogany).

Appendix III

This contains about 170 species that are listed after one member country has asked other CITES parties for assistance in controlling trade in a species. Trade in these species is only permitted with an appropriate export permit and a certificate of origin (e.g. two-toed sloth, African civet, alligator snapping turtle).

The legal and ecological importance of intervention around threatened and endangered species is evident in the sheer scale of this environmental crime. For example, it has been estimated that in the early 1990s:

> ... the value of legally traded wildlife products was US$160 billion per annum, legal wood exports were worth US$132 billion, and legal seafood exports were valued at US$50 billion. The value of the illegal trade in wildlife products is harder to estimate, but is likely to be worth between US$10 and US$20 billion per year, second only to the international drugs trade in the ranks of illegal exchange.
>
> (Duffy 2010: 9–10)

Others likewise observe that the illegal harvest, shipment and sale of protected animals and plants has been estimated to follow only the illicit drugs and arms trades in overall commercial value. In the specific area of illegal wildlife trade it has been noted that the extent of exploitation is driving many species to the brink of extinction (see, for example, the websites for Traffic, the International Fund for Animal Welfare, World Wide Fund for Nature, Humane Society International and similar organisations). Thus, there is lots of money to be made, but the consequences are devastating from the point of view of biodiversity and overall ecological resilience on a world scale.

Reduction in species includes both animals and plants. With regard to the latter, for example, it has been observed that every year some 10 million hectares of forest are destroyed, that industrial timber exports total around US$150 billion per year, and that estimates are that illegal logging accounts for about 25 per cent of removals worldwide (Setiono 2007: 27). Much of the illegal logging necessarily involves the involvement of corrupt government officials, including law enforcement officers, as well as banks and financial backers, and business people who import timber or wood-based products. Bribery and 'goodwill' payments, smuggling, illicit trafficking, money laundering and forging of documents are all part of the illegal logging industry (Setiono 2007).

Deforestation is not only due to logging, however. Land clearance is also due to agricultural exploitation (as discussed in greater depth below), cattle farming, mining, oil and gas installations, and hydroelectric dams (see Boekhout van Solinge 2008a and b, 2010; Khagram 2004). There is also the phenomenon of 'conflict timber', associated with west Africa, for example, in which deforestation is linked to the funding of civil wars and armed conflicts (Boekhout van Solinge 2008a).

The ecological impact of logging and land clearance is thus something that transcends the legal–illegal divide insofar as vast amounts of forest are subject to destruction in many different locations – from Peru and Brazil, and Liberia and Sierra Leone, to Indonesia and Australia. The purposes and motivations may vary, depending upon the social context and industry interests, but the result is further depletion of many different kinds of trees and varieties of forests.

The concern of eco-global criminology is not just with legality, since many of the most damaging environmental activities are legal or have yet to be criminalised. Nor is it with conservation as such, since the quality of life for species-level and individual animals, for example, is also of concern, as expressed in the notion of species justice (White 2008a). It is this wider conception of harm that marks off eco-global criminology from both mainstream criminology that deals with environmental issues (see Wellsmith 2010) and 'conservation criminology' as variously conceptualised (Herbig and Joubert 2006; Gibbs *et al.* 2010a).

Moreover, given the emphasis on ecological constructions of well-being and harm, a further feature of eco-global criminology is the importance attached to big picture constructions of the issues – for instance, consideration of illegal trade in endangered species within the context of, and as only one contributing factor towards, loss of biodiversity. Accordingly, the concern is with not only traditional criminological concerns with illegal activity or with nature as an exploitable resource, but also those harms arising from both legal and illegal human interventions. Some of these interventions are explored in the following sections.

Biodiversity and plants

Many different forces and factors are involved in potential biodiversity loss in relation to plants. For example, bioprospecting (the worldwide search for plants with special properties, such as for medicinal use) that is unregulated and inappropriate can be considered a form of overexploitation which has the potential to degrade ecosystems and increase biodiversity loss, as well as impacting on the rights of the communities and states from which the resources are taken (see, for example, Mgbeoji 2006). Probably the biggest single threats to biodiversity are those associated with contemporary agricultural methods and climate change.

Biodiversity and agriculture

The corporatisation of agriculture has been accompanied by significant changes in land use. For example, there has been a major expansion in cropland worldwide. 'Viewed in a wider historical context, more land was converted to cropland in the 30 years after 1950, than in the 150 years between 1700 and 1850' (UNEP 2007: 86). The environmental impact is loss of habitat and biodiversity; soil water retention and regulation; disturbance of biological cycle; increases in soil erosion, nutrient depletion, salinity and eutrophication. For humans, there is greater exposure to agrochemicals in air, soil and water.

In addition to the corporatisation of agriculture, food production is increasingly influenced by localised changes in biodiversity, and by the overarching effect of global warming. Climate change is altering the physical and biological world in a number of ways. For instance, two-thirds of the North Sea's fish species have shifted in both latitude and depth (BioSecurity New Zealand 2006). This example signals a more general issue, namely, a large-scale shift in plant and animal species that is invasive to the endemic or native population of particular geographical areas (see Secretariat of the Convention on Biological Diversity 2010). Simultaneously, local species may be placed under threat due to changes in temperature, moisture, wind and carbon dioxide that may diminish their ability to withstand hitherto familiar pathogens, much less competing species newly invading their spaces.

The threats to biodiversity are many, and profound. They have major ramifications for food production now and into the future. Particular threats to biodiversity in the Western Cape of South Africa, for example, include: population growth; pollution (industrial emissions that cause acid rain); global climate change (the greenhouse effect and destruction of the ozone layer); habitat destruction (burning or felling of old-growth forests); overexploitation of natural resources (illegal trade of fauna and flora); and invasion of introduced species (NatureCape 2010). Research has claimed that the risk of extinction for many species may have been underestimated (McGrath 2008), a situation likely to be made worse by the consequences of climate change (Secretariat of the Convention on Biological Diversity 2010). Moreover, as local climates and temperatures change, greater pressure will be placed on local environments as local producers convert land to industrial uses (e.g. agriculture, forestry and pastureland) in response to phenomena such as desertification (United Nations Development Programme 2010).

Ironically, one of the greatest threats to biodiversity is in fact the industrialisation of agriculture (incorporating the use of seed and other patents) since this is one of the greatest causes of erosion of plant genetic and species diversity. The basic means of life of humans is being reconstituted and reorganised through global systems of production (Croall 2007: 206) and in many cases we still do not know the longer-term effects of new developments in the food area.

As discussed in Chapter 3, changes in climatic conditions are putting new and additional pressures on existing global food stocks. One response by governments and agribusiness has been to foster ever greater reliance upon large-scale agricultural techniques and methods, and on new technologies such as the use of genetically modified organisms (GMOs). GMOs are the by-product of splicing genes from one species into the DNA of another. According to New Zealand's Royal Commission on Genetic Modification (quoted in Walters 2004: 152), genetic modification can be defined as the use of genetic engineering techniques in a laboratory that involves:

- the deletion, multiplication, modification, or moving of genes within a living organism; or
- the transfer of genes from one organism to another; or
- the modification of existing genes or the construction of novel genes and their incorporation in any organism; or
- the utilisation of subsequent generations or offspring of organisms modified by any of the activities described above.

The application of GM technologies to food production is perhaps one of the most publicly recognised, and fear-inspiring, uses of such technology. Countries that have been reluctant to adopt GM crops have been subjected to intense pressures to do so.

The turn towards use of GMO crops has involved converting land to industrial forms of agricultural production, and the application of practical restrictions on what is being grown and how. These, in turn, have implications for biodiversity.

As stated above, the use of genetic modification technologies in food production is perhaps one of the most publicly recognised and feared responses to world hunger. One consequence of the industrialisation of agriculture, combined with and intensified by application of GMO technology, is that biodiversity is systematically reduced.

> Today, a mere four crops account for two-thirds of the calories humans eat. When you consider that humankind has historically consumed some 80,000 edible species, and that 3,000 of these have been in widespread use, this represents a radical simplification of the food web.
>
> (Pollen 2007: 47).

It has been estimated that 75 per cent of crop diversity has been lost over the past century (French 2000: 61). In other words, there is a tendency towards monoculture, since uniformity means ease of cultivation and harvest, and higher yield, which translates into higher profit.

This simplification of production generates paradoxical harm from the point of view of biodiversity and potential threats to future food production. That is, to feed the world (at least in this scenario) means depleting the genetic plant pool and prioritising certain species over others, and this, in turn, creates further problems.

> One consequence of the erosion of plant genetic diversity is that the capacity of the economically preferred plants to resist pests and diseases is compromised. The marketability of plant produce is not necessarily coterminous with the inherent superior quality of the plants to be marketed or selected for mono-cropping. Given the potential utility of plants that market forces may erroneously dismiss as economically useless, the short-sighted depletion of the plant genetic pool can be both costly and dramatic.
>
> (Mgbeoji 2006: 181)

Put simply, 'over the ages farmers have relied upon diverse crop varieties as protection from pests, blights and other forms of crop failure' (French 2000: 61). Reducing this diversity affects the inbuilt mechanisms that helped to protect the soil and the vitality of the overall agricultural process. Moreover, intensive use of land and soils that rely upon chemical additives to ensure productivity, rather than for example traditional methods of crop rotation, further diminishes longer-term agricultural viability. Contemporary farming practices that feature biodiverse fields (based upon up to 12 different types of seed crops) have been found not only to be more resilient to frost, drought and variations in rainfall, but also to produce more food and cash earnings than that of corn monoculture (Shiva 2008). Diversity is strength.

Ironically, given their social impact, the gaining popularity of biofuels has been used to legitimate the further spread of genetically modified crops. GMO soy, for example, has been touted as perfect for biofuel.

Biodiversity and biofuels

Indeed, the push towards biofuel production reflects the interests of large agricultural businesses, who can patent the monocultural crops designed as 'energy crops'. Powerful interests, including car manufacturers and grain farmers, have benefited from the search for energy alternatives to fossil fuels. The shift to biofuel is seen as a key source of green fuel supply for the world's car manufacturers. Greater demand for biofuel crops such as corn, palm oil or soya also means that farmers are finding the growing of such crops very lucrative economically. The hybrid car is the flavour of the month for all concerned.

However, the trend towards biofuel is generating its own paradoxical harms (see Chapter 3). First, the use of crops for fuel is leading to food price rises and food shortages (Mitchell 2008). This was made evident, for example, when Mexicans protested in the streets about the price of cornflour that is used to make tortillas; a situation brought about by US corn growers selling an increasing portion of their harvest for the purpose of making corn-based ethanol (a diesel-type fuel made from plants). Less corn for food equals higher food prices.

Second, the profitability of biofuel production is leading to the establishment of large-scale plantations in places such as Indonesia and Brazil. This process has seen the clearing of rainforests and in some instances the forcing of Indigenous people off their lands. This deforestation process has been going on for a number of years, and has been supported by organisations such as the International Monetary Fund. Clearing of land for export-oriented cash crops has been touted as a key strategy to lift developing countries' economic performance (see French 2000). Biofuels provide yet another avenue to accelerate this process. Cutting down trees also, of course, has a direct bearing on global warming. It has been estimated that by 2022, biofuel plantations could destroy 98 per cent of Indonesia's rainforests and that 'Every ton of palm oil used as biofuel releases 30 tons of CO_2 into the atmosphere, ten times as much as petroleum does' (Shiva 2008: 79).

Third, there is evidence that the nitrogen-based fertiliser used in corn production is causing environmental harm in its own right. Millions of kilograms/pounds of those nitrates end up in the Gulf of Mexico each year, where it is causing a massive algae bloom. This bloom impacts negatively on the ecology of the Gulf:

> When the algae dies it sinks to the bottom, where it absorbs oxygen as it decays. In recent years that oxygen depletion has created an aquatic 'dead zone' covering about 8,000 square miles in which shrimp, fish, oysters and crabs cannot survive.
>
> (Reliable Plant 2007)

Biodiversity is lessened due to the replacement of food crops, and a diversity of food crops, with monoculture designed for an export market (e.g. Argentina and soybeans). Moreover, the intensive use of Roundup (the brand name of a systemic, broad-spectrum herbicide produced by Monsanto) tends to make the earth sterile by destroying the microbial flora essential for soil fertility, and the disappearance of certain bacteria makes the earth inert (see Robin 2010: 265). Biofuels are thus not quite the panacea to environmental and energy crises that some supporters claim.

Maize for biofuels accounted for 25 per cent of US production in the 2007/08 crop year, and the use of global vegetable oil supplies for biodiesel production is on the increase:

The largest biodiesel producers were the European Union, the United States, Brazil and Indonesia, with a combined use of vegetable oils for biodiesel of about 9 million tons in 2007 compared to global vegetable oils production of 132 million tons ... The estimated increase in vegetable oils use for biodiesel was 6.6 million tons from 2004 to 2007, which would attribute 34 percent of the increase in global consumption to biodiesel.

(Mitchell 2008: 5)

Biofuel production in places such as the United States and the European Union is encouraged through strong incentives (e.g. tax credits) and mandates such as energy legislation (e.g. mandatory blending requirements). As indicated, the advent of biofuels has helped to push up global grain prices, and to bolster the prospects of the grain producing countries. It has, however, been accompanied by ecological costs in the form of degraded environments and social costs in the form of high prices for food, especially in less developed and import-dependent countries (Roberts 2008). It has also pushed up feedstock prices, thus affecting the pastoral industries as well as the agricultural.

According to some commentators (see Tilman *et al.* 2009; Rist *et al.* 2009), the search for beneficial biofuels should focus on feedstocks that:

* do not compete with food crops;
* do not lead to land clearing;
* offer real greenhouse gas reductions;
* maximise social benefits.

However, land, water and energy resources have effectively been put to the goal of producing biofuels rather than production of food for human consumption (Pimental *et al.* 2009). This is important insofar as, while it may seem beneficial to use renewable plant materials for biofuel as well as crop residues and other biomass, food and biofuels are dependent upon the same resources for production. Given the problems of biofuel production (including the release of large quantities of carbon dioxide associated with the planting and processing of plant materials for biofuels), and given that nearly 60 per cent of humans in the world are currently malnourished, the blunt conclusion is that 'There is simply not enough land, water, and energy to produce biofuels' (Pimental *et al.* 2009: 9).

Transnational environmental crime and plants

Some of the biggest problems with GMO and biofuel crops relate to poor regulation and the social justice impacts of their introduction on local communities. These have been noted by the affected communities themselves. For example, the use of terminator seed technology has been objected to by Indigenous people, such as a group of Indigenous farmers from Peru who filed a submission on their concerns to the Fourth Meeting of the Working Group of the International Convention on Biological Diversity of the UN Environment Programme in January 2006:

'Andean and Amazonian biodiversity, both domesticated and wild, is put at risk for contamination through gene flow from Terminator crops, and, as Terminator seeds would not be 100% sterile in the second generation, this risk is great' (quoted in Engdahl 2007: 297). GMO invasion of endemic species and crops is seen to be capable of destroying unique genotypes, thereby creating the potential for a threat to food security (i.e. diminishing diverse genetic material).

Such fears are not unfounded. Scientific study has reported two issues of concern: first, that genetic contamination is occurring; and second, that transgenes are unstable, meaning that once the GMO cross-pollinates with another plant, the transgene splits up and is inserted in an uncontrolled way – the displaced DNA could be creating utterly unpredictable effects (Robin 2010: 247). The potential size of the problem is considerable. Over the past decade the use of GMO crops has rapidly increased, for a number of reasons.

In 2007, transgenic crops (90 percent of which, it should be recalled, have genetic traits patented by Monsanto) covered about 250 million acres: more than half were located in the United States (136.5 million acres), followed by Argentina (45 million), Brazil (28.8 million), Canada (15.3 million), India (9.5 million), China (8.8 million), Paraguay (5 million), and South Africa (3.5 million).

(Robin 2010: 4)

Almost all of these crops were 'legally' planted, but the genetic and species consequences are potentially of a huge scale in terms of negative ecological impact.

What is also of especial concern, however, is those crops which have not been distributed through such means. For instance, traditional corn has been found to be contaminated in Mexico by GMO corn; this is despite the fact that in 1998 Mexico had declared a moratorium on transgenic corn crops in order to preserve the extraordinary biodiversity of the plant. As noted above, contamination is indeed occurring and crossing national boundaries. The way in which this is occurring has, however, directly criminological implications.

Indeed, the illegal sowing of GMO crops is a strategy, a successful one at that, for introducing it into formerly GMO-free zones. For example, in Paraguay, where (as of 2007) no law authorises the cultivation of GMOs, 'From 1996 to 2006, surfaces devoted to soybean cultivation went from less than 2.5 million acres to 5 million acres, an increase of 10 percent a year' (Robin 2010: 275). To avoid losing markets, by ensuring proper labelling of crops for markets such as the European Union, the Paraguayan government ended up simply legalising the illegal crops. Much the same thing happened in Brazil and Poland (Engdahl 2007), and for much the same reasons (namely EU rules on traceability and labelling of GM foods intended for human and animal consumption) (Robin 2010). Illegal smuggling of GMO seeds is lucrative for those wishing to promote particular industries and types of farming, much less for the companies that own the patents.

The spread of GMO seeds has also been associated with corruption of government officials and other types of crimes. Engdahl (2007: 269–70) states that:

> In Indonesia, Monsanto was forced to plead guilty to criminal charges of paying $50,000 in bribes to a senior Indonesian Government official to bypass controls on screening new genetically modified crops. Court records revealed that the bribe had been authorized in the US headquarters of Monsanto. Monsanto later was found guilty and forced to pay a fine.

The lucrative market for biofuels and GMO crops has been linked to the forced takeover of communal lands, using armed men and bulldozers, as well as fraudulent claims of land title (see Robin 2010). Moreover, given that the focus of the UN mechanism for Reducing Emissions from Deforestation and Forest Degradation (REDD) is on minimising carbon emissions caused by the destruction of living forest biomass, there will be greater pressures to convert or modify other ecosystems, especially savannahs and wetlands, for food or biofuel (Sutherland *et al.* 2009). In other words, forests are privileged over other types of ecosystems, and the result could well be the loss of biodiversity associated with destruction or conversion of these 'less valued' non-forested ecosystems. Again, compulsory takeover of such land is not uncommon.

Biodiversity and animals

The conversion of land for commercial purposes is relevant to the well-being and survival of animals too. For example, the native woodlands demolished for cash crops such as GMO soybeans in Argentina have a major impact on the habitats of animals such as pumas, jaguars, Andean cats and tapirs, which cannot live outside this particular ecosystem (Robin 2010: 271). Similar events are happening in places such as Indonesia, where deforestation is putting pressure on the Sumatran tiger and the orangutan (Boekhout van Solinge 2008b).

Simultaneously, GMO technologies are also being applied to animals, including fish, with potentially dire consequences. To put this into context it is useful to consider several other interrelated factors that are putting pressures on animal species around the world. One of these is the relationship between pollution and endangerment. For example, PCBs (polychlorinated biphenyl – a toxic persistent organic pollutant) have been found in whales, seals and polar bears, with sea mammals such as killer whales especially vulnerable and threatened with extinction caused by PCBs (Robin 2010). Building resilience is part of the agenda of GMO animal production. But this, in turn, can generate a 'Frankenstein effect' – the construction of superspecies that pose dangers to those around them. Shiva (2000), for example, tells the story of GMO fish which, as invasive species, have had a devastatingly negative impact on endemic fish species.

The point of technological inputs into animal production processes, whether this is through GMO genetic manipulation or through hormone injections, is to increase production. The emphasis on profits lends itself to a 'succeed at all costs' mentality that occasionally includes various immoral and criminal activities such as bribery and theft. In Canada, for example, a senate inquiry into the use of bovine growth hormone in milk production involved interviews with six Canadian government scientists who tried to stand up to pressure to approve a product they believed was unsafe. A local newspaper, the *Ottawa Citizen*, reported that:

> The senators sat dumbfounded as Dr. Margaret Haydon told of being in a meeting when officials from Monsanto, Inc., the drug's manufacturer, made an offer of between $1 million and $2 million to the scientists from Health Canada – an offer that she told senators could only have been interpreted as a bribe.
>
> (cited in Smith 2003: 77)

Dr Haydon also told the senators how notes and files critical of scientific data provided by Monsanto were stolen from a locked filing cabinet in her office (Smith 2003).

Wild and domestic animals

The question of what is 'native' and what is 'invasive' and the relationship between the two is a perennial one in zoology and animal studies. Attempts to categorise animals according to environment and/or human service are difficult to do well due to the complexities involved. Different criteria inevitably provide different ways in which to categorise different types of species (see O'Sullivan 2009; Herbig and Joubert 2006). While this method is not unproblematic, Table 4.2 provides an attempt to distinguish animals according to two main criteria (wildlife/domesticated), and within each of these categories according to how the animal is perceived relative to human needs (service to/service for).

Human intervention in the lives of both wild and domesticated animals has major ramifications for species survival and biodiversity. Consider for example the phenomenon of assisted colonisation, which involves the moving of species to sites where they do not currently occur or have not been known to occur in recent history. This is happening in response to climate change, and usually is directed at species in the wild. 'In the UK, two native species of butterfly were recently translocated approximately 65 km northward into areas identified by modelling as climatically suitable for occupancy by the butterflies' (Sutherland *et al.* 2009).

The problem is that non-native species moving into new ecosystems are already recognised as a major conservation problem (see Secretariat of the Convention on Biological Diversity 2010). This is evidenced, for example, by the rapid expansion in the numbers of Indo-Pacific lionfish along the east coast of the United States and in the Caribbean to the detriment of native coral reef fish (Sutherland *et al.* 2009). Assisted colonists could be viewed as invasive and

Table 4.2 Animal categories

Wildlife
- *Introduced wild*
  - o Invasive/pests (e.g. cane toad in Australia)
  - o Valued (e.g. trout in Tasmania)
  - o Ambiguous (e.g. camels and wild donkeys in central Australia)
- *Native species with a value of their own*
  - o Avian (e.g. kookaburras, cockatoos)
  - o Marine (e.g. whales, sharks)
  - o Aquatic (e.g. Murray river cod, marron)
  - o Terrestrial (e.g. koala, kangaroo)
- *Economic wild animals*
  - o Recreation (e.g. fish)
  - o Food (e.g. mutton birds)
  - o Eco-tourism (e.g. birdlife, crocodiles)
  - o Collectables (e.g. lizards, exotic fish)
- *Wild animals as threat/pest*
  - o to agriculture (e.g. kangaroos)
  - o to pastoral industry (e.g. dingos)
  - o to surfing/recreation (e.g. sharks)
  - o to angling (e.g. galaxia fish)

Domestic animals
- *Economic animals (humans doing something to them)*
  - o Farm animals (e.g. pigs, cows, chickens)
  - o Aquaculture animals (e.g. fish, prawns, oysters)
  - o Research animals (e.g. rats, mice)
  - o Exhibited animals (e.g. lions, tigers, bears)
- *Economic animals (animals doing something for humans)*
  - o Law enforcement (e.g. dogs)
  - o Industrial/transportation animals (e.g. oxen, horses)
  - o Recreation/racing/rodeos (e.g. horses, dogs)
  - o Performing animals/circuses (e.g. lions, monkeys)
- *Non-economic animals (other human purposes)*
  - o Companion animals (e.g. cats, dogs, exotic fish, rabbits)
  - o Hunting/sport companions (e.g. horses, dogs)

---

as constituting a potential danger to existing ecosystems and their inhabitants. Classic cases where considerable damage has resulted include the introduction of the cane toad into Australia. Its subsequent spread has had colossal impacts on native species. With no or few natural predators, it has proliferated and continues to take over more and more territories previously held by other endemic species.

Invasive species are not the only threat to animal biodiversity. So too is the corporatisation of animal production, as is evident in egg and poultry production, piggeries and cattle production.

> ... while Australia's 'beef' cows have traditionally been raised by small town farmers on vast grasslands, almost one-third now spend part of their

lives confined in feedlots owned by large corporations, where they can be efficiently fattened and prepared for market.

(Sharman 2009: 39)

What better way to make this efficient than to feed them GMO grains? The industrial processing of one species is thus (literally) feeding into the industrial processing of another. Meanwhile new industrial processes associated with fisheries are in their own way contributing to biodiversity loss. For example, the growth of aquaculture has been associated with the use of fish inputs that are more than the fish outputs (Shiva 2000).

Certainly a major area of governmental concern and criminological examination relates to issues pertaining to endangered species, usually referring to 'wild' animal species. The International Union for the Conservation of Nature categorisation of the status of species is provided in Table 4.3.

Various laws and agreements are in place to prevent the illegal trade in endangered species. Ironically, the focus on protection can in some situations make the threatened species even more attractive to criminal syndicates or private collectors, since it confirms the scarcity (and thus 'value') of the species in question.

The illegal trade in plants and wildlife not only involves transnational environmental crime but also threatens biodiversity more generally. The threat

Table 4.3 Survival status of species

Extinct: the last remaining member of the species has died, or is presumed beyond reasonable doubt to have died (e.g. thylacine, dodo, passenger pigeon)

Extinct in the wild: captive individuals survive, but there is no free-living, natural population (e.g. Alagoas curassow, dromedary)

Critically endangered: faces an extremely high risk of extinction in the immediate future (e.g. mountain gorilla, Javan rhino)

Endangered: faces a very high risk of extinction in the near future (e.g. blue whale, orangutan)

Vulnerable: faces a high risk of extinction in the medium term (e.g. polar bear, cheetah, komodo dragon)

Conservation dependent: not severely threatened but must depend on conservation programmes (e.g. spotted hyena, leopard shark)

Near threatened: may be considered threatened in the near future (e.g. tiger shark, blue-billed duck)

Least concern: no immediate threat of the survival of the species (e.g. wood pigeon, house mouse)

here is not only to endangered species directly but also to the economic viability of industries such as agriculture, forestry and fisheries.

> Illegal exports of wildlife and wildlife products from Australia pose a threat to the protection of endangered species. Illegal imports are accompanied by the potential for the introduction of pests and diseases which could have a dramatic impact on agriculture, conservation of the environment, and specialist industries, such as aviculture.
>
> (Halstead 1992: 1)

Thus, the smuggling of wildlife across national borders has the potential to threaten the viability of endangered species, whether flora or fauna, as well as to provide a potential vehicle for the introduction of pests and diseases into formerly unaffected areas (Herbig 2010).

Illegal trade is not the only threat to particular 'wild' animal species. The intense competition for food worldwide is also evident in the ways in which commercial fishing takes place. The issue here is not only that of biodiversity, but of wholesale destruction of major breeding grounds and fishing beds.

The greatest negative impact to the long-term sustainable management of global fisheries is a combination of illegal, unreported and unregulated (IUU) fishing (see Wilson and Tomkins 2007). IUU fishing may involve huge factory ships that operate on the high seas, and which process thousands of tons of fish at any one time. Alternatively, it may be organised around dozens of smaller vessels, each of which is contracted to provide a catch that ultimately brings reward to the originating contractor. In other words, such production can be organised according to the economies of scale (e.g. factory ships) or the economies of scope (e.g. small independent fishers). In each case, however, there is a link to legitimate markets (e.g. for abalone, for lobsters, for Patagonian toothfish) for the value of the commodity to be realised in dollar terms.

In each case, as well, the damage is manifest in phenomena such as overfishing and destruction of habitat that, in turn, affect subsequent market prices for the commodity in question. Scarcity is a major motivator for illegal as well as legal forays into particular kinds of harvesting and production activity.

Differences and hierarchies of value

The regulation of the welfare of wild animals is arguably more complex than that for domesticated animals, given the more complicated property status of wild animals and the significance of nature conservation legislation in framing a species-wide, rather than individual, conception of welfare. Despite this complexity, a close examination of wild animal regulation reveals the same irrationalities and inconsistencies found in relation to the welfare regulation of other categories of animals, including companion, farmed and research animals. The regulation of wild animal welfare in Australasia is marked by a distinct stratification, with introduced wild animals at the bottom of the protection hierarchy, common native wild animals in the middle, and endangered or rare native wild animals at the top.

(S. White 2009: 258)

The ways in which animals are valued are perhaps more complicated than this quotation suggests (see Table 4.2, and Franklin 2006). There are often distinctions made between 'good' and 'bad' invasive/native species, as illustrated by the welcome and protection afforded to (introduced) trout in the lakes of Tasmania, to the detriment of their local cousins. Nonetheless, the discussion of stratification is indeed an important one. Beirne (2009), for example, outlines the many different legal definitions given to the term 'animal' across different jurisdictions in the United States. What is defined, and what is valued, when it comes to animals is highly variable and subject to ongoing contestation at the level of philosophy as well as at the level of legislative practice (see Beirne 2009; Sankoff and White 2009). This has important consequences for intervention practice.

Table 4.4 outlines in cryptic form the ways in which harm against different species of animal is socially constructed. On the one hand, harm can be distinguished as being intentional or non-intentional. The use of the term 'non-intentional' rather than 'unintentional' is a conscious distinction. The latter implies no knowledge or awareness of effect or consequence. However, non-intentional connotes the idea of collateral damage. Even if knowledge or awareness of the harm is there, the primary activity that generates it continues. The harm is not intended, but it may be accepted regardless. The status of specific animals is related to whether or not the problem is one of threatened extinction, or one relating to the status of the species vis-à-vis productivity as a resource.

It would seem that the 'value' of a species is shaped by its utility vis-à-vis human needs and services, and its relative abundance as a species. For example, certain types of fish, and elephants, may be assessed in terms of their value as a resource. The central issues are those of scarcity and suitable regulation of

Table 4.4 Harm and species decline

	STATUS	
	Resource issues	*Survival issues*
HARM		
Intentional	illegal harvest of fish, birds and game animals	illegal trade related to elephants, reptiles and exotic species
Non-intentional	direct harm to organism through use of chemicals in soil that affects bacteria	indirect harm that affects environment of polar bear, koala, orangutan

trade. The problem is construed in terms of illegal (or unreported or unregulated) use of the species as resource (e.g. as a food, as an ornament). From a crime prevention perspective, the tendency is towards various kinds of trade-related measures (see for example Lack 2007 in relation to fish) and market reduction strategies (see Schneider 2008 in regards to illegal wildlife trade) as a means to combat illegal use of the resource.

In other cases, the status of the species is defined in terms of biodiversity. For example, polar bears and certain types of microbes may suffer unintentional harms, and thus species decline, due to unintentional acts that impinge upon their environments. The key issue is that of extinction or diminishment of habitation, whether this is associated with climate change (for example, the melting of Arctic ice in ways that affect the environment of the polar bear) or other forms of human-generated harm (such as overuse of pesticides in soils that kills bacteria as a result). Aside from dealing with fundamental matters such as global warming and use of GMO-related agricultural technologies, there is little recourse other than attempting to soften the blow by prohibiting overt direct harms to species such as polar bears (by putting them on the endangered list, for example). What gets criminalised is the end point of a much larger and more complicated social and ecological process.

Different animal species are also valued in terms of general service to humanity. This applies especially to companion animals such as dogs and cats, but also, to some extent, to domesticated animals used for food, such as chickens and cows. Here the key issue is not one of preservation or conservation but prevention of abuse. It is animal suffering and animal welfare that is of concern. The response of the law and criminal justice system, therefore, is to regulate human–animal interaction in ways that are welfare enabling for the animal, but that do not necessarily challenge the logic of using animals in particular kinds of human service.

Simply stated, it is the perceived value of a species that determines the regulation of human behaviour in relation to that species. This extends to law enforcement and crime prevention measures, as well as incorporating how 'crime' is institutionalised in relation to specific kinds of animals. What activities (and omissions) get criminalised depends upon how value is construed at any point in time. This will vary as well depending upon the species in question.

Conclusion

The point has been made that: 'Illegal logging, fishing, and wildlife trade are almost invariably carried out at unsustainable levels, running down the natural capital from which poor people derive their livelihoods' (Brack, quoted in Schmidt 2004: A97). Transnational environmental crimes of this kind thus negatively impact upon local workers and residents, as well as animals and environments. As this chapter has demonstrated, the question of legality is in fact only one part of the story when it comes to sustainability. The complete picture is one that views plants and animals in the wider context of biodiversity. The threats to this are manifold and many. Furthermore, as shown in Table 4.5, they are frequently accompanied by a wide range of more conventional criminal activities.

Thus, in the end, the diminishment of biodiversity sets in train a long line of offences and infringements that, in turn, reinforce the basic problem – namely, the rapid deterioration of biodiversity across the plant and animal kingdoms. In the context of climate change, such developments are life-threatening to all species insofar as resilience and adaptation demand versatility and difference.

Table 4.5 Transnational environmental crime and biodiversity

Environmental offences

Subject of offence	Nature of offence
Forestry	Illegal felling of trees
Genetically modified organism	Unauthorised release of organisms
Pesticides	Misuse of pesticides
Water pollution	Entry of polluting matter into controlled waters
Wildlife crime	Trade in endangered species
Unauthorised developments	Threat to endangered species
Collecting eggs	Harming threatened species

Associated offences

Subject of offence	Nature of offence
Corruption	Bribing of government officials
Public order offences	Conflict over local land use
Theft	Water theft
Folk crime	Poaching of local wildlife
Trespass	Encroachment on privately and publicly owned reserves
Piracy	Alternative sea-based income generation
Money laundering	Illegal financial transactions

5 Waste and pollution

Introduction

Toxic wastes and emissions are affecting human, ecosystem and animal well-being in many if not most parts of the planet today. This chapter explores the issues surrounding the production and commodification of waste, again reflecting the major concern of eco-global criminology with ecological issues that are global in their reach and effect.

Production and disposal of waste is a matter of significant concern to academic researchers interested in questions of environmental harm. Systematic analysis in this area is evident in a range of studies, many of which are associated with matters pertaining to environmental justice. Relevant examples of such research include:

- the role of organised criminal syndicates in the dumping of waste, including toxic waste (Block 2002; Ruggierro 1996);
- inequalities associated with the location of disadvantaged and minorities communities near toxic waste sites (Saha and Mohai 2005; Pellow 2007; Pinderhughes 1996);
- the use of medical and epidemiological evidence in demonstrating the nature and dynamics of toxic crimes (Lynch and Stretesky 2001);
- the global trade in electronic waste as a form of environmental crime that is of particular concern at the present time (Gibbs *et al.* 2010b; Interpol 2009);
- the social and cultural context within which local residents come to perceive what it is that pollutes their neighbourhoods and local rivers (Natali 2010);
- environmental racism linked to social status of being poor, part of a minority group or indigenous community (Bullard 1994; Brook 1998);
- specific incidents in which toxic materials have been dumped into developing countries by unscrupulous companies (White 2009c).

In addition to this kind of work, discussions of waste disposal today are also driven by non-government organisations and United Nations agencies concerned with matters of environmental justice. These bodies are highlighting issues such as the massive growth in 'e'-waste associated with the microchip revolution, and the way in which old computers, televisions and other electronic products are being dumped in regions such as Africa and South-East Asia (Pellow 2007; White 2008a; Gibbs *et al.* 2010b; Interpol 2009). Social and environmental harm is being caused by both legal and illegal transfers of hazardous waste, and it is the poor and vulnerable of the world's population who are paying the price (Clapp 2001). Particular environments are being denuded and both human and animal health are suffering, as toxic materials permeate specific areas and become embedded in local landscapes.

Waste and pollution

The definition of waste is itself highly contentious because substances can change in content, form and impact over time. In part this is reflected in waste management strategies that talk about the need to reduce; reuse; recycle; recover waste by physical, biological or chemical processes; and landfilling, incineration or other disposal method (Meyers *et al.* 2006). Things change over time – and what is considered waste today, or in one manifestation, may well be considered a 'resource' tomorrow or in another social application. Consider as well the diverse categories of waste. The following list is taken from a European Commission list (see Meyers *et al.* 2006: 506):

- production or consumption residues not otherwise specified below;
- off-specification products;
- products whose date for appropriate use has expired;
- materials spilled, lost or having undergone another mishap, including any materials, equipment, etc. contaminated as a result of the mishap;
- materials contaminated or soiled as a result of planned actions (e.g. residues from cleaning operations, packing materials, containers, etc.);
- unusable parts (e.g. reject batteries, exhausted catalysts, etc.);
- substances which no longer perform satisfactorily (e.g. contaminated acids, contaminated solvents, exhausted tempering salts, etc.);
- residues of industrial processes (e.g. slags, still bottoms, etc.);
- residues from pollution abatement processes (e.g. scrubber sludges, baghouse dusts, spent filters, etc.);
- machining/finishing residues (e.g. lathe turnings, mill scales, etc.);
- residues from raw materials extraction and processing (e.g. mining residues, oilfield slops, etc.);
- adulterated materials (e.g. oils contaminated with polychlorinated biphenyls, etc.);
- any materials, substances or products whose use has been banned by law;
- products for which the holder has no further use (e.g. agricultural, household, office, commercial and shop discards, etc.);

• contaminated materials, substances or products resulting from remedial action with respect to land; and any materials, substances or products which are not contained in the above categories.

In addition to this kind of list approach, we might add categories of waste that deserve further reflection, such as medical or clinical waste, radioactive waste and so on.

Waste production is associated with growth. Built into the logic and dynamics of capitalism is the imperative to expand (see White 2002). Capitalism is always searching for the things which can be transformed from simple use-values (i.e. objects of need) into exchange-values (i.e. commodities produced for exchange). This extends to 'nature' as it does to other kinds of objects. Thus, every aspect of human existence is subject to transformation insofar as capital seeks the transformation of existing or potential use-values into exchange values through commodification of all types of human activity and human requirements (e.g. water, food, entertainment, recreation). For example, what may have been formerly 'free' (e.g. tap water) is now sold back to the consumer for a price (e.g. bottled water or metered water). Effectively consumption has been put at the service of production in the sense that consumer decisions and practices are embedded in what is actually produced and how it is produced. Yet it is via consumption practices, and the cultural contexts for constantly growing and changing forms of consumption, that production realises its value.

The obvious implication of an expanding system, one based upon ever-increasing production and consumption, is for constant and escalating pressures on the world's non-renewable resources. Competition and the wastes associated with global capitalist production have a huge impact on the wider environment, on humans and on non-human animals (in the form of pollution, and in toxicity levels in air, water and land). The same processes pose major threats to biodiversity and in the narrowing of species generally (related both to legal and illegal trade in species, as well as production-related issues such as industrial production and GMO technologies). At the heart of these processes is a political culture which takes for granted, but rarely sees as problematic, the proposition that continued expansion of material consumption is both possible and will not harm the biosphere in any fundamental way (Foster 2002). Profitability very often means commodification. It also means vast amounts of waste and pollution.

Basically, production and destruction are interlinked. Waste is both a by-product of production and the refuse left over from consumption. The raw materials that go into making goods and in the provision of services are fundamentally determined by the producers, not the end consumers. This involves exploitation of environments, humans and non-human animals alike. Similarly, the waste by-products of production and the refuse left over from consumption are ultimately determined in the production process itself, according to the dictates of profit-making interests. For example, plastic wrappers entice consumers to buy, and then become part of the waste which must be disposed of afterwards.

There are extensive international agreements relating to the transportation, storage and disposal of waste and pollutants (see Table 5.1).

Applied to the study of waste and pollution, an eco-global criminology insists upon a global analysis of the problem and a focus on the notion of 'harm' as central, rather than 'crime' as such. Yet, the notion of crime is still relevant insofar as much that does occur when it comes to waste disposal is indeed criminal. In a similar vein (as will be elaborated on below), there is a need to go beyond the legal/illegal nexus to examine how 'harm in practice' works, but the nexus is nevertheless still significant analytically. To understand waste, we have to understand where it comes from, and where it is going. In this context, an analysis of product chains is also valuable.

Table 5.1 Selected international agreements pertaining to waste and pollution

---

Stockholm Convention on Persistent Organic Pollutants is an international environmental treaty that aims to eliminate or restrict the production and use of POPs.

Vienna Convention for the Protection of the Ozone Layer encourages international cooperation in research and modelling on causes, effects and trends in ozone depletion.

Montreal Protocol on Substances that Deplete the Ozone Layer (1987) prohibits member states from trading ozone-depleting substances with any state that is not a party.

The Convention on Long-Range Transboundary Air Pollution (1979) sets up the scientific framework for a better understanding of the environmental problem, its causes, and the extent of the effects of air pollution.

International Convention for the Prevention of Pollution from Ships (1973), as modified by the Protocol of 1978 relating thereto (MARPOL 73/78) aims to preserve the marine environment through the complete elimination of pollution by oil and other harmful substances and the minimisation of accidental discharge of such substances.

The Convention on the Prevention of Marine Pollution by Dumping of Wastes and Other Matter (1972) controls pollution of the sea by dumping and encourages regional agreement supplementary to the Convention.

Basel Convention on the Transboundary Movement of Hazardous Wastes and Their Disposal (1989) is organised around a set of principles. First, generation of hazardous waste should be minimised. Second, hazardous waste should be disposed of in a location as close to where it is generated as possible. Finally, transboundary movement of such waste should be tightly regulated.

Rotterdam Convention on the Prior Informed Consent Procedure for Certain Hazardous Chemicals and Pesticides in International Trade (1998) is a multilateral treaty to promote shared responsibilities in relation to importation of hazardous chemicals.

Waste and commodification

A key moment in the history of waste is its commodification on a large scale. This commodification of waste is linked to growth of waste removal companies in the post-World War II period (Field 1998). One consequence of this trend is that waste becomes an aggregate rather than specific substance. Many different and specific wastes are brought together by the one company or brought to the one depot. That is, specific waste from specific sites is mixed up together and the cash-nexus arrangement means that waste is sought after and collected in bulk. Whereas waste disposal was previously linked to immediate production sites such as around a factory, and affected all classes who lived in proximity to the site including workers, managers and owners, its commodification allows for two things: first, the amalgamation of many wastes into an indistinguishable generalised waste; and second, the transportation of waste off-site, to new and specific places for waste disposal, which, in some cases, simply includes dumping at sea; later, it includes transference to less developed countries in the Caribbean, Africa and Asia. In other words, there is a separation of waste product from the producer of waste.

There are also dramatic changes in the content of waste generally in the post-war period. For example, chemicals and other toxic waste such as persistent organic pollutants (POPs) proliferate. Specifically, the rise and rise of the chemical industries means that many different types of toxic waste are produced, and gathered up and put together into the same dump sites (e.g. rivers and lakes and ocean outlets). Much of this occurs without adequate precaution or scientific testing. This accelerates in the post-war period (until people like Rachel Carson [1962] started to write about the 'silent spring' and the environmental movements begin to crank up). The extent of the chemical revolution cannot be underestimated:

> Every living thing on the earth has been exposed to some level of human-made toxic substances. Lead, strontium-90, pesticides, and persistent organic pollutants (POPs) pervade our environment and reside in all of our bodies. This is a relatively new phenomenon, occurring mainly after World War II, as the production and use of hazardous substances increased exponentially in warfare, agriculture, electronics, and a range of industries, including transportation and housing.
>
> (Pellow 2007: 26)

The phenomenon of 'e'-waste now presents itself as yet another type of waste that requires critical scrutiny (as does the notion of 'recycling' when it comes to its international transfer). Just as nylon represents the front end of the chemical revolution (and the pervasive presence of plastics in the environment) so too the microchip initiates a whole new era of commodity production (and its expansion into every realm of social life).

Electronic waste or 'e'-waste consists of things such as discarded computers, TV sets and mobile phones. It is notable that 'The electronics industry is the world's largest and fastest growing manufacturing industry, and as a consequence of this growth, combined with rapid product obsolescence, discarded electronics or e-waste, is now the fastest growing waste stream in the industrialized world' (Basel Action Network and Silicon Valley Toxics Coalition 2002: 5). According to the United Nations, about 20 million to 50 million tons of 'e'-waste is generated worldwide annually (United Nations Environment Programme 2006). The waste contains toxins such as lead and mercury, or other chemicals that can poison waterways if buried, or release toxins into the air if burned. Much of this waste ends up as transfers from rich countries to the poor (Gibbs *et al.* 2010b; Interpol 2009).

The specific value and character of waste is partly shaped by circumstance and social utility. In general, the value of waste depends upon how it can be processed, that is, the labour power embedded in the disposal process (including technology). The different stages of disposal include collection, classification or sorting, transport, and treatment. Each stage itself involves diverse processes: treatment for example can include reuse, recycling, incineration, and landfill (Van Daele *et al.* 2007).

Waste removal and externalising harm

Waste disposal is big business that today involves large transnational corporations as active players (Beder 2006). As such, it is about profit-making and keeping costs down. This is associated with several different ways in which the costs for waste management have been externalised.

Transferring waste

Externalising harm frequently takes the form of transferring waste from Europe, the United States and Japan to non-metropole countries and regions such as Latin America, the Caribbean, Africa and South and South East Asia. Pellow (2007: 8–10) argues that there are four principal reasons for this shift:

- an exponential increase in the production of hazardous waste and the emergence of more stringent environmental regulation in industrialised nations, i.e. incentive for worst polluters to seek disposal sites beyond national borders;
- widespread need for fiscal relief among southern nations – construed as either 'economically efficient' or 'garbage imperialism' depending upon economic interests;
- the power of economic globalisation, that also includes hazardous waste management companies – that must access global markets and labour forces, increase automation and improve efficiencies: they must access buyers and markets where the prices result in increasing their profits and reducing their costs; and

• racist and classist culture and ideology within northern communities and institutions that view toxic dumping on poor communities of colour as perfectly acceptable.

The specific mechanisms for the transfer of hazardous waste from the North to the South vary, and are ostensibly governed by international conventions and protocols. However, the dynamic nature of hazard transfer is enabled both by the inbuilt limitations of domestic or national laws (Collins 2010) and through the sidestepping of existing international regulation through strategies such as the renaming of the process as recycling (Clapp 2001).

Socialisation of harms

Externalisation of the costs of waste also takes the form of socialisation of the harms, and of who pays to address the harms. If everyone is a victim of poor waste disposal, then everyone, via the state, is expected to pay to address what is deemed to be a communal rather than a private problem.

Particular firms and companies create the risks and problems, and reap the economic rewards from their activities. However, it is the public in general who suffer the health consequences (e.g. of air and water pollution, toxic landfill, loss of biodiversity, atmospheric changes). It is the state that frequently has to step in to clean up the privately caused mess (e.g. the pollution of Sydney Harbour by industrial factories).

At a concrete material level, harm is frequently constituted by the cumulative impact of many different operations, involving many different companies, and, as such, questions of blame and liability are diffused (see Gunningham *et al.* 1995). One political consequence of this is the idea that governments ought to pay (financially) for specific harms that have a collective impact, such as global warming and carbon emissions. The problem may originate neither from the public nor the state, but its resolution nevertheless still takes the form of broad sweeping measures that abrogate specific responsibilities (e.g. legislation and replacement costs for new 'greener' materials and energy sources). The people pay the penalties for individual private-sector activities.

Action or inaction on environmental threats has also been legitimated one way or the other by claims of scientific uncertainty. The uncertainty has been due to both lack of data and a more general problem of indeterminacy. The latter refers to processes and systems that cannot readily be captured by the methods of science as such. This is illustrated in the following passage:

> When nutrients accumulate in shallow waters, or when toxic chemicals bio-accumulate in tissues, systems approach a phase-change threshold where conditions can suddenly and dramatically change. This chaotic, inherent un-predictability in natural processes, combined with the conditional and erratic influences of social behaviour, creates contingency in all scientific assessment.
>
> (Scott 2005: 60)

Moreover, research on scientific decision-making makes it clear that there are inherent political choices being made in risk assessment (see Scott 2005). This extends across the past, present and future. Indeed, the socialisation of harms and costs is also achieved by discounting them to the future. The idea here is to act now, pay later – by circumventing the precautionary principle and ignoring concerns about intergenerational equity. A profound and challenging example of this is the continued reliance upon coal-based energy sources in the face of its well-known ecological consequences.

Point of production

Another form of externalising harm is to do so at the point of production rather than via transfer of waste per se. Several decades of neo-liberal ideology and free-market politics have provided the groundwork for the transfer of production from the centre to the periphery. This kind of free trade may lead to the alteration of a country's relative production of pollution, that is, production of clean goods relative to production of dirty goods (the latter produce more pollution per unit than the former).

This transformation of economies and environments is called a composition effect, which describes changes in the importance of polluting industries in a country once free trade is introduced (Grafton *et al.* 2004; Cole and Elliot 2003). The composition effect requires a wider range of goods to be produced in the home country, thereby increasing its pollution. Pollution may also be affected by the scale effect, that relates to the increase in overall pollution created by an increase in the level of economic activity; and technique effect, that refers to changes in production methods and, later, how increases in income result in a greater willingness to pay higher abatement costs. The composition effect dominates the technique and scale effects and so free trade will increase overall pollution.

Specific factors that affect the extent of pollution include differences in capital–labour endowments (for example, levels of capital-intensive development relative to capacities of the labour force) and differences in environmental regulations. Conventional economic analysis indicates that increased trade liberalisation can have mixed results insofar as, depending upon the pollutant, it can lead to either a reduction in per capita emissions or increased emissions (Cole and Elliot 2003). The state of the global economy will also obviously have consequences for how trade liberalisation impacts upon the environment, as it directly affects levels of income (and thus the support and capacity to provide for pollution abatement measures).

Disconnection between production and consumption

Another way in which harm is externalised is through the disconnection between production and consumption relations in ways that sustain unequal trade and waste-producing relations.

The nature of capitalist production and consumption tends to sever the connection between consumption and waste. The commodity appears as outside human agency, as alienated from production as such. This is evident in a culture of disconnection that marks the relationship between consumer and producer (O'Brien 2008). This refers to the dissociation between the harm derived from the production and later disposal of a commodity, and the act of consumption, a process in which 'every good and service is, in its material totality, a link in an economically infinite chain of harms' (O'Brien 2008: 46). Thus, there is no sense of communal ownership in relation to the costs as well as the benefits of the exploitation of human and natural resources (Pepper 1993).

Waste production and climate change

It is also important to consider how responses to climate change are impacting upon practices relating to waste and waste disposal. Here again we see a number of examples of paradoxical harm (see Chapter 3).

Disposal of radioactive waste

The notion that 'business can profit by protecting the environment' (Baer and Singer 2009: 181) is frequently linked to the idea of technological fixes vis-à-vis climate change, such as the development of hybrid cars, more technologically efficient appliances and lighting sources such as fluorescent bulbs. Burying the problem is also touted as a solution – whether this is in regard to radioactive waste or carbon pollution.

Uranium is not a renewable energy source, yet nuclear power is high on the list of preferred energy sources in the era of global warming. But nuclear energy also means nuclear waste. High-level waste (HLW) is so radioactive that it generates heat and corrodes all containers. It must be stored above ground for 50 years so it can cool before being transported and disposed of. Intermediate-level waste (ILW) arises mainly from the reprocessing of spent fuel and from general operations and maintenance at nuclear sites. It is typically packaged by encapsulation in cement in highly engineered stainless steel drums or in high-capacity steel or concrete boxes.

In the UK alone, 365,000 cubic metres of high- and intermediate-level radioactive waste will soon have been accumulated from its existing post-war nuclear programme (Clarke 2009). The decision in 2009 by the US government to end development of the Yucca Flat, Nevada repository for permanent disposal of radioactive waste has also highlighted waste issues in that nation. As of 2009, the United States has been left with some 60,000 metric tons of spent reactor fuel in need of a permanent storage facility, but with no viable facility on the drawing board, and no indication of when – if ever – the situation will be resolved (see Pickard 2010). Problems in developing a suitable response relate to technical and scientific issues, the NIMBY (Not In My Back Yard) effect, and who is, or ought, to carry the financial burden over time.

Nuclear waste in the US is currently stored at 121 temporary sites in 39 states across the country (Clarke 2009). Yet, 'Sixty years into the nuclear era there is no universally agreed upon strategy for the disposal of high level nuclear waste. Significantly more is being produced each year by nuclear powered electricity generation. But the power so generated is needed' (Pickard 2010: 713). At present, the only reasonable course of action, and moral obligation, is to bury this type of waste in deep underground repositories, rather than leaving the waste on the surface for an indefinite period – where each day might bring an incident that disperses it into the biosphere (Pickard 2010).

The biggest difficulty, across the board and pertaining to many different countries, is finding a site that is both geologically secure and also accepted by the local community. This is compounded by the problem of capacity relative to need. In South Korea, for example, the large increase in projected nuclear power will inevitably accelerate the accumulation of spent fuel – but if the direct deposit option is pursued, South Korea would not be able to secure enough suitable sites for disposal, given its geographic profile (Ko and Kwon 2009). Meanwhile, most countries are still in the planning stages for HLW repositories. In Japan, for example, the government has not yet started work on its HLW repository, even though the first experimental reactor was initiated in 1963 (Zhang *et al.* 2009).

Then there is the effect of global warming on preventive storage strategies. For example, the near-surface facility and geological repository are both likely to be affected by the consequences attending to global warming – the landscape and hydrogeological regime at and around a disposal facility may change, as might the biosphere receptors, and the animal and human habitats. When considering the long-term evolution of the disposal system, major climate change (e.g. future glacial periods) should be assessed (Van Geet *et al.* 2009: 473). Global warming will have a major influence over short and long periods of time, as in the case of changing water infiltration through the multilayer cover of a waste disposal site. The phenomenon of the 2010 summer fires in Russia also points to the vulnerability of nuclear plants to climate-related 'natural' disasters, in much the same way that recent seismic and volcanic activity in Iceland or Indonesia can be seen as threats to underground storage facilities.

Yet, the environmental crisis stemming from climate change is providing major impetus for a huge and rapid expansion of the nuclear power industry. The crime and safety implications of these combined issues include: illegal disposal of radioactive waste; unsafe containment of existing and immediate future waste; and externalisation of costs and wastes from core to peripheral countries. There is the accusation, for example, that French nuclear waste gets shipped to northern Africa and dumped in the desert sands (Bridgland 2006). This allows for a clean, green image within France to be maintained, because the real problem has been exported away. The demand for new forms of energy, within a context of reducing carbon emissions, may well open the door to new types of dumping and new forms of transference of harm worldwide.

Meanwhile, the capture and disposal of carbon dioxide raises issues that are also relevant to discussion of the use of deep underground depositories for radioactive waste. Suzuki (2007: 122) expresses this eloquently:

> We know virtually nothing about this living underworld – how many species there are and how they are distributed, how they interact with other life forms, how they are involved with the movement of heat and nutrients from the planet's core, or even how they contribute to soil. Yet today, in order to reduce CO_2 emissions contributing to climate change, 'carbon sequestration' is held out as a solution. The proposal is to pump hundreds of millions of tonnes of carbon dioxide into the ground where we have no idea how it is held, what kind of bonding occurs, where it is retained, how long it will remain underground and what it will do to the life forms that exist there. As creatures that live on Earth's surface, we regard the dark underworld as a lifeless, uniform matrix that we can use to sequester carbon without concern. It is time we learned to recognize our ignorance and acquire the humility to be very careful when we don't know enough.

This, too, highlights the importance of the adoption of the precautionary principle, in practice, now, to protect for the future. And yet governments, such as is happening in Canada, continue to tout the idea that the answer to greenhouse gas emissions from big projects (such as the tar sands project in Alberta) is to capture the carbon dioxide, compress it, and inject it deep under the Canadian prairie (Smandych and Kueneman 2010).

Compact fluorescent light globes

The replacement of incandescent light globes with compact fluorescent light globes (CFLs) also poses a paradoxical harm relating to disposal. Mercury is the most toxic pollutant after radioactive substances on the Environmental Protection Agency list of industrial pollutants. We are replacing one type of light globe with another in order to save energy (climate change agenda), but the new CFL globe contains mercury and there are already serious questions about the mass waste disposal of such globes (pollution agenda).

For example, compact fluorescent lamps, used mostly in homes, are required under a new Australian standard to have a maximum of 5mg of mercury. This is nonetheless seen by some as a major looming problem. For instance, 99 per cent of used fluorescent tubes and HID (high-intensity discharge) lamps, which contain mercury, are currently dumped in public landfill sites, causing a serious and ever-increasing mercury pollution problem. The CEO of the Australian Council of Recyclers, Ms Anne Prince, says that the move to fluorescent tubes without corresponding legislation governing their disposal is an ecological disaster in the making: 'We need to be smart enough to avoid creating a mercury pollution problem in order to fix a carbon pollution problem – we need another system, and fast' (Australian Council of Recyclers 2007). Governments are in the process of consulting with various stakeholders over how best to respond.

It has been pointed out that the mercury emitted over a CFL's life – by power plants to power the CFL and by leakage on disposal – is still less than the mercury that can be attributed to powering the incandescent light globe (Ramroth 2008). That is, the contribution of a CFL to reduction of mercury emissions from power stations (through lower energy consumption) is actually greater than the amount of mercury in a CFL. This observation implies an overall lowering of both power needs and the production of harmful substances.

It is argued that where coal-fired plants play a major role in producing electricity for a given region, the benefits of using CFLs are therefore increased proportionately (Ramroth 2008). About 53 per cent of Australia's electricity is produced by burning black coal and about 21 per cent from the burning of brown coal. CFLs use only about 20 per cent of the electricity which incandescent bulbs use to produce the same amount of light. Overall approximately 20 per cent of the coal therefore needs to be burnt to produce the same amount of light, resulting in an overall reduction in mercury emissions of about 80 per cent (Department of the Environment, Water, Heritage and the Arts 2010). Such logic, however, further rationalises the continued use of coal-powered plants, a major source of carbon emissions and thus global warming.

There are three disposal scenarios for CFLs – recycling, incineration and landfilling. The issues that arise in the disposal of CFLs are listed below (Equipment Energy Efficiency Committee 2009: 76).

• Waste collectors and processors may be exposed to mercury as CFLs enter the waste stream, and that this exposure is likely to increase as more CFLs enter the waste stream.
• Mercury from lamps in landfills can be converted to methyl mercury. Methyl mercury is more toxic than elemental mercury and, when emitted to air, may be a risk to landfill workers.
• If CFLs are processed in Alternative Waste Treatment facilities the mercury they contain may contaminate compost and render it unusable.
• Mercury can also escape from landfills into the environment harm or into ground water as leachate.
• Mercury escaping from landfills in various forms can contribute to overall mercury pollution that can bioaccumulate in the environment and affect human health and animal health.

Recycling is seen as one of the best answers to this, but this, too, raises issues of where the waste is to be recycled, under what conditions and by whom (see Basel Action Network and Silicon Valley Toxics Coalition 2002; White 2008a, 2008b). In some cases recycling is simply used as a cover for the transfer of toxic waste to developing countries (Clapp 2001, 2002).

Waste and the legal–illegal nexus

To explain the specific mechanisms by which environmental harm is transferred through time and space we need to appreciate the particularities of the waste industry generally. There are big differences between local dumping and the transnational movement of waste, between corporate behaviour and that of the individual perpetrator. Lynch *et al.* (2002: 111) are worth quoting at length on this point:

> To overcome the limits of the legal definition of toxic crimes, we define toxic crimes *as corporate behaviors that unnecessarily harm or place humans and the environment at risk of harm through the production and management of hazardous waste in the course of a legitimate business enterprise.* We include the word 'corporate' in our definition to exclude behaviors individuals perform that threaten human and environmental health. Individuals, for example, may illegally dump oil or radiator fluids they flush from automobiles, or paints or household solvents by disposing of these chemical in their trash, or by pouring them down the drain. While these acts are serious and illegal (as defined in federal and state regulations), *the harms they create pale in comparison to the organized production and disposal of hazardous wastes by legitimate businesses.* In addition, we focus on corporate behavior to illustrate the organized nature of corporate efforts to deceive the public about the extent of harm caused by corporate production and disposal of toxic chemicals [emphasis in original].

On the other hand, there is often overlap between the harmful actions of legitimate businesses and those of criminal syndicates. More extensive discussion would need to include analysis of local dumping (of things such as rubbish, fertilisers, landfill) and the transnational movement of waste (especially 'e'-waste), via both legal mechanisms (for example, under the guise of recycling, or as dictated by the Basel convention) and illegal mechanisms (involving illegal activity on the part of both mainstream companies, including waste companies themselves, and organised criminal syndicates such as those that operate in Naples). For now, the concern is to point to the key drivers for the harmful disposal of waste.

The dearth of adequate regulatory, enforcement and prosecution agencies and resources at the local, regional and international levels means that little incentive exists from a cost–benefit perspective to desist from illegal dumping, however it is organised. Yet, much of the criminality associated with waste disposal has its origins in the regulatory apparatus of the state. To understand this, we need to explore several interrelated issues.

First, waste disposal is a lucrative area in which to make money. Huge profits are there to be made in cases where waste is a product with an inelastic price – that is, an increase in price does not equally reduce demand for the service (Van Daele *et al.* 2007: 35). This has made waste disposal attractive to organised criminal syndicates while simultaneously opening the door for legal waste management companies to increase their profits by utilising illegal practices:

Available estimates indicate that profits from illegal waste management are about three to four times higher than those for legal activities. For hazardous wastes, the profit differential is even higher. It is possible that commercial entities' creative cost reduction beyond what is allowed is encouraged by these factors and that corporate culture considers the environment less important than profits. Beyond this, the growing use of subcontractors may decrease transparency, reducing the risks of detection of illegal waste management practices.

(Van Daele *et al.* 2007: 36)

Second, the impetus to bend rules and merge practices stems from the costs of waste disposal themselves. These comprise two major components (Dorn *et al.* 2007):

- high costs of legal waste management – related to industry standards, international conventions, government regulation, application of suitable technologies;
- high costs of compliance – traceability, labelling, automation and book-keeping procedures.

Subcontracting is one means to be legal and also be the beneficiary of illegal waste management.

There are other methods used to circumvent regulations and cut costs and increase profits as well. These revolve around issues of 'risk', and constructions of 'evidence', 'thresholds' and 'harms'. To take three examples, we can consider the following:

Mixing of hazardous waste with non-hazardous waste

This provides opportunities to mask hazardous waste proportions. These mirror entries define certain waste streams as hazardous only when their concentration in liquids exceeds a certain level. By keeping the hazardous waste degradation under legal limits, collection, transport and treatment become less regulated.

(Van Daele *et al.* 2007: 35–36)

Relabelling waste, not for disposal, but for recycling

The adoption of these national and international rules that sought to control the transnational trade in toxic waste [e.g. Basel Convention] resulted in a significant reduction in exports of toxic waste for disposal in developing countries by the early 1990s. At the same time, however, a new problem emerged. It soon became apparent that instead of exporting waste for *disposal*, waste exporters shifted their business toward the export of toxic wastes to developing countries for *recycling*. There was, in effect, a loophole in the rules that allowed waste transfers to continue – legally – under the auspices of recycling.

(Clapp 2002: 143)

Transferring of waste embedded in weapons to new international destinations

[Depleted uranium] has been given away to military industries at no cost to the manufacturer of arms and ammunition. In its own way, this represents one means to dispose of what is legally considered 'waste'. It also ensures the transnational movement of the waste when military operations take place in other parts of the world – such as the Middle East and the Balkans – which do not produce such products (and waste) to begin with.

(White 2008b: 34)

The methods used to circumvent regulations and to minimise labour and other costs will vary depending upon the players involved. Distinctions can be made, for example, between bourgeois (large capitalist) and petty bourgeois (small business) class situations, whether this is in regard to legal business activity or criminal organisations (such as the so-called eco-mafia in Italy). The size and dynamics of the group will influence how specific problems are tackled at the practical level. Issues to consider here include, for instance, pressures at the local level to dump waste because of the prohibitive costs of waste removal for small businesses. The petty bourgeoisie, as a class, frequently get squeezed by state regulation and fiscal crisis, and cutting corners financially is part and parcel of adjusting to this. On the other hand, the costs of waste removal for big business in a strict regulatory regime (as in Europe) can be analysed in terms of corporate efforts to increase profit margins by transferring waste, more cheaply, to offshore non-metropole sites. It is useful in this regard to track the record of specific companies, especially those that have a history of corporate corruption and illegal dumping (see Chapter 6).

Conclusion

As indicated in Table 5.2 there are a number of environmental and associated criminal offences linked with pollution and waste issues. To understand and respond adequately to these, we need to put waste disposal into its wider political economic context.

The apparent severing of the link between specific waste and its specific production means that responding to the 'waste problem' (which is socially constructed via the activities of environmentalists, local residents and concerned citizens, as well as through particular and spectacular instances of harm – e.g. Love Canal in the US) is no longer a case of blaming the producer (since we do not necessarily know how much and what kind of waste each individual producer supplies to the waste removal company). And the waste removal company, while liable to some extent for certain types of harm (depending upon how and where

Table 5.2 Transnational environmental crime and pollution/waste

Environmental offences

Subject of offence	Nature of offence
Air pollution	Emissions of dark smoke
Contaminated land	Unlawful pesticide spraying
Drinking water quality	Supplying water unfit for human consumption
Hazardous substances	Offences related to storage, transportation and disposal of regulated substances
Industrial pollution	Unlicensed pollution
Waste management	Illegal waste disposal
Water pollution	Entry of polluting matter into controlled waters

Associated offences

Subject of offence	Nature of offence
Threats of harm	Protection rackets, stand-over tactics
Public order offences	Conflicts over local land use
Trafficking	People smuggling
Theft	Water theft
Corruption	Graft, illegal commissions
Violent offences	Homicide, gang warfare
Fraud	Misrepresenting carbon emission trading

they dispose of waste), is not a key target for social action (perhaps due to the disconnection between production, consumption and waste disposal). As a result, the 'waste crisis' is often constructed as a generalised problem of society (it is 'our' waste, since it cannot be ascribed to any particular individual or company) and, accordingly, it is up to 'society' (read, the state) to clean things up. In other words, the waste crisis is reconstructed as a social problem, rather than one stemming from individual producers and their waste removal partners. Add to this the urgency of clean-up (and the delays associated with litigation and criminalisation) and pressure is on the state to intervene and do something concrete.

One consequence of unsustainable environmental practices is that it puts more pressure on companies to seek out new resources (natural and human) to exploit as existing reserves dwindle due to overexploitation and the contamination of nature from already produced waste. Nature itself is used as a dumping ground, particularly in the invisible spaces of the open seas and less developed countries (White 2008a). Waste is both an outcome and a driver of the production process. Simultaneously, the social consequence of no work, no income and no subsistence livelihood for significant numbers of people worldwide means that waste-producing and toxic forms of production (including recycling) are more likely to be accepted by the vulnerable. The imposition of such victimisation is embedded in the wider systemic pressures associated with global capitalism. Profitability very often means adopting the most unsustainable practices for short-term gain.

We conclude this chapter with the observation that activity in the regulatory sphere (e.g. greater enforcement of the Basel Convention and European concerns to tighten up procedures relating to waste production and waste treatment) provides impetus to cut costs by bypassing the formal waste treatment economy and adopting illegal methods of disposal, including entering into partnerships with corrupt or failed governments (e.g. Somali warlords, Ivory Coast politicians) or with organised criminal syndicates (e.g. that will secretly dispose of the problem or buy the right people off). The global financial crisis and subsequent recessions exacerbates this tendency. In the end, the disconnection between production and consumption, and the implicit distinction between well-being in the North versus well-being in the South, ensures the continuation of global environmental degradation that puts all in peril.

6 Perpetrators

Introduction

This chapter is about the challenges of assigning blame or responsibility when it comes to activities that threaten environmental rights, ecological justice and non-human animal well-being. This is no easy task. Dealing with the perpetrators of transnational environmental crime will always be fraught with controversy and conflict to the extent that fundamental interests clash and questions of justice come to the fore.

For eco-global criminology, system-level structures and pressures that commodify all aspects of social existence, that are based upon the exploitation of humans, non-human animals and natural resources, and that privilege the powerful over the interests of the vast majority are clearly problematic. It also acknowledges that those who determine and shape the law are very often those whose activities ought to be criminalised for the sake of planetary well-being. Yet, when all is said and done, we still want to know who, specifically, is to blame for environmental wrongdoing. As this chapter demonstrates, more abstract considerations of causal factors or causal forces often beg this question or provide limited and unsatisfactory answers.

While important, discussions of systemic processes and global institutions do not really get to the nub of the issue when it comes to perpetrators. Clearly major cultural and institutional changes are required if the shift from climate change producing conditions to ecological sustainability is to be achieved. This will, indeed, require massive changes at a global systems level across the whole of the world's political economy. This is a crucial agenda for all those who believe that things must change fundamentally if the full impacts of global warming are to be successfully mitigated – or if we are collectively to survive climate change, full stop.

Yet, we need to make a distinction between the general causal problems that underpin what is happening on such a grand scale, and issues of specific accountability and specific responsibility. In other words, we need at some stage to be able to fix culpability or blame to actual persons (including, somewhat ironically, the corporation as a legal entity). Things do not just happen by chance, and particular individuals and firms are especially complicit in perpetrating environmental harms. The notion of a distinct offender is essential, for otherwise no 'guilt' can be assigned and no prosecution undertaken (see also Chapter 8). But more often than not the perpetrator is not in fact subjected to criminalisation or treatment as an offender. This, too, needs explanation. Regardless of how perpetrators are dealt with by criminal justice systems the question of 'responsibility' matters.

Systemic perspectives on responsibility

Consideration of who is responsible for environmental harm can be approached by acknowledging that the answer, in part, depends upon the level of abstraction one applies. Even though intrinsically linked, there are major differences between explanations that focus on systemic answers and those that examine immediate situational causes of harm or risk. Here we might consider several of the more general explanations for ecological calamity that point to particular sorts of 'perpetrator' as the source of the problem.

Humans are responsible

The argument here is that humans are responsible for much of the destruction of ecological systems and, as such, are the key agents of environmental harm in the contemporary time period. The argument is that the problem lies in how humans as a whole transform their immediate environments for their own purposes. The net result is to the detriment of both human and non-human, but the causal force for environmental degradation is ultimately human. This is not to deny observations on the powerful shaping of human society by 'nature' and natural phenomena (such as river systems, naturally burning forests and so on). But at a gross, historical level it is what humans do *en masse* that reshapes landscapes, pollutes air, water and soil, leads to species decline among plants and animals, and changes the content of the atmosphere and the level of the seas. The moral responsibility for this lies with humans (White 2007: 32).

There are several ways in which 'humans' can be seen to be responsible: as a species, and as distinct individuals. The idea of blaming the human species, however, can be subjected to counter-factual analysis. That is, if all humans are implicated in the harm, then all humans must by their own 'human' nature be destructive. Yet we know from accounts of Indigenous relationships with nature, to take one example, that some humans have lived countless years in harmonious relationship with their local ecosystems (see Robyn 2002). We also know that some contemporary communities in places such as India are actively reconfiguring their relationship with nature in ways that are ecologically sustainable and that promote biodiversity (see Shiva 2008). It is only at a very high level of abstraction, then, that we can place blame on humans. The more grounded the analysis becomes – the more reflective of specific groups and communities – the more tenuous the sweep of the generalisation.

Individuals are also the target of responsibility arguments. For example, knowing of the ecological harms associated with oil-based economies, and the specific contribution of the motor vehicle to these, it might be argued that the person driving a car is engaging in harm against the environment. According to this view, individuals who do so should be seen as responsible for their actions, and thus responsible for the environmental harms in which they are implicated. A very different perspective emerges, however, if we analyse closely the mode of production and the power relations embodied in this mode. Individuals as workers and consumers are shaped by systemic forces and tendencies which affect the basic ways in which they can, 'should' and do live their lives. In response to the problem of 'car drivers', for instance, we need to ask the broader sociological questions about the state of public transport infrastructure, the privatisation of mass transit systems and the huge amounts of money being spent upon tollways and freeways, and how these infrastructural elements of transport affect who drives cars, and why. Individual choices tend to reflect wider societal and political decisions.

Responsibility can, to some extent, be shunted down to the level of the individual. How each person lives their life involves a specific relationship with those around them, including environments and non-human animals. However, analysis of broad trends indicates that it is systemic imperatives and historical transformations that ultimately shape what it is that individuals do in and with their lives and their environments (see White 2002).

Technology is responsible

Another perspective places the emphasis on technology as a perpetrator or facilitator of environmental harm. 'Climate change is a consequence of the transition from biodiversity based on renewable carbon economies to a fossil fuel-based non-renewable carbon economy. This was the transition called the industrial revolution' (Shiva 2008: 130). Again, while factually correct, the question of responsibility tends to get lost in the form of a global analysis that can obscure specific causal links and specific social processes. The spread of industrialisation and specific means of production is not merely a technical process or one that stems solely from technological determinants. Two hundred years of industrial revolution has been driven and underpinned by powerful forces (nation states, companies, armies) pursuing sectional interests. This has been achieved through global imperialism, colonialism and militarism that have served to entrench a dominant world view and the material basis for certain types of production, consumption and reproduction.

The idea that technology is the root of all evil necessarily has to be pitched at a very general level. It is the technologies associated with industrialisation that are seen as the problem, for example, not the social system underpinning this industrialisation as such. In this scenario, technology is seen as that which creates the risks and harms. It is the motor car, the factory, the tractor, the coal-fired power station, the dam, the fertiliser, that is the problem. In response, proposals to downshift to a low-tech future might be interpreted as a 'blame the technology' kind of argument.

Against this is the acknowledgement that the technology question is inherently about the social character of collective practice. Davison (2004: 144) points out that 'Technologies of genetics, biology, energy, matter and information cannot be neatly sorted into good and bad, or sustainable and unsustainable, piles'. What counts is the specific social and ecological conditions under which technologies are utilised and applied. On the one hand, as Shiva (2008: 130) observes, 'Dirty nuclear power is being redefined as "clean energy". Non-sustainable production of biodiesel and bio-fuel is being welcomed as a "green" option.' On the other hand, we cannot assume that by their very nature renewable energy technologies are inherently positive and good. Depending upon the social context, for example, 'sustainable forms of agriculture and other "green" techniques may reduce some forms of ecological risk, but they may also help to prop up, to sustain, an unsustaining social whole' (Davison 2004: 144). The social context of technological use and development is therefore crucial.

Population is responsible

Overpopulation is frequently touted as the most important factor or variable in ecological destruction. Put simply, there are too many people on the planet for the planet to be able to sustain them. In ecological terms, this is often expressed in the language of ecological footprint. Thus:

> As a result of the growing competition and demand for global resources, the world's population has reached a stage where the amount of resources needed to sustain it exceeds what is available ... humanity's footprint is 21.9 ha/person, while the Earth's biological capacity is, on average, only 15.7 ha/person, with the ultimate result that there is net environmental degradation and loss.
>
> (UNEP 2007: 202/Box 6.1).

The solution is to reduce the number of people if we are to survive.

Again, while it is true that the many billions of humans on the planet are contributing to global warming, loss of biodiversity and increased waste and pollution, to blame population per se risks pitching the problem at too abstract a level of explanation. As seen in Chapter 3, for instance, the bulk of consumption is generated by consumers in the advanced industrialised nations, the metropoles rather than the periphery. Moreover, it is the displacement of the poor and the profound social inequalities between North and South (and within these) that make for desperate people doing what they can to survive.

But population numbers and the composition of populations vary greatly around the world. In the developed countries, the key issue is one of structural ageing, as the older live longer and the proportion of the young shrinks relative to the overall population. In less developed countries and, importantly, disadvantaged communities within the advanced industrial countries, the issues pertain to big families, young families and use of family size as a hedge against little or no social welfare supports. Population growth is substantively linked to economic, social and political circumstance insofar as the more affluent one is the less proclivity there is to reproduce to the same extent as those who have little. Again, the question of power (and inequality) looms large, since it is those who 'have' who are most likely to favour controlling population policies in regards to those who do not. This takes the form of immigration restrictions, security against potential climate-induced migrations and support for the imposition of birth control measures on 'them'. Interestingly, the population debate also raises important questions regarding the relative importance of ecological security versus human rights.

Capitalism is responsible

Even a cursory examination of dominant world political economic trends reveals the close link between capitalism as a system and environmental degradation and transformation generally. The key aspects of contemporary political economy include (White 2010c):

- expansion – growth as progress, accumulation as economic engine, exploitation of natural resources, non-human animals and people;
- privatisation – from common property to private property, concentrated ownership and management, reliance on market mechanisms rather than government controls;
- commodification – transformation of use-value into exchange-value, more and more aspects of social life and environment are commercialised;
- massification – mass production including for niche markets, simplification of consumables including foods as well as goods and services to a narrow range of choices;
- globalisation – monopolisation of control over production via takeovers and mergers worldwide, penetration of the transnational corporation into local markets and practices.

While a system can be seen to be to blame (in the sense of being instrumental) for environmental degradation, it is nevertheless perplexing when it comes to assigning specific responsibility. Systems are deemed to be blameworthy, but they are not responsible insofar as there is no single 'controlling mind'. Systems may be subjected to social and moral condemnation, and they may invoke substantive movements towards reform and revolutionary change. But there is no perpetrator as such. A simplistic blaming of capitalism, therefore, provides little more than rhetorical shorthand for 'something is wrong' rather than providing a guide to who, precisely, is doing what within the overarching parameters of global capitalism.

Writing in the context of governing climate change, Bulkeley and Newell (2010: 68, emphasis added) comment that 'Conceiving of accountability as involving both *answerability* – the need to justify and explain positions and actions adopted – and *enforceability* – the ability to impose sanctions for non-compliance – can help to examine the complex questions raised by transnational climate governance'. In a similar vein, when it comes to perpetrators of environmental harm we need to move beyond the more abstract systemic causes to a level of investigation and analysis that will allow us to make someone or something accountable for the harm they have caused. This means drilling down from seeming universals (humans, technology, population, capitalism) to the particular and the concrete. In this regard, the fundamental position of the transnational corporation on the world stage cannot be ignored.

Corporations are responsible

As with blaming capitalism for everything there is also a temptation to blame transnational corporations (TNCs) for everything. While there are certain 'truths' to this, it is nonetheless important to be able to specify which TNCs are harming the environment, how exactly they are doing so and in which jurisdictions.

Such a study is easier said than done. A sizeable literature exists that spells out the many ways in which TNCs escape or minimise negative media coverage for acts or omissions that cause harm (Lynch *et al.* 2000), proactively use greenwashing techniques to make them seem environmentally responsible or good corporate citizens (Beder 1997), threaten critics and environmental activists with lawsuits (Beder 1997; White 2005) and generally make life difficult for those trying to expose their wrongdoing (White 2008a). The powerful have many ways in which to protect their interests.

We also have to bear in mind that not everything that TNCs do is bad or wrong, and that not every TNC necessarily engages in things that harm the environment. This complicates analysis of perpetrators as well. For example, there is great variability between and within TNCs in terms of core activities, nature of executive decisions, and relationship to workers, consumers and environments. Again, more precision is needed in analysing the actual role and behaviour of specific companies, rather than relying upon stereotype and overgeneralisation (contrast, for example, Braithwaite and Drahos 2000 and Bakan 2004).

Given that the top private corporations are economically more powerful than many nation states, and given that they own and control great expanses of the world's land, water and food resources, TNCs individually and collectively are a formidable force. On occasion, as well, business competitors may combine to use their collective muscle to influence world opinion or global efforts to curtail their activities. For example, analysis of how big business has responded to global warming reveals a multi-pronged strategy to slow things down (Bulkeley and Newell 2010). Some of these have included:

- challenging the science behind climate change;
- creating business-funded environmental NGOs;

- emphasising the economic costs of tackling climate change;
- using double-edged diplomacy to create stalemates in international negotiations;
- using domestic politics (particularly in the United States) to stall international progress;
- directly influencing the climate change negotiations through direct lobbying.

It is only continuous pressure from below (grass-roots groups and global activists) and the occasional exercise of political will from enlightened politicians from above (as is evident in some Latin American countries such as Bolivia) that moderates TNC power.

However, due to the sheer size and scale of the modern TNC, many can do pretty well what they like. They also have the leverage. Consider for example the importance of water to human existence. On the other hand, consider as well the growing profitability of (legal) waste disposal and pollution control (see Chapter 5). The human need for clean drinking water combined with the increasing scarcity of such equates to huge profits for private water suppliers and managers. Simultaneously, the proliferation of 'e'-waste generated by the disposal of tens of thousands of computers and other equipment, and the quantities of household rubbish that require disposal, equates to huge profits for private waste disposal companies. In some cases, as illustrated in Table 6.1, the water corporation and the waste corporation are one and the same.

The concentration of economic power into fewer and fewer hands, on a world scale, means that transnational corporations wield enormous influence across the globe. It is not only the size of companies that gives them such power, nor their

Table 6.1 The world's major water and waste corporations

Corporation	Water subsidiary	Country base	2003 total revenue (euros)	2003 water revenue (euros)
Veolia Environment 70	Veolia Water	France	28.4 billion	11.2 billion
Suez 71	ONEDO	France	39.6 billion	6.5 billion
RWE 72	Thames	Germany	43.9 billion	2.85 billion
Bouygues 73	SAUR	France	21.8 billion	2.45 billion

Corporation	Waste subsidiary	Country base	2003 total revenue (euros)	2003 waste revenue (euros)
Waste Management Inc 76		US		11.6 billion
Veolia Environment 77	Onyx	France	28.4 billion	6.0 billion
Suez 78	SITA	France	39.6 billion	5.5 billion
RWE 79	RWE Umwell	Germany	43.9 billion	2.0 billion

Source: drawing from Beder 2006: 99–100

monopolisation of particular industries and financial sectors. Their power is also related to the nature of the corporate form itself.

For example, the origins of the modern corporation lie in efforts to facilitate the gathering of investment capital for large-scale ventures by the selling of shares in particular companies. The corporate form was invented in order to separate the corporate identity from that of the shareholder. If the venture succeeded, the shareholder acquired dividends and the shares would tend to rise in value; if the venture failed, leaving large debts, it was nothing to do with the shareholder, who had no responsibility. Historically, the duty of company directors was to maximise the interests of shareholders (i.e. to increase their return on investment); they had no duty to advance, or even consider, any other interest, economic or social.

The corporate form is associated with a number of legal fictions that serve to protect the company and its directors and shareholders – the so-called 'corporate veil' (see Glasbeek 2004). For example, shareholders are rendered legally immune from any wrongful, illegal and criminal acts the corporation might commit in their search for profits. Moreover, when it comes to such activity, in a large corporation it is immensely difficult to prove intention on the part of the company and hence to convict. In part because of these legal fictions and protections, Glasbeek (2004) argues that the corporation has been legally designed as a criminogenic creature, and is thus prone to criminal behaviour.

Some lifting of the corporate veil has nonetheless occurred. This has taken the form, for example, of shareholder groups that attempt to call companies to account for things such as toxic spills or environmentally destructive practices. Corporate reporting has steadily included reference to environmental matters, as well as financial probity and community engagement. Recent legal reforms, including in the area of environmental law, have also acknowledged the need for some sort of direct accountability, usually through concepts such as strict liability and nominated responsible officers. All of these developments and more indicate that the relationship between TNCs and transnational environmental crime deserves close and detailed attention.

Studying perpetrators

Methodologically, the study of perpetrators of transnational environmental crime will generally involve investigation of the chains of harm. That is, we need to know the links between diverse players at different stages in any particular criminal process. Trade in wildlife, for instance, involves transactions involving the thieves through to those who arrange the sale of the product on the market. This has implications for prevention of such crime as well as for identification of perpetrators as such. This is illustrated in Table 6.2. By understanding the social dynamics pertaining to the particular crime in question it becomes apparent who the perpetrators are (as a class or category of offender) and how they are linked into other stakeholders if a crime is to be successfully achieved.

Table 6.2 Focus for market reduction approach to wildlife crime

Focus	MRA/Wildlife
Who	Hunter, poacher, handler, consumer
What	Animals, plants and/or by-products
Location	Country of origin (range area), country of consumption
Date	Seasonality, mating season
How	How things are harvested, processed, shipped
Why	Demand

Source: drawing upon Schneider 2008: 279

This kind of network analysis provides a general scoping of the likely perpetrators and likely processes associated with the criminal activity. In other words, for any particular type of crime and particular type of criminality, there is a need to undertake an industry scan in order to identify who the key suspects might be. For example, in regards to illegal logging there are a number of potential players linked to specific kinds of activities (Setiono 2007):

*   financial backers of illegal logging activities;
*   corrupt forestry officials, police and military officers who allow illegal logging practices to occur;
*   international shipping companies which are complicit in the smuggling of illegal logs;
*   international timber traders who are engaged in forgery of timber permits;
*   international and local timber traders involved in illicit trafficking;

A similar exercise can be undertaken with regard to other types of illegal activity such as IUU fishing.

For other sorts of crimes, the investigation may involve other kinds of causal chain analysis. For example, the dumping of toxic waste in the Ivory Coast in 2006 involved a sequence of connected events, as shown in Box 6.1. The concern of this analysis is less that of networks than of temporal development that can link the originator of the problem to the final criminal act.

Another way to approach the study of perpetrators is to identify who the key players are in specific industry areas. For example, in the case of GMO crops, the overwhelming majority of such crops (and their accompanying fertilisers, seeds and herbicides) are produced by four chemical corporations – Monsanto, Syngenta, Du Pont and Bayer. These companies control not only GMO crop production through share of market, but also the GM technologies, built into the crops, through the use of patents. Under the guise of free trade, and with the support of the US and the World Trade Organisation, these companies are active in their efforts to monopolise crop production around the globe (Walters 2005).

In the case of energy and oil, again a short list of names serves to identify who dominates the industry. Just five global oil corporations – Exxon Mobil, BP Amoco, Shell, Chevron and Texaco – produce oil that contributes some 10 per

Box 6.1 A chronology of events associated with toxic dumping in the Ivory Coast

- Amsterdam Port Services (APS) had initially agreed to dispose of the waste for $15,000.
- However, when a subcontractor pumped the waste to an unloading ship, it was evident the washings were more concentrated than expected.
- APS took a sample from the 'waste water' and it proved to be a highly lethal cocktail of petroleum, caustic soda and other agents.
- People around the docking area complained about feeling ill and about the smell, and the waste was pumped back into the original ship, the *Probo Koala*.
- The port authorities reclassified the tank contents as toxic waste and then instructed the ship's captain to take the waste to a special facility and dispose of it, at a cost of $650,000.
- The ship's owners, Trafigura, refused to pay and mindful of 'significant financial time penalties' if it waited to resolve the issue in Amsterdam, the *Probo Koala* left.
- An independent Dutch committee ordered by the city of Amsterdam to investigate the handling of the *Probo Koala* was subsequently to find that the ship could have been detained at the port of Amsterdam.
- A later study of events by independent lawyers for Dutch MPs said that transport ministry officials did not dare to stop the ship leaving Dutch waters because Trafigura had threatened to sue for damages if the ban proved to be groundless.
- The ship then travelled on to Estonia, where it turned down an offer to dispose of the waste for $260,000.
- The next port of call was Nigeria, where no agreement for disposal of the waste was possible after negotiations with two local waste disposal firms.
- Both Estonia and Nigeria have ratified an international ban on the shipping of hazardous waste from rich to poor countries, but Ivory Coast had not.
- In Ivory Coast, Trafigura 'found' a local company called Tommy which agreed to dispose of the waste for roughly the original price.
- Tommy was an off-the-shelf company that was quickly formed between two French commodity traders and executives of a waste disposal company in Ivory Coast.
- From the beginning, however, no company in Ivory Coast had the facilities to deal with this specific kind of waste.
- More than a dozen trucks contracted by Tommy simply poured the tons of waste out at multiple sites across the city, after midnight of 19 August 2006.
- On the night of 14–15 September 2006, further dumpings were reported to have taken place.

Source: White 2009c

cent of the world's carbon emissions (Bruno *et al.* 1999: 1). These companies are responsible for more greenhouse gases than most countries. But several of these have also been involved in prominent events involving considerable harm to the environment – such as the Exxon Valdez oil spill off the coast of Alaska, and the BP oil spill in the Gulf of Mexico, not to mention the continuing civil strife and social unrest associated with Shell's operations in Nigeria.

Specific company profiles can be developed through close examination of the history of that company. For example, Monsanto has come under scrutiny by those who are concerned about genetically modified organisms. Study has revealed not only the huge extent of Monsanto's reach and power in this area, but also specific breaches of the law, including major acts of environmental harm (Engdahl 2007; Robin 2010; Smith 2003). Companies such as Trafigura likewise exhibit a dubious criminal history (White 2009c), and investigation of major events such as the Bhopal incident in India reveals a company history, in this case of Union Carbide, that involved overt and conscious risk-taking that inevitably led to disaster (Engel and Martin 2006).

While beyond the scope of the present work, a future task of eco-global criminology is to identify the major corporations underpinning and dominating specific industries (such as waste, water, food, oil, nuclear) and to undertake a sustained analysis of how specific companies do what they do. Such analysis would have to consider a wide range of activities – including mergers and takeovers within the specific industry, the corporation's relationship to local communities and to specific national/regional governments, and the social conflicts associated with their core business (such as disputes over land use). An integral part of this analysis is to identify those environmental harms that may well be perfectly legal (at the moment) but that are ecologically disastrous.

It is also important to document those few, but significant, instances when big corporations are subjected to legal action. Street offenders have criminal track records that dog them for life. Yet when it comes to corporate wrongdoing and criminal activity, the story is different. While legally a 'person', somehow the biography of this corporate person magically changes (or disappears) as the company name changes, or once the latest amalgamation takes place, or the Chief Executive Officer is replaced with one more palatable to the public at large, as seen in the recent case of BP following the Deepwater Horizon oil spill in the Gulf of Mexico. Tracking illegal, criminal and harmful activity over time means digging into the background of specific personnel and the corporate forms and guises of contemporary TNCs. It also means investigating the links among corporate directors, and between business and government leaders (see Beder 2006).

Responsibility and accountability

So, in the end, who is responsible for environmental crime? In the case of individuals, it is relatively easy for prosecutors to establish criminal intent or negligence, and thus to establish blameworthiness which would lead to a prosecution. In a similar vein, legal research has demonstrated that when it comes to prosecution of environmental crime it is small businesses that generally bear the brunt of state intervention. This is not only due to politics and the capacity to defend oneself, it is also related to organisational features. For example, Fortney (2003: 1620) observes that in the United States 'generally the *mens rea* required for felony convictions is easier to prove in a small or close corporation setting, without resort to judicial strict liability constructs'. In other words, the mental element of criminal law is easier to establish in smaller firms.

Those most responsible for the vast majority of environmental violations, namely the large corporations, are also the least likely to suffer prosecution except in extraordinary circumstances. One reason (among many) for this is because intent or negligence is much harder to establish in the case of corporations. When it comes to corporate criminal liability, for example, the central question is, in what circumstances are companies to be held to account for the acts of their employees?

> It had been thought that such corporate liability would only be established where the employees responsible were of sufficient seniority to act as the 'controlling mind' of the company. The problem is that many pollution incidents are the responsibility of operational staff who are far removed from the 'controlling mind'. The Courts [in the UK] have held that the actions of employees will create corporate criminal liability where it is clear that the relevant statutory purposes would be defeated if a company could not be prosecuted for the acts of its employees.
>
> (Bell and McGillivray 2008: 288)

Thus one response to these legal dilemmas is recourse to the notion of 'vicarious liability'. This is where it is argued that to make legislation effective, there is a necessary implication that companies should be liable for the acts and omissions of all of their employees as opposed to simply the senior employees who are the 'controlling minds'.

In the United States, a similar concept is expressed in the notion of 'collective knowledge', which stems from the fact that the size and complexity of large corporations lead to greater delegation of responsibility that is spread among more and more subordinates. This has led the courts to 'develop a theory under which the aggregate knowledge of the subordinates could be imputed to the corporation without requiring proof that any individual agent had actual knowledge of all of the operative facts' (Brickey 2008: 49). Establishing organisational liability is about imputing certain acts to the corporation and thus deeming it responsible in its own right for the environmental harm.

In addition to this, individual directors and managers can also be prosecuted individually. This relates to the concept of 'responsible corporate officers' that holds corporate officers personally liable for crimes arising from business processes over which they hold ultimate authority or responsibility. Responsibility, here, is tied to specific organisational responsibilities in relation to particular company practices (see Brickey 2008). In the UK, for example, to establish personal liability for directors, there must be:

- an offence committed by the company; and
- consent, connivance, or neglect by the individual.

(Bell and McGillivray 2008: 289)

Yet, once again, there are major issues surrounding how to interpret key concepts such as neglect or indeed whether or not an offence has occurred.

Part of the difficulty is that 'doing business' frequently involves a cost–benefit trade-off (see Chapter 8). The perpetration of environmental harm is often simply part of the normal operations of industry. Insofar as this is the case, the matter of intent can become conflated with the issue of harm. This extends to analysis of environmental victimisation as well. For example, in a strict legal sense, accusations of environmental racism demand proof of intentional discrimination. But regardless of intent, the consequence of existing social practices is that people of colour do live near toxic waste sites (see Stretesky and Hogan 1998). This can involve either direct or indirect discrimination: for instance, is the waste put near poor people and people of colour or do poor people gravitate to the cheaper housing near toxic sites? Trying to establish intent can in fact distract from the main issues at hand, although ultimately issues of accountability do need to be addressed.

Particularly in the case of corporations a central issue is whether perpetrators should be judged on the basis of *mens rea* (the guilty mind), on the basis of *actus reus* (the actual conduct), or a combination of the two. The legal subject is the corporation, but there can be designated responsible officers among the executive who would actually have to suffer the sanctions associated with company actions. So, depending upon the circumstances and the jurisdiction, to whom specific blame should be assigned is in fact possible to ascertain.

In addition to the use of notions such as a designated responsible officer, corporate criminality can also be addressed through strict liability provisions. According to Bell and McGillivray (2008: 283) there are four main arguments for the use of strict liability. The imposition of strict liability:

- promotes the public interest goal inherent in environmental legislation;
- acts as a deterrent, which improves the quality of environmental risk prevention measures;
- increases the ease of prosecution, which increases the deterrent effect;
- accords with the polluter pays principle.

They also observe that 'The use of strict liability can be justified by reference to both trivial offences (through ease of prosecution) *and* serious offences (by acting as a deterrent and through the polluter pays principle)' (Bell and McGillivray 2008: 283). However, questions are raised as to whether the imposition of strict liability, in turn, leads to lenient sentences and low prosecution rates (because of the perceived harshness of strict liability regimes). This is highly problematic given the already low rates of conviction for environmental crimes, and weak sanctioning regimes (see Chapter 8).

According to Williams (1996) it is important to phrase a definition of crime or harm as 'consequence of' rather than 'caused by'. This is because of the technical difficulties in proving causation in many instances of environmental harm. In the light of this it is not surprising that there are frequently deliberate denials of causal links, and hence the avoidance of liability and responsibility by perpetrators. Williams (1996: 26) argues that these are particularly important issues in relation to the environment insofar as 'the *complexity* of establishing causation creates an easy escape for perpetrators, and the *scale* of remediation is usually immense and so the incentive to avoid liability is great'. Coupled with systematic use of techniques of denial of harm, of responsibility, and of victimisation, and clever manipulation of legal discourse in court (Du Rees 2001; de Prez 2000), this means that few perpetrators are prepared to accept responsibility and fewer still are found to be legally responsible in any meaningful way.

State–corporate collusion

The nature of the state as a site for, and facilitator of, transnational environmental crime also warrants further explicit consideration within the eco-global criminology framework. To put the current thinking on its head, there is a need to move from concern about the state of (environmental) crime, to concern about crimes of the state, which whether by omission or enablement allow the harms to occur. In essence, in many different parts of the world, local political elites are working hand in glove with large corporations in ways that negatively impact upon the environment (and on workers and local residents). This occurs in many different ways, and at different scales.

For example, at a global level we might consider the intersection of global warming, government action or inaction and corporate behaviour (Lynch and Stretesky 2010) and how these contribute to the overall problem of climate change. In this instance the state is itself implicated as a perpetrator of harm. Government subsidies for coal-fired power stations and government approval of dams that destroy large swathes of rainforest constitute substantial crimes against nature. In the light of the existing scientific evidence on global warming, continued encouragement of such activities represents intentional harm that is immoral and destructive of collective public interest in the same moment that particular industries and companies benefit.

Given the stakes involved, we might well ask, should the impending destruction of ecosystems, and the human collateral damage associated with this, be thought of as a form of environmental genocide – ecocide? If so, then it is state leaders and government bureaucrats, as well as corporate heads and key shareholders, who should ultimately be held responsible for this crime. But how do we make them accountable for their actions (or non-actions)? In many cases, the answer lies in political mobilisation, both against (or for) specific projects and as a wider political movement in support of environmental politics (see Chapter 9).

The exploitation of Canada's Alberta tar sands provides another case in point. This massive industrial project involves the active collusion of provincial and federal governments with big oil companies. The project is based upon efforts to extract and refine naturally created tar-bearing sand into exportable and consumable oil. One result of the project is a wide range of different types of harm to the ecosystem, animals and humans. For example, it has been pointed out that the tar sands oil production is the single largest contributor to the increase of global warming pollution in Canada. It will lead to the destruction of vast swathes of boreal forest, it contributes greatly to air pollution, and it is having negative health impacts on aquatic life and animals, and for humans who live nearby (see Smandych and Kueneman 2010).

For those who study this type of environmental degradation, one that is associated with considerable social and ecological harm, the concept of state–corporate environmental crime is considered entirely appropriate as a descriptor (Smandych and Kueneman 2010). Placed within the larger global context of climate change, the scale and impact of this project also fit neatly with the concept of ecocide. The role of the federal and provincial governments is crucial to the project, and in propelling it forward regardless of manifest negative environmental consequences.

The political economic relations of global capitalism are crucial in any discussion of environmental harm insofar as how, or whether, certain human activity is regulated and facilitated is still primarily a matter of state intervention. The ways in which nation states (and varying other levels of government) attempt to deal with environmental concerns is contingent upon the class interests associated with political power. In most cases today the power of TNCs finds purchase in the interface between the interests and preferred activities of the transnational corporation and the specific protections and supports offered by the nation state. The latter can be reliant upon or intimidated by particular industries and companies. Tax revenue and job creation, as well as media support and political donations, may depend upon particular state–corporate synergies. This of course can undermine the basic tenets of democracy and collective deliberation over how best to interpret the public or national interest.

The structure and allocation of societal resources via the nation state also has an impact upon how environmental issues are socially constructed. Spending on welfare, health, transportation, education and other forms of social infrastructure makes a big difference in people's lives. Recent fiscal crises (especially noticeable in European countries such as Greece, Ireland and Spain) and the global economic crisis have had the global impact of making ordinary workers extremely vulnerable economically. Under such conditions, there is even greater scope to either reduce environmental protection, or to increase environmentally destructive activity, to the extent that existing state legislation and company practices are seen to put fetters on the profit-making enterprise. This is so whether the activity is in the metropole countries or in the periphery.

Politically, the problems generated in and through economic restructuring are also reflected in the scapegoating of environmental activists, immigrants and Indigenous people, who are frequently portrayed as impeding the immediate job prospects of workers in industries associated with resource exploitation (e.g. logging, mining), industrial production (e.g. manufacturing) and project development (e.g. tourist resorts). Intensified competition between workers for jobs thus has major implications for environment-related politics.

The study of the perpetrators of transnational environmental crime needs to incorporate sustained analysis of the role of the nation state, operating at many different levels (international through to local), and pursuing particular projects and protecting particular interests. Specific types of transnational environmental crime are associated with the nature and extent of state intervention (or non-intervention). Some acts of harm are perfectly allowable, and receive the approval of state authorities. Others are illegal but, without adequate state response, are in effect allowed to occur as a matter of course. In some instances, the local government simply does not have the resources to police environmental crime and so the problem is not political as such, but related to availability of resources and expertise. The nature of state–corporate collusion (or conflict) thus varies in substantially different ways, and so needs to be examined in detail in any particular instance. Whether it be related to corruption or connivance, compliance or enforcement, the specific terms of the arrangement between government and business do in fact matter.

Conclusion

From the point of view of eco-global criminology there is a big difference between perpetrators and offenders. Perpetrators include those individuals, groups and corporations that engage in or who are behind environmentally harmful activities (acts or omissions) that affect humans, specific ecosystems and animals. Those who perpetrate environmental harm do so in ways that vary according to the size of the organisation and the nature of the specific harm in question. They also vary in the legitimacy or otherwise granted by the nation state in relation to particular activities. In many instances, the harm is not conceptualised as a crime as such. It will simply be seen as part of the cost of doing business. The harm, nonetheless, occurs.

Environmental offenders, on the other hand, include perpetrators who actually get caught committing a specified crime and who are formally processed through some kind of regulatory or criminal proceedings. The distinguishing element here is application of the law such that someone or something is actually to be held accountable for the harm they have caused. How offenders are dealt with is discussed in further depth in Chapter 8. This kind of treatment remains the exception, however, since most environmental harm, and the most harmful of such, is perpetrated by firms and companies that are more likely to be seen (and to present themselves) as good corporate citizens rather than deviant organisations engaging in criminal offences.

There is of course overlap between perpetrators and offenders. Perpetrators of environmental harm on a large scale tend to engage in activities that are inherently and structurally prone to environmental destruction and degradation, yet are legal. This is partly why perpetrators are not considered criminal or bad, insofar as it is only in exceptional circumstances that the risks of what they do come to public attention. It is when 'accidents' happen that companies may be seen, temporarily, as offenders. However, it is the specific act that is seen to be wrong (e.g. dumping of toxic waste), not usually the company as such. In other cases, the harm may be fully intended (for example clearing land for the growing of GMO crops) and backed by state sponsors. In these cases the perpetrator will not be seen or treated as an environmental offender, regardless of the extent of ecological destruction.

7 Environmental victims

Introduction

Questions of inequality, disadvantage and subordination are never far from the surface when we talk about environmental victims. Such questions are at the centre of eco-global criminology given its concern with varying forms of eco-justice.

The notion of environmental victim implies that someone or something is being harmed through the conscious or neglectful actions of another. As discussed in Chapter 2, environmental harm itself can be conceptualised in several different ways that incorporate consideration of the non-human as well as the human. From a green criminology perspective, environmental harm is best seen in terms of justice, based upon notions of human, ecological and animal rights, and egalitarian concerns. The key issue is weighing up of different kinds of harm and violation of rights within a broad eco-justice framework, and stretching the boundaries of conventional criminology to include other kinds of harm than those already deemed illegal.

For the purposes of this chapter one specific strand of green criminology is particularly relevant. This is the approach that focuses on environmental rights and environmental justice, in which environmental rights are seen as an extension of human or social rights. However, this specific focus – on humans – has several implications that need to be acknowledged.

For instance, environmental justice issues tend to be examined in terms of effects on human populations, including the ramifications of certain practices on competing industries (e.g. negative impact of clear-fell logging on tourism). The use of pesticides, to take another example, may have dramatic impacts on animal species (in that, for example, their use seems to have coincided with the spread of a tumour disease amongst the Tasmanian devil population in recent years) and on specific environments (the pollution of coastal waters in north-eastern Tasmania). But the damage is often framed in terms of human loss (of a Tasmanian tourism icon; of the destruction of oyster farms), rather than of loss to biosphere or non-human animal per se. Environmental justice movements are largely focused on redressing the unequal distribution of environmental disadvantage, and in particular on preventing environmental hazards being located in their local area.

In the specific area of environmental victimology, the literature to date has likewise tended to focus on humans as victims rather than on other species or particular environments (see, for example, Williams 1996). Moreover, the complexities and development of victimology as a specific sub- or associated discipline of criminology have primarily been due to attention given to the dynamic nature of relationships between human actors as perpetrators, as victims, and as observers (Rock 2007; Fattah 2010).

The aim of this chapter is to explore the nature of environmental victimisation in ways that emphasise victimisation as an active social process involving relations of power, domination and resistance. In doing so, it explores the varying ways in which human agency is played out in instances where environmental harm affects individuals, groups and communities. As will be demonstrated, environmental victimisation is not a socially neutral process in that some people suffer more than others when it comes to poor environmental living conditions and/or events that are disastrous to their lives. Before considering humans as victims, however, there are others, as well, that deserve recognition for the harms done to them.

The other victims

We begin in fact with the acknowledgement that, while generally absent from mainstream criminological concerns, there has been work done on non-human animals as 'victims' (or at the least as objects of harm) and this, too, is of relevance and concern to eco-global criminology. Two types of literature are particularly prominent here. The first tends to look at questions of animal abuse from the point of view of the 'progression thesis' that looks at how the torture and killing of animals by humans leads to or is associated with criminal behaviour generally among the perpetrator population (Dadds *et al.* 2002; Ascione 2001; Beirne 2004; Hackett and Uprichard 2007). In much of this literature the concern appears to be less with the rights of the animal as such than with the implications of animal cruelty for later harms against humans, by humans.

The second and developing strand of work locates questions of harm to animals within wider philosophical frameworks that go to the heart of concerns with species justice (Beirne 2009; Sollund 2008). This involves dedicated discussions about the 'value' of non-human animals, and the judgements made by humans as to their 'worth' as living creatures (see also Chapter 4). In strict legal terms, it is pointed out that:

> Animals have for centuries been characterised by the common law as the property of humans and, in accordance with the law governing such property, they could be treated in any way their owners saw fit. Humans could breed them, sell them, kill them – even torture them – without running afoul of any law.

> (Sankoff and White 2009: 1)

Recent commentary and research on animal rights and animal welfare direct attention to the changing nature of 'animal law' and the ways in which the conception of animals as property is being challenged by alternative conceptions of animals as 'persons' and/or as rights holders in their own right (Sankoff and White 2009; Beirne 2009). Radical positions declare much of current practice and attitudes towards animals as fundamentally immoral and wrong, as a form of non-human oppression (see Svard 2008).

The fact that environmental victimisation is generally and explicitly defined in terms of *human* interests and in terms of injury to *humans* is not, therefore, without controversy. There are long-standing debates and antagonisms between those who adopt an 'environmental justice', an 'ecological justice' and a 'species justice' perspective on the nature of harm (see White 2008a; Sandler and Pezzullo 2007). For present purposes we will not revisit these debates, although they do provide an important backdrop to issues of morality and activism, as well as those that relate to victimisation.

Abolitionism as a political and philosophical position provides an important, abstract discussion of the human–animal relationship. It involves debates that are far-reaching and that will continue well into the future. These hinge upon the nature of 'rights' as these pertain to animals, and the application and applicability of human laws and conventions to non-human species. It also involves analysis of the place of animals in wider systems of production and consumption – including how animals relate to one another as well as to humans (Munro 2004; Cullinan 2003).

The animal-centred discourse of animal rights shares much in common with the environment-centred discourse of green criminology, but certain differences, as well as commonalities, are also apparent (Beirne 2007; Svard 2008). For example, non-human animals are frequently considered in primarily instrumental terms (as pets, as food, as resources) in environmental criminology, or categorised in mainly anthropomorphic terms (such as 'wildlife', 'fisheries') that belie the ways in which humans create and classify animals as Other. From an animal rights theoretical framework, one key issue revolves around how rights are constructed: via utilitarian theory that emphasises the consequential goal of minimising suffering and pain; via rights theory that emphasises the right to respectful treatment; and via feminist theory that emphasises the ethic of responsible caring (Beirne 2007).

At a more concrete and pragmatic level, green criminology has raised a number of immediate questions that continue to search for an answer. These are well summarised by Beirne (2009: 200):

If violation of animals' rights is to be taken seriously, I recommend that activists and scholars could profitably examine why some harms to animals are defined as criminal, others as abusive but not criminal, and still others as neither criminal nor abusive. In exploring these questions, a narrow concept of crimes against animals would necessarily have to be rejected in favor of a more inclusive concept of harm. Without it, the meaning of animal abuse will be overwhelmingly confined to those harms that are regarded as socially unacceptable, one-on-one cases of animal cruelty. Certainly, those cases demand attention. But so, too, do those other and far more numerous institutionalized harms to animals, where abuse is routine, invisible, ubiquitous, and often defined as socially acceptable.

Be this as it may, the type of analysis provided in this area – frequently framed in terms of animal abuse or cruelty to animals – provides a very different perspective to that provided within victimology as such.

The absence of animal considerations within mainstream victimology is due in part to the absence of legal status as 'persons' and thus the treatment of non-human animals as outside the usual realms of ordinary law and legal decision-making. The difference in analytical approach is also due to species differences in the exercise of agency, relating to issues of consciousness, response and social dynamics (including for example victim-precipitation). Humans may be treated like animals (i.e. treated badly), but traditional victimology would nonetheless see human victims less in terms of being objects of harm (e.g. victims of cruelty) than subjects with rights (i.e. victims of human rights violations). Again, the distinction between species, and their relative status in legal and philosophical terms, is crucial.

The remainder of this chapter is preoccupied with exploring environmental victimisation from the point of view of human victims. This is not simply a biased conceptual emphasis based upon privileging human welfare and well-being over particular environments or other animal species, although this is a matter of substantial concern and will have to be taken up elsewhere in greater depth. Rather, the contribution of the chapter lies in not only analysis of the harm done to particular individuals and groups, but also the ways in which these individuals and groups respond to their victimisation. Thus, the question of human agency looms large, as much as anything because it is this agency that creates space for political responses to environmentally harmful activity more generally. In other words, we study human victims not only to assess the damage and the social processes behind victimhood but also for the potential for change embodied in some instances of victimisation. This, too, is a mandate of eco-global criminology; namely, the necessity of not only understanding the world, but also analysing ways in which it can be transformed in positive directions.

Environmental victimology

Environmental victimology, as such, is less concerned with non-human animals and specific biospheres than with the interests and well-being of humans in specific circumstances.

The seriousness or lack thereof of how environmental victims are treated is reflected in how the UN *Declaration of Basic Principles of Justice for Victims of Crime and Abuses of Power* has been interpreted and used in practice, with much less attention being given to those suffering abuse of power compared with victims of traditional crime. Indeed, Fattah (2010: 56) makes the telling comment that:

> ... the new victimologists have been extremely selective in the types of crime they denounce and the groups of victims whose cause they champion. They chose to focus their attention and to concentrate their political efforts and action on traditional crime and its victims, on crimes that cause individual harm rather than ones that cause collective harm. As a result, victims of white-collar crime and its depredations have been once again relegated to the shadow, to the background.

Replace the phrase 'white-collar crime' with 'environmental crime' and the result is pretty much the same. This is a situation that eco-global criminology wants to change.

Who is an environmental victim?

According to Williams (1996: 21) the term 'environmental victim' represents the idea of injury caused by a deliberate or reckless act or omission. Environmental victims are:

> ... those of past, present, or future generations who are injured as a consequence of change to the chemical, physical, microbiological, or psychosocial environment, brought about by deliberate or reckless, individual or collective, human act or act of omission.

Environmental victimisation can be defined as specific forms of harm which are caused by acts or omissions leading to the presence or absence of environmental agents which are associated with human injury (Williams 1996). This is portrayed in Table 7.1. Again, for present purposes, the intention is to restrict discussion to

Table 7.1 Environmental victimisation

	Act	*Omission*
Presence of environmental agent	e.g. the presence of methyl-isocyanate caused by an act of polluting and poisoning (Union Carbide–Bhopal)	e.g. the presence of excess lead in water supplies caused by an omission of the duty to provide safe drinking water
Absence of environmental agent	e.g. the absence of food and micronutrients leading to malnutrition and brain injury resulting from land degradation caused by the act of dumping toxic waste	e.g. the absence of iodine caused by an omission of failing to iodise salt in accordance with the law (India)

Source: Williams 1996: 22

humans rather than to extend the concept of victimisation to non-human animals and specific environments. In part this is because a major concern of this chapter is to consider victims as actors exhibiting varying types of social agency, which has important implications for social action and social change.

It is important to distinguish between environmental issues that affect everyone, and those that disproportionately affect specific individuals and groups (see Williams 1996; Low and Gleeson 1998). In some instances, there may be a basic equality of victims, in that some environmental problems threaten everyone in the same way, as in the case for example of ozone depletion, global warming, air pollution and acid rain (Beck 1996).

As extensive work on specific incidents and patterns of victimisation demonstrates, however, it is also the case that some people are more likely to be disadvantaged by environmental problems than others (see also Chapter 5). For instance, studies have identified disparities involving many different types of environmental hazards that adversely affect especially people of colour, ethnic minority groups and Indigenous people in places such as Canada, Australia and the US (Bullard 1994; Pinderhughes 1996; Langton 1998; Lynch *et al.* 2004, 1999; Brook 2000; Rush 2002). There are thus patterns of differential victimisation that are evident with respect to the siting of toxic waste dumps, extreme air pollution, chemical accidents, access to safe clean drinking water and so on (see Chunn *et al.* 2002; Saha and Mohai 2005; Williams 1996). It is the poor and disadvantaged who suffer disproportionately from such environmental inequalities.

There are also differential risks within 'at risk' populations. This is particularly apparent when it comes to socially differentiated characteristics such as age (the very young, the very old), gender (women tend to experience greater suffering than men in circumstances of famine and disaster) and general health (mental, physical, as well as ability/disability). For instance, a particular suburb or city may be placed in circumstances that heighten risks to well-being and health for everyone (e.g. dumping of toxic waste in Abidjan, Ivory Coast; the spraying of chemical pesticides in New York City). However, particularly where heightened risk is deemed to be 'acceptable' in terms of cost–benefit analysis (as in the use of pesticides to prevent the spread of disease borne by mosquitoes) there are 'hidden' costs that may not be factored in. For instance, children and those with chemical sensitivities will suffer disproportionately if chemicals are sprayed, since they are more vulnerable than others to ill effects arising from these toxins. In such circumstances, the crucial questions are not only 'how many will be harmed?' but also 'who will be harmed?' (Scott 2005: 56). To appreciate this, we need to be conscious of differences within affected populations.

Who is a victim is also inclusive of differing degrees of harm, injury and suffering. Death from environmental catastrophe is only one manifestation of how victimisation can occur. Whether the affliction is or incorporates a disease or permanent injury or prolonged mental illness and psychological distress, a large proportion of 'victims' are in fact 'survivors'. They sometimes sustain injuries that significantly alter the course and quality of their lives and that are economically onerous in terms of health care. So, too, the breaking up of communities, the displacement of individuals, the loss of economic livelihood and dispossession of land all constitute varying forms of harm to human populations.

Vulnerabilities to victimisation

As indicated above, one of the truisms of victimology is that being and becoming a victim is never socially neutral. This holds true for environmental victimisation as it does for other sorts of victim-making. Fattah (2010: 46) makes the comment that:

> In most instances victims are not chosen at random, and in many cases the motives for the criminal act develop around a specific and nonexchangeable victim. Therefore, an examination of victim characteristics, of the place the victim occupies, and the role the victim plays in these dynamic processes is essential to understanding why the crime was committed in a given situation, at a given moment, and why a particular target was chosen.

This should not be interpreted as suggesting that somehow the victim is responsible in some way for their targeting. Rather, it is an acknowledgement that the more one examines specific actions that produce and involve environmental victims, the greater the consensus that those who suffer harm do so because of their specific relationship to the perpetrators of the harm. Largely these consist of relations of power, domination and exploitation. It is the social, economic and political characteristics of the victim populations that make them vulnerable to victimisation in the first place.

Accordingly, environmental justice discourse places inequality, and inequalities in the distribution of environmental quality, at the top of the environmental agenda (see Julian 2004; Harvey 1996). After all, environmental victimisation generally involves on the one hand powerful players such as corporations and nation states, and on the other less powerful groups such as Indigenous people, ethnic minorities, the poor and those less able to take care of their own interests (such as the elderly and the very young).

Consider for example the effect of mining on the environment near the Ok Tedi River in Papua New Guinea. Over a period of many years, the BHP mine operators discharged 80 million tons of tailings, overburden and mine-induced erosion into the river system each year. This caused widespread harm to the 50,000 people who live in the 120 villages downstream of the mine. The main beneficiaries from the mine have been BHP, the PNG government and the clan that holds ownership of the land on which the mine is built. Experts have predicted that it will take 300 years to clean up the toxic contamination (see Kirsch 2006; Low and Gleeson 1998).

Another illustrative example is persistent pollution in the surrounding areas of a residential community. In the historic African American community of Mossville, Louisiana, it has been documented that residents have an average level of dioxins in their bodies that is three times higher than the average level of dioxins in the general US population. Dioxins are the most toxic chemicals known to science, and can cause cancer, reproductive damage and extensive harm to foetal and child development. Independent analysis of government data has demonstrated that six local industrial facilities are the sources of the elevated dioxin levels in the Mossville community – yet, government agencies continue to issue permits which allow the industrial facilities to increase the amount of toxic pollution, including dioxins, which they release into the local community. The facilities release millions of tons of toxins into the air, water and land each year (Mossville Environmental Action Now 2007).

Such instances of blatant disregard for human health and well-being have been labelled environmental racism. For those who engage in systematic study of such questions, it is clear that, regardless of intent, the practical outcome of corporate and government action has been to ensure that disadvantaged groups end up living in the most hazardous and environmentally poor areas (Pellow 2007). This is so whether it is in the United States (Bullard 1994), Canada (Chunn *et al.* 2002), India (Engel and Martin 2006) or Australia (Walker 2006). Moreover, it is these kinds of communities that also suffer most from the extraction of natural resources. Specifically, in many places around the globe where minority or Indigenous peoples live, oil, timber and minerals are extracted in ways that devastate local eco-systems and destroy traditional cultures and livelihoods (Scholsberg 2004, 2007).

The context of global warming, declining oil resources and food crises puts even more of the world's ecological and economic burdens on the backs of the poor. As Shiva (2008: 5–6) observes:

> First, they are displaced from work; then they bear a disproportionate burden of the costs of climate chaos through extreme droughts, floods, and cyclones; and then they lose once more when pseudo-solutions like industrial biofuels divert their land and their food. Whether it is industrial agriculture or industrial biofuels, car factories or superhighways, displacement and forced evictions of indigenous peoples and peasants from the land are an inevitable consequence of an economic model that creates growth by extinguishing people's rights.

Displacement from homeland is accelerating through the acquisition of large areas of arable land in developing countries by foreign governments and private companies (see also Chapter 4). Thus:

> Parcels of several hundred thousands of hectares are being bought or leased in Africa, Central and Southeast Asia, and Eastern Europe by food-importing countries with domestic land and water constraints but abundant capital, such as the Gulf States, and by countries with large populations and food security concerns, such as China, South Korea and India.
>
> (Sutherland *et al.* 2009: 5)

These land acquisitions are having major negative impacts on local people, who are losing access and control over the resources on which they depend, and which are the rightful inheritance of future generations.

These problems are compounded in some case by the ways in which 'conservation' is being foisted upon these same communities. As Duffy (2010: 11) points out:

> When wildlife reserves are established, local communities can suddenly find that their everyday subsistence activities have been outlawed and they have been redefined as criminals ... Some of the world's best-known pristine wilderness areas are, in fact, engineered environments. Creating a national park means drawing up new conservation rules which outlaw the everyday subsistence activities of local communities, such as hunting for food and collecting wood.

Victims can thus be transformed into offenders. Another example of this is the climate-induced subsistence activities that do further harm to the environment. The plight of the dispossessed and disadvantaged means that often any environmental destruction brought about by their actions (cutting down of forests, fishing in protected areas or in another state's exclusive economic zone) is best remedied by social justice initiatives rather than criminal justice interventions. Similarly, the person with no land and no natural resources already faces a huge and daunting task to survive – to be subjected to ill treatment and placed in prison (i.e. detention centres) constitutes an additional harm that violates their very being.

From a historical perspective, the imposition of colonial power was intrinsically a matter of resource colonisation, a phenomenon that affected many different Indigenous peoples in places such as South America, North America, and Australasia, as well as the native inhabitants of Africa, Asia and beyond. In places such as Australia, Indigenous territories were considered frontier lands that were unowned, underutilised and therefore open to exploitation. The prior ownership rights, interests and knowledges of Indigenous inhabitants were treated as irrelevant by the European invaders. Such complete disregard for the physical and cultural well-being of Indigenous people and their connection to 'country' was also evident in how they and their lands were treated when it came to nuclear testing, as well in establishing mining interests (White and Habibis 2005). Environmental victimisation has been central to dispossession and maltreatment of Indigenous peoples over many continents and over a period of several centuries.

Such processes continue today albeit under various new guises. For example, one consequence of climate change has been the policy search in the West for Band-Aid solutions to carbon emissions. There are two kinds of disparities associated with this. First, most of the emissions of the North are 'luxury' emissions and contrast sharply with the 'survival' emissions of the South. Second, while not the main perpetrators of the problem, it is the people of the

South who suffer the most the effects of disasters related to climate change (see also below).

Moreover, there is the emerging issue of carbon colonialism as a form of climate injustice. This relates to interest in the role of forests as carbon sinks (on the part of businesses in the developed countries) for which credits might be earned and finance provided to developing countries, particularly biodiverse countries such as those in Latin America. The governments of those countries may gain financially from such arrangements, at the expense of local communities. For example, it has been alleged that a Norwegian company operating in Uganda leased its lands for a sequestration project that is said to have resulted in 8,000 people in 13 villages being evicted (Bulkeley and Newell 2010: 48). According to Bulkeley and Newell (2010: 77), Frances Seymour of the Center for International Forestry Research claims that:

> as payments for conserving forests for carbon storage become increasingly likely, state and non-state actors alike will have strong incentives to passively ignore or actively deny the land and resource rights of indigenous, traditional and/or poor forest users in order to position themselves to claim compensation for forest stewardship in their stead.

The effects of the commodification of carbon (that is, its extraction from local contexts and circulation in global markets) will thus put pressure on communities that are home to these resources.

Those who are most vulnerable to the effects of climate change are those who are most likely to be vulnerable to events such as droughts, floods and cyclones. The conventional approach to disasters is to see them as 'natural' (and to include such things as earthquakes, volcanoes and floods) or human-caused (relating to fires, explosions and oil spills) (see Picou *et al.* 2009). This type of approach is reflected in Table 7.2 that outlines one particular way in which to categorise disasters.

In the context of major global changes in climate change, biodiversity and pollution, this presumption may no longer be warranted.

Table 7.2 Erikson's classification of disasters

Toxicity	Cause	
	Human (technological)	*Nature*
Non-toxic	Fires, dam collapses, aeroplane crashes, explosions	Hurricanes, floods, tornados, earthquakes
Toxic	Oil spills, toxic chemical spills, radiation leaks, toxic waste contamination	Radon gas, na-tech (nature-technology) scenarios, natural disasters that cause a technological disaster

Source: Picou *et al.* 2009: 284.

In a similar vein, Williams (1996) argues that when formulating a definition of environmental victim it is usually necessary to exclude those who are more accurately defined as 'environmental casualties', as this relates to those who have suffered as a result of natural disasters. This suffering, it is argued, is the result of chance. However, he goes on to point out that 'Some circumstances that appear natural may, if analysed in greater depth, be a consequence of human acts' (Williams 1996: 19). Thus, 'Environmental suffering that has affected many generations, such as iodine deficiency, might not be seen as victimization until power relationships are examined. Why are the communities that suffer iodine deficiency forced to live on land that cannot sustain human life properly?'(Williams 1996: 19).

The same logic extends to the impact and causes of specific events. Again, those least responsible for climate change are worst affected by it.

> Peasants, indigenous peoples, and artisans who live outside the industrialized globalized economy, who have caused no harm to the earth or other people, are the worst victims of climate chaos. Over 96 percent of disaster-related deaths in recent years have taken place in developing countries. In 2001, there were 170 million people affected by disasters around the world, of which 97 percent were climate-related.
>
> (Shiva 2008: 3)

These vulnerabilities to victimisation are not only due to geographical location as such. Many countries have coastal areas that are vulnerable to sea-level rise, for example. But the Netherlands has the technological and financial capacity to protect itself to a greater extent than Bangladesh. Thus, not only are poorer countries less responsible for the problem, they are simultaneously least able to adapt to the climate impacts that they will suffer because they lack the resources and capacity to do so.

This raises matters of justice surrounding three key questions: the question of responsibility (e.g. the North owes the South an 'ecological debt'); the question of who pays for action on mitigation and adaptation; and the question of who bears the costs of actions and inactions (see Bulkeley and Newell 2010).

Victim mobilisation

From the point of view of activism and mobilisation, the fact that environmental victims frequently consist of those drawn from the ranks of the poor, the disadvantaged and the minority has significant ramifications. For example, many such victims fit into the category of 'socially expendable victims' (Fattah 2010). That is, no one really cares what happens to these specific individuals and groups, since they are already devalued in wider community terms. As Engel and Martin (2006: 479) put it: 'If victims are perceived as degraded in some sense, then it does not seem so unfair when bad things happen to them.'

This is on top of the existing stigmatisation that 'ordinary' victims endure.

The term 'victim' is a word that 'evokes strong images of submissiveness, pain, loss of control and defeat … Victims are riddled with taboos' (Rock 2007: 41). To be judged on preconceptions based upon race or income adds further fuel to the debasement associated with victimisation processes. To (re)act against perpetrators of environmental harm (which, typically, includes powerful forces and organisations) often means first throwing off the chains of servitude and underprivilege that, in turn, undermine confidence and tactical wherewithal.

Differential victimisation relates to the subjective disposition and consciousness of the people involved in other ways as well. The specific groups who experience environmental problems may not always describe or see the issues in strictly environmental terms. This may be related to lack of awareness of the environmental harm, alternative explanations for the calamity (e.g. an act of God) and socio-economic pressures to 'accept' environmental risk in return for economic reward (see Julian 2004). Waldman (2007), for instance, describes a local community in South Africa that saw the contamination effects of asbestos as 'natural'. This was due to a combination of religious beliefs (that stressed a passive stance to the world around them) and the fact that often harms that are imperceptible to the senses only exist as a problem if they are constituted as such in public discourse (and, in particular, the public discourse of the village community). Otherwise, what is, simply is as it is.

This last point is important in another respect as well. Those who study disasters often make a distinction between 'human-made' (or technological) disasters and 'natural' disasters (Picou *et al.* 2009). The latter are seen as 'acts of God', and are responded to very differently compared with the former. Something that is seen to be 'naturally' caused or created tends not to generate the same anger, angst and conflict as that which is perceived to be due to human error and/or conscious intervention. On the other hand, human-caused disasters frequently end up in drawn-out resolution processes that, in their own way, likewise stifle or diminish victim resolve over time.

Nevertheless, environmental justice movements have historically tended to stem from specific instances of environmental victimisation (see Bullard 1994). Such movements largely focus on redressing the unequal distribution of environmental disadvantage. Action may also be taken to prevent environmental hazards being located in particular local areas. For example, in the 1990s the communities of the lower Fly Region in PNG sued BHP and received an out-of-court settlement, which was the culmination of an enormous public-relations campaign against the company by environmental groups. In January 2007 another lawsuit was lodged on behalf of other villagers seeking billions of dollars in damage.

There are, however, different types of environmental victimisation (for further elaboration and examples, see Stevens 1996; White 2009a and 2010a). Environmental victimisation may be direct or indirect, immediate or long-lasting, local or regional. It may involve lead in soils, dioxins in water, radioactivity in the atmosphere. It may be based upon routine industrial practices or stem from specific events. The threat may be realised (due to actual presence or absence of something in the environment) or be potential (as in for example a proposed privatisation of drinking water, or development plans to build a dam or pulp mill). Children are much more vulnerable to some types of environmental harm (e.g. toxic chemicals) than adults; in other cases, victimisation is more a question of proximity to the harm (e.g. death and maiming related to explosions).

Just as environmental victimisation differs concretely in its manifestation, so too victim responses vary greatly. In broad terms, different events, in different countries, have given rise to responses that vary from the passive to the confrontational, and from those involving collaborative activities aimed at redress to those based upon violence (Williams 1996).

Detailed analysis of specific events, over time, has revealed that there may be stages in the struggle for justice by victims, involving spontaneous and organised actions. The issues may be centred upon justice and/or on relief. The effectiveness of specific struggles, such as that related to events in Bhopal, India or the Cape region in South Africa (Waldman 2007) can also be analysed in terms of who defines the issues, who fights for or against on the issues, who owns the struggle and how the struggle is shaped and carried out in regards to local and international participants (see Sarangi 1996; Waldman 2007; Engel and Martin 2006). Examination of victim responses needs to take into account the type and extent of networking and coalition-building, but also the lack of participation and the marginalisation of some victim groups within a wider victim movement (Waldman 2007).

Then there is the issue of how NGOs from somewhere else (i.e. the metropoles of the North) impact upon the status and livelihoods of those in certain parts of the world (i.e. those who actually live in the South). Duffy (2010) recounts a number of stories where effective transnational NGO action has translated into the criminalisation of local residents and alienation from their own lands and natural resources. There is a 'dark side' to conservation that is based upon cultural ignorance and that can, in its own right, create more harm than good and lead to both human misery and unsustainable ecological solutions.

Table 7.3 provides an overview of key dimensions of environmental activism from the point of view of limited and expansive focuses on the part of victims and victim groups.

This type of analysis of victim response illustrates the idea of conflicts over priorities within victim circles, and how self-interest in a victim context is socially and politically constructed.

The politics of knowing and knowledge

At the heart of investigations of transnational environmental crime is the question of whose knowledge of 'wrong' is right? In other words, whose voices are going to be heard, and to what kinds of evidence do we lend credibility? It is rare that scientific evidence is uncontested and that proof of environmental harm is simply a matter of 'let the facts decide'. What counts as 'science', what counts as 'evidence', who counts as being a 'scientific expert' and what counts as

Table 7.3 Key dimensions of environmental victim activism

Limited focus	Expansive focus
Spontaneous	Organised
Exclusive to survivors/victims i.e. 'ownership'	Inclusive of outsiders i.e. 'alliances'
Localism i.e. focus on specific issue or event	Globalism i.e. worldwide connections
Material relief e.g. compensation	Abstract principle i.e. rights and justice
Top-down leadership, including charismatic leadership i.e. 'voices on behalf of'	Democratic and participatory forms of engagement i.e. 'voices of/by'
Rectification i.e. addressing what was	Transformation i.e. looking to what ought to be
Appeals to authority i.e. calling on government for answers and information	Self-governance i.e. reliance upon do-it-yourself research and analysis
Action motivated by loss i.e. informed by 'nothing left to lose'	Action motivated by future i.e. informed by 'a world to gain'
Victim focus as such	Victim interests linked to new social movements and wider struggles

Source: White 2010e

'sensible' public policy are all influenced by factors such as economic situation, the scientific tradition within a particular national context, the scientific standards that are used in relation to specific issues, and the style and mode of government (White 2008a and b).

In investigation and prosecution of environmental crime there is inevitably a range of social interests and 'discourses' that contribute to the shaping of perceptions and issues (see Hannigan 2006). This implies differences in perspective and a certain contentiousness of knowledge about the nature of the harm or crime. Assessment of victimisation usually involves responding to a series of interrelated questions:

- How are 'harm' and 'risk' defined, and by whom?
- How do we distinguish 'risk' (potentials) from 'harm' (actuals)?
- At what point does 'risk' or 'harm' actually occur?
- At what point does 'risk' or 'harm' occur to an extent warranting action or intervention?
- Who has the responsibility for proof?
- Why has the harm occurred and why was it done?
- Is responsibility in the hands of those harming, or of those being harmed?

- What is acceptable as evidence?
- What are the histories of 'risk' or 'harm'?
- What are the immediate signs of 'danger' or 'harm'?
- How do we stop the harm from occurring again?

The answers to these questions will frequently vary depending upon the stakeholder involved. Consider for example the variety of players who might be associated with disputes over toxic landfill in a residential community that is related to a nearby mining operation. In essence, victimisation is a contestable social process that engages a wide range of individuals. It is important therefore to undertake identification of stakeholders and specific stakeholder interests (e.g. workers and jobs; residents and amenity). It is also useful to explore the diverse narratives around 'risk' and 'harm' from different stakeholders (e.g. medical risk vis-à-vis the health department; loss of livelihood in the case of farmers; limited perception that there is a problem from local miners).

Moreover the marshalling of particular types of evidence is usually driven by very specific requirements (and forms of evidence) related to institutions and groups. Who says what and why is linked to specific social purposes and particular discursive domains. The language of crime and victimisation is reflective of how a social problem (in this case toxic landfill) is socially constructed depending upon how it is being considered and by whom. Table 7.4 sketches out diverse discourses that collectively contribute to both an understanding of, and differences in opinion over, particular issues.

Table 7.4 Matrix of discourse diversity

Legal discourses
- how the law defines the issues (e.g. crime, liability, responsibility)
- different pieces of legislation covering different aspects of the environment (e.g. health, environment, water, occupational health and safety)

Policing and regulatory discourses
- including Environmental Protection Agency (EPA) (e.g. proof of wrongdoing)
- assigning institutional responsibility for doing something

Scientific discourses
- including competing expertise (e.g. toxicology versus medical practitioners)
- in-house science and independent scientific review

Community/lay discourses
- competing claims regarding the 'best interests of the community'
- including local 'experts' (e.g. GP, local residents, Indigenous people)

Occupation discourses
- related to specific types of activities (e.g. farmers, fishers, loggers, oyster farmers)

Litigation discourses
- claims over damages from environmental victims (e.g. repairing the harm)
- claims over damages to reputation and production by industry (e.g. SLAPPs)

Media discourses
- investigative journalism
- current affairs shows and sensationalistic accounts

The sources and nature of different types of knowledge and information vary greatly. Each has implications for how victimisation is understood and conceptualised. The following vignettes provide a survey of diverse ways of thinking about and intervening in the world.

Science-based risk levels

The risk assessment process by which 'safe levels' of exposure to chemicals and other pollutants are assessed is highly problematic, and incorporates a range of ideological and moral assumptions. As Field (1998: 90) comments, 'The use of the apparently reasonable scientific concept of average risk, for example, means that data from the most sensitive individuals, such as children, will not be the basis for regulation, but rather data from the "statistically average" person.'

Indigenous knowledge and technologies

The concept of 'Indigenous knowledge' refers to the unique, traditional local knowledge existing within and developed around the specific conditions of women and men indigenous to a particular geographical area. Such IK systems, including management of the natural environment, have been a matter of survival to the peoples who generated these systems. Simultaneous with this is the concept of 'Indigenous technology', which is defined in terms of hardware (equipment, tools, instruments and energy sources) and software (a combination of knowledge, processes, skills and social organisation) that focus attention on particular tasks (Robyn 2002).

Knowledge from the periphery

Much of what we know is promulgated through Western media and Western academic institutions. This tends to privilege such knowledge over and above that which is organic to non-metropole regions and sites. Moreover, such knowledge production can implicitly and explicitly serve to prop up the hegemony of the metropole, often under the rubric of the claim to universal knowledge or universal values (e.g. individualism versus the collectivity). Yet, '… colonised and peripheral societies produce social thought *about the modern world* which has as much intellectual power as metropolitan social thought, and more political relevance' (Connell 2007: xii). This is evident, for example, in the rejection of GMO crops by the Zambian government on the grounds that not only was precaution required in the face of scientific uncertainty, but local varieties of maize and local agricultural practices needed to be protected from foreign imports that would, literally, change the regional landscape (Walters 2005).

Localised knowledge and experience

It may well be that it is local residents, local workers and laypeople generally who are more conscious of environmental risk than the scientist or the politician. Some indication of this is provided in a study of interaction between scientists and English sheep farmers in the wake of the 1986 Chernobyl nuclear accident in the Ukraine (Wynne 1996). The study highlighted the accurate, detailed and contextual knowledge of the farmers, even though the scientists considered this layperson knowledge to be lacking in precision. Those who are closer to the 'coalface', and who have lived and worked in the same area for years, are frequently those who notice the small changes that are the harbingers of things to come.

Studying up rather than down

Instead of middle-class academics studying 'down' on the poor, the marginal and the troubled, the notion of 'studying up' concentrates on the rich, the corporate sector and the metropolitan states as the key focus for research and critique (Connell 2007). The work of Beder (2006) provides a concrete illustration of how Internet resources and publicly accessed information can be compiled, interpreted and pieced together to show the networks and policy influence of powerful individuals and institutions internationally.

Alternative data sources for criminological purposes

Lynch and Stretesky (2001) argue that harm exists where evidence can be presented that the products/processes in question are reasonably expected to harm human health (e.g. medical data); that toxic harms can be placed into context by comparing them with other harms that society considers serious (e.g. assault rifle homicide versus pesticide exposure deaths); and that criminal responsibility exists where there is evidence that corporations have had knowledge of the risks they create, or are indifferent to these risks (e.g. silence or rejection of alternatives). Importantly, any claims along these lines are not reliant upon traditional criminological evidence (the usual crime data sets and criminal justice statistics) to be empirically substantiated. Medical records and epidemiological data can be drawn upon to establish the reality of the harm and to raise the possibility of criminal action against the perpetrators.

Victim accounts and stories

The actual stories and accounts provided by victims are an often neglected source of data and information. This is somewhat surprising given that very often it is biographies or specific histories featuring particular individuals that can have a major impact upon public opinion and legal proceedings. For example, the narrative accounts of asbestos victims in Australia, which inevitably make mention of the committed work of Bernie Banton in relation to the James Hardie Corporation, highlight both the work of victims as activists and the importance of their stories to public debate over environmental harms (see, for example, Peacock 2009).

Denial and affirmation

State crime is rarely something that is affirmed by states – rather, it is precisely the locus of denial (Cohen 2001). Accordingly, information and data that may make denial more difficult are likely to be made scarce or couched in language that masks the harm by the very agencies capable of producing it. On the other hand, regardless of humanitarian sentiment, passionate commitment and ideological predilection, those who claim that something is environmentally harmful (e.g. the use of depleted uranium in war weaponry) may do so with very little systematic evidence (see White 2008b). Responding to this situation ultimately means sifting through various types of evidence, listening to diverse voices of authority, and considering differing methods of investigation. For issues relating to environmental harm, there are serious practical challenges in relation to dealing with matters that are intrinsically multidisciplinary in nature, interconnected with other issues, highly politicised and global in scope.

Conclusion

Discerning who or what the environmental victim is, is partly subjective (it is 'in the eyes of the beholder') and partly objective (it is based upon evidence of some kind). Ultimately the construction of victimhood is a social process involving dimensions of time and space, behaviours involving acts and omissions, and social features pertaining to power and collectivities.

As this chapter has demonstrated, the transnational environmental victim is 'made' in the crucible of global polarisation, varying degrees of mobilisation, differing levels of ecological consciousness and major differences in the discourses of understanding. The majority of victims of environmental degradation – stemming from global warming, loss of biodiversity and increased waste and pollution – are, generally speaking, the poor and the dispossessed. While all are threatened by global environmental disaster, there remain large social differences in the likelihood of injury, harm and suffering. For those who disproportionately bear the brunt of worldwide changes, big questions arise as to who will compensate them for their suffering, now and into the future.

For the privileged few in both North and South, environmental victimisation could likewise be inevitable, but social interests and material comforts provide protection, thereby precluding the thought of 'being a victim' for some time yet. For the time being, victimisation will indeed be experienced by these people as a matter of unlucky chance – until the day when chance is all that defines the moment.

8 Criminal justice responses

Introduction

Eco-global criminology is not only concerned with crime or harm; it is also intrinsically interested in the ways in which the institutions of criminal justice currently or potentially engage with and prosecute issues pertaining to the environment. For the purposes of this chapter the main concern is with those perpetrators who actually get caught and are actually processed in and by the criminal justice system. As discussed in Chapter 6, the fact remains that many of the perpetrators do not end up being treated as offenders, nor do they suffer any negative consequences for the harms that they cause, facilitate and/or create.

How criminal justice institutions respond to environmental crime is still important, because it reflects the contemporary value placed upon these sorts of social and ecological harms. To change the criminal justice system as it stands will require a significant shift in general court attitudes towards environmental harms and in the specific values attached to different types of environmental harm. Certainly the present track record in this regard is less than encouraging, especially if we consider what is occurring in countries such as the United States (see, for example, Collins 2010). As this chapter discusses, there is a need to firm up regulatory and enforcement capacities if environmental crime is to be adequately dealt with by relevant government agencies and courts.

A key challenge in this area is how to conceptualise and structure an international system of criminal justice to deal with transnational environmental crime. This will require transborder cooperation between police and other types of environmental law enforcement agencies, as well as suitable forums and legal expertise in the prosecution of indicted offenders. This poses questions relating to the nature and possibilities for global policing regimes and networks, and the role of international courts. Furthermore, any discussion and analysis of global institutions immediately raises issues about global norms and values, especially if worldwide action is to be effective.

Environmental law enforcement

Many different agencies, at many different levels, deal with environmental crimes. For some, the central mandate of the agency is driven by the specific type of crime. For example, environmental protection agencies (or their equivalent) often focus on 'brown' issues pertaining to pollution and waste. Forestry commissions or national parks authorities (or equivalent) tend to concentrate on 'green' issues and so deal with matters of conservation, animal welfare and land use. Bodies such as the Royal Society for the Prevention of Cruelty to Animals (or equivalent) are charged with the responsibility to intervene in cases of harsh treatment of, particularly, domesticated animals (such as companion animals or those destined to be food). Customs services typically are on the lookout for trade in illegal fauna and flora, as well as the international shipment of toxic wastes and banned substances. Police services may have a general duty to protect animals and monitor the environment, while in some cases being vested with the lead role in wildlife offences. The regulation and policing of fisheries may involve specific fisheries management authorities and specially trained fisheries officers. Health departments may be the key authorities when it comes to disposal of radioactive and clinical waste. Park rangers could be tasked with the job of preventing the poaching of animals from national parks and private reserves. And so the list of agencies that have some role in environmental law enforcement goes on.

Part of the conundrum of responding to environmental offenders is figuring out who precisely is going to deal with them. Again, this is partly a function of the alleged offence, since this will often dictate the agency deemed to be responsible for a particular area. For the ordinary member of the public, however, this can be confusing. In addition, there are important cross-jurisdictional differences in who does what, even within the same nation state (see Tomkins 2005). Different personnel have different powers, and different agencies will use their specific powers in different ways, including powers related to sanctions (such as on-the-spot fines). Legislation usually sets out the mission parameters of a government agency, but what the law says is not necessarily what transpires at the ground level of practice.

There are also significant differences in how each nation state organises its environmental law enforcement efforts. Consider the police, as just one of the many agencies responsible for environmental law enforcement. In some contexts and situations, members of a police service may be trained up to be specialist environmental police. In Israel, for example, an environmental unit was established in 2003 within the framework of the police. It is financed by the Ministry of the Environment and includes police officers who form the 'Green Police'. These police carry out inspections, investigation and enforcement under a variety of laws in areas such as prevention of water source and marine pollution, industrial and vehicular pollution, hazardous substances, and prevention of cruelty to animals. Each year they carry out thousands of inspections of factories, landfills and sewage treatment sites, in the process liaising with regional officers of the Ministry of the Environment.

Research on 'conservation police' (a term that broadly refers to what are known as fish and wildlife officers, wildlife management officers, game wardens, park rangers, and natural resources police) in the United States has noted the complexity of the task for these officers, who have authority to deal with both conventional crime and environmental crime. In places such as Florida, for example, the fish and wildlife law enforcement officers possess general law enforcement authority, and so officers can investigate and enforce all state laws, not only those that relate specifically to fish and wildlife issues (Shelley and Crow 2009). In this case, what first appears as a specialist position is in fact expanding outwards to incorporate more generalist policing concerns.

By contrast, in the Netherlands, all police are trained and expected to actively deal with issues pertaining to environmental crime – it is built into the routines of everyday operational policing. In the United Kingdom, there are wildlife officers in most constabularies, and police in places such as Scotland are taking greater interest in environmental law enforcement, particularly as this relates to wildlife crime (Fyfe and Reeves 2009). Again, it is the specific nature of the offence that determines how active (or reactive) the police engagement actually is in regards to any particular environmental crime.

Within a particular national context, there may be considerable diversity in environmental law enforcement agencies and personnel, and police will have quite different roles in environmental law enforcement depending upon the city or state/province within which they work. In a federal system of governance, for example, such as with the USA, Canada and Australia, there will be great variation in environmental enforcement authorities ranging from police operating at the local municipal level (such as the Toronto Police Service) through to participation in international organisations (such as Interpol or Europol) (Tomkins 2005).

Specific kinds of crime may involve different agencies, depending upon the jurisdiction. For example, the policing of abalone poaching in Australia is generally undertaken by civilian fisheries authorities (with mandated coercive powers), except in Tasmania and the Northern Territory where it is in the hands of marine police. The transborder nature of illegal fishing operations – across state as well as international boundaries – means that often a local police service (such as Tasmania Police) will necessarily have to work collaboratively with national agencies (such as the Australian Federal Police) that, in turn, will have relationships with regional partner organisations (such as Interpol).

In the Australian context, Blindell (2006: 1, Note 2) defines environmental law enforcement agencies as all those agencies that enforce environmental protection legislation, for example:

- water resource agencies;
- parks and wildlife agencies;
- planning and development agencies;
- native vegetation protection agencies;
- environmental protection agencies.

As stated by the Australian Federal Police (AFP), the protection of the Australian environment is an issue that the Australian government and the AFP ostensibly takes very seriously. The AFP identifies a number of Australian government departments that have a role to play in the detection and enforcement of laws designed to protect the environment, including the AFP, Department of the Environment, Water, Heritage and the Arts, Australian Customs Service, Australian Fisheries Management Authority, Australian Maritime Safety Authority, Australian Quarantine and Inspection Service, and state agencies such as environmental protection agencies (AFP website 2008).

There are, then, many diverse agencies engaged in some form of environmental law enforcement. Some of these are engaged in both regulation and enforcement, and individual agencies may be charged with either or both. As illustrated in Table 8.1, agencies dealing with environmental matters work in and across different jurisdictions and deal with a myriad issues.

The plethora of players and laws demands an approach to environmental law enforcement and compliance that necessarily must be collaborative in nature. Dealing with global environmental harm will demand extraordinary efforts to relate to one another across distance, language and cultural borders; to understand specific issues; to coordinate actions; to enforce international laws and conventions; and to gather and share information and intelligence.

Table 8.1 Agencies at different tiers dealing with environmental law enforcement: Australia

Geo-political scale	Examples at the operational level
Local councils	• Urban and metropolitan councils • Regional or rural (shires)
State	• Environmental protection agencies • Local government association • State police services • Royal Society for the Prevention of Cruelty to Animals (RSPCA) • Parks and wildlife
National	• Australian Fisheries Management Authority • Australian Federal Police • Australian Customs and Border Protection Service • Office of Consumer Affairs • Department of Sustainability, Environment, Water, Population and Communities
National/state bodies	• Australian Crime Commission • National Pollutant Inventory • The Australasian Environmental Law Enforcement and Regulators Network (AELERT)
International	• Interpol • International Network of Environmental Enforcement and Compliance (INECE)

Among the many issues pertaining to the proliferation of agencies dealing with environmental crime and environmental harm is that each may be driven by different aims and objectives, different methods of intervention, with different powers, and exhibiting different levels of expertise and collaboration with others. Another issue relates to the need to distinguish between organisational affiliation (which may be formal and policy oriented) and inter-agency collaboration (which refers to actual operational practices and linkages). In some cases, there is a clear need for capacity building in order for collaboration and, especially, for rapid response, to be successfully institutionalised as part of agency normal practice. There can also be agency differences in defining and interpreting just what the crime is and how it should be responded to – as in the case of breaches versus crime, customs offences versus fisheries offences, and so on. Powers of investigation, particularly in relation to the gathering of suitable evidence for the specific environmental crime, will inevitably be shaped by state/provincial, federal and international conventions and protocols, as well as by availability of local expertise, staff and resources.

How environmental law enforcement is carried out in practice is shaped by agency mission and organisational capacities. Blindell (2006: 3) observes that:

> a major organisational enforcement challenge is that while police agencies have an existing and extensive pool of expertise and resources to enforce the criminal law, they have little experience or expertise in the enforcement of EPL [Environment protection legislation]. On the other hand, environment agencies have a very limited pool of expertise and resources to enforce EPL, coupled with substantial advisory, regulatory and compliance responsibilities – creating at the very least, a perception that environment agencies have conflicting roles.

Whether the issue is one of conflicting roles, or the emergence of multifaceted roles among environmental regulatory agencies, these are important questions when it comes to dealing with offenders. So, too, is the matter of resources and capabilities more generally.

For example, in a scoping analysis of law enforcement practices and institutions in Brazil, Mexico, Indonesia and the Philippines, in relation to a variety of environmental issues, Akella and Cannon (2004: 19) identified the following common problems across different sites:

* poor inter-agency cooperation;
* inadequate budgetary resources;
* technical deficiencies in laws, agency policies and procedures;
* insufficient technical skills and knowledge;
* lack of performance monitoring and adaptive management systems.

In a national study of crime in the Australian fishing industry, Putt and Anderson (2007: 54) likewise found 'the survey of fisheries officers as highlighting insufficient sharing of information by agencies and of collaboration across jurisdictions'. They observed that:

- The lack of formal agreements was seen as a major problem;
- Protocols to enable the sharing of information that does not breach privacy provisions would clearly be of benefit (subject to some degree of agreement on the purpose of sharing the information and what the expected benefits are to all parties);
- Differing priorities will continue to affect the success of joint operations, as well as the willingness of agencies to collaborate with information and resource commitments.

Tomkins (2005) also clearly identified the need to share intelligence and to develop cooperative enforcement structures to deal with environmental offenders. Who does what, and how, remain important practical issues.

In addition to questions of resources, staffing, recruitment of the right people, and training, a big factor that impacts upon agency performance is how well it interacts with other relevant agencies in the field. Related to organisational matters, the dynamics of environmental crime are such that new types of skills, knowledge and expertise need to be drawn upon as part of the law enforcement effort. For example, crimes related to toxic waste and pollution require the sophisticated tools and scientific know-how associated with environmental forensics (Murphy and Morrison 2007; White 2008a). Investigatory methods and powers, particularly in relation to the gathering of suitable evidence for specific environmental crimes, will inevitably be shaped by state/provincial and national laws and regulations, and influenced by regional and international conventions and protocols. The availability of local expertise, staff and resources will determine how investigation is carried out in practice.

Global issues demand global responses. This pertains to environmental law enforcement as much as it does to laws, policies and overall environmental strategies. Dealing with global warming, and the specific contributing factors to global warming (including both legal and illegal carbon emissions, legal and illegal logging practices, systematic reductions in biodiversity, extinction and endangering of species, etc.), for example, ultimately will call forth concerted coercive action to combat environmental harm. The role and capacity of environmental law enforcement agencies is essential in responding to harms of a global nature. This is complicated by the fact that most intervention occurs locally. To be effective, agencies need to be able to harness the cooperation and expertise of many different contributors and liaise with relevant partners at the local through to the international levels.

Penalties and remedies

The continuing degradation of the environment is linked to the broad regulation and enforcement framework itself. Thus, too often there is preference for education, promotion and self-regulation (with limited success) rather than directive legislation and active enforcement and prosecution (White 2008a). While environmental law enforcement capacities and interventions need to be ramped up, these will count for little if not accompanied by changes in attitudes towards regulation and penalties.

Put bluntly, to be effective those in charge of regulation and enforcement must be willing to utilise the 'big stick' and to monitor compliance systematically and diligently. Consider, for example, the impact of enforcement activities on compliance with the Canadian Environmental Protection Act and Canadian Fisheries Act amongst the anti-sapstain industry, pulp and paper industry, and the heavy-duty wood preservation industry (Commission for Environmental Cooperation 2001).This study demonstrated that intensive enforcement is directly correlated with effective regulation and dramatic change in the harmful activity (see Figure 8.1).

In this case, persistent and continuous inspections, accompanied by substantive operational powers (including use of criminal sanctions), led to rapid positive changes. In the instance of the federal Fraser River Action Plan, this strategy meant that discharges of acutely lethal effluent immediately fell off, and there was a 94 per cent reduction in effluent levels from 1991 to 1998 (Commission for Environmental Cooperation 2001).

There are special challenges for agency responses to transnational environmental harms in that many different jurisdictions have to be mobilised

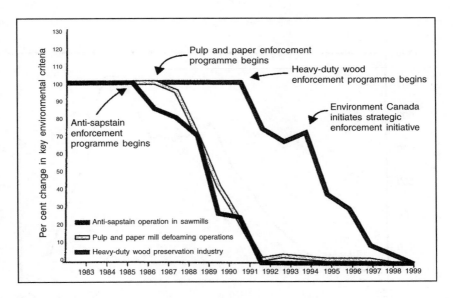

Figure 8.1 Normalised graphs of responses by three British Columbia forest sector industries to environmental law enforcement programmes

Source: Commission for Environmental Cooperation 2001

simultaneously around the same aims and objectives. Enforcement practices in these circumstances must be inclusive and comprehensive. This is achievable if there is enough consensus and political will. This is illustrated in Figure 8.2.

In this particular case of international law (and enforcement) the banning of ozone-depleting substances actually worked to address the environmental problem. It may have worked due to vested interests not being threatened by the proposed changes; it may have worked due to a conjunction of particular political circumstances. Whatever the answer, it does demonstrate what can be achieved by countries working in concert.

However, the multiple demands on specific environmental protection agencies by different sections of government, business and community, and the varied tasks they are required to juggle (e.g. compliance, education, enforcement), may lead to a dilution of their enforcement capacities and activities in both the national sphere and the international arena. This by no means derogates the importance of a 'bottom line' when it comes to compliance with environmental laws and rules.

> 'Speak softly and carry a big stick' is an appropriate aphorism for today's environmental regulator, but to be effective there must be certainty that the big stick can and will be used and the how, why and where of its use. It is the anticipation of enforcement action that confers the ability to deter.
>
> (Robinson 2003: 11)

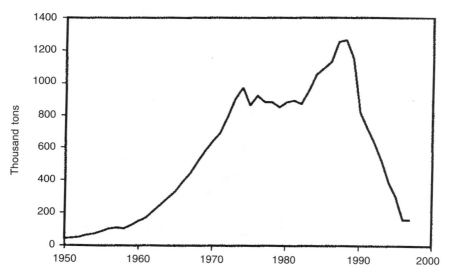

Figure 8.2 World production of chlorofluorocarbons, 1950–97

Source: French 2000

This of course raises the question of what types of sanctions in the enforcement toolbox are most effective and how they differ or are similar in effectiveness across different industry domains and types of harm, and when and how they might be applied.

Range and appropriateness of sanctions

Legislative change and law reform may provide abstract solutions to environmental harm, but it is through the grounded activities of enforcement officers and courtroom practices that the law in theory becomes the law in practice. A range of penalty types, approaches and mechanisms is identified below in regards to environmental sanctions (White 2010c). They fall into the broad categories of civil, administrative and criminal justice responses:

- prosecution as a central tool in enforcement and compliance activities, which means using the full application of criminal laws and criminal sanctions strategically and in proportion to the nature of the offence, including the use of imprisonment;
- alternative sentencing mechanisms which involve the compulsory contribution of offenders to an environmental project that requires restoration or enhancement of the environment;
- civil penalties for less serious breaches of environmental law, which ensure timely and efficient application of sanctions appropriate to the nature of the offence;
- imposition of stricter liability regimes (and use of nominated accountability) given the technical and resource difficulties in prosecuting large companies, which criminalises actions in ways that allow courts to sidestep some issues of *mens rea* in cases of corporate crime;
- tailored enforcement approaches that take into account organisation type, which means that sanctions such as fines are suited to the firm-type rather than the offence committed;
- restorative justice and enforceable undertakings approaches that can involve the offender, victim and community mutually discussing the nature of the offence and suitable remedies, as a prosecution alternative, and which are aimed at repairing the harm at a substantive level.

The sanctioning process for environmental offences at present covers a broad range of strategies, with new possibilities on the horizon. Bell and McGillivray (2008), for instance, mention the use of cumulative penalties, as for example in the case of points systems in motoring offences, so that a penalty infringement notice (PIN) does not become 'routine' or permit wealthy operators the 'right' to pollute.

The recent trend in countries like Australia towards alternative sentencing options reflects both the difficulties of prosecution in relation to corporations, and a shift in thinking away from the offender towards the nature of the offence.

For instance, the range of sentencing options around the country, whilst varying from jurisdiction to jurisdiction, includes an increasing number and type of orders (Preston 2007):

- orders for restoration and prevention;
- orders for payment of costs, expenses and compensation;
- orders to pay investigation costs;
- monetary benefits penalty orders;
- publication orders;
- environmental service orders;
- environmental audit orders;
- payment into environmental trust or for other purposes;
- orders to attend training;
- orders to establish training course;
- orders to provide financial assurance.

How this burgeoning range of sentencing options translates into particular sentencing outcomes warrants ongoing and close scrutiny. This is not only a matter of how the tension between compliance and facilitation is reconciled within specific institutional settings (such as an Environmental Protection Agency); it also goes to the heart of the processes of prosecutorial and judicial intervention on issues pertaining to environmental harm, and the valuing of environmental harm in and by the criminal justice system.

Measuring the value of environmental harm

Research is necessary to investigate how 'value' is perceived by magistrates and judges in relation to particular environmental offences, as reflected objectively in sentencing outcomes (i.e. sentencing patterns over time in relation to various environmental offences). These kinds of issues are being addressed in various ways. For example, Interpol provides information to support the work of prosecutors of environmental crimes, while in England a substantial toolkit has been prepared to guide magistrates in assessing the seriousness of environmental offences, determining sentencing criteria for environmental offences, and working through specific types of cases (Interpol Pollution Crime Working Group 2007; Magistrates' Association 2009).

From a legal perspective, the value of environmental harm is linked to the seriousness of environmental offences (see Table 8.2). Achieving consistency in sentencing for environmental offences is a special concern of the Land and Environment Court of New South Wales, which has been at the forefront of work to establish an environmental crime sentencing database (Preston and Donnelly 2008a and b). This remarkable database provides detailed sentencing information including judgements, recent law, publications, conferences, notes on evidence, and so on. Analysis comprises sentencing statistics for environmental offences dealt with by the Land and Environment Court, including data on offences,

Table 8.2 Criteria to determine seriousness of environmental offences

Immediate and direct impact of the environmental crime
- Environmental impact (e.g. dead fish from polluted water)
- Social impact (e.g. air pollution and health problems)
- Economic impact (crops damaged by pollution)

Wider effects in environmental, social and economic terms
- Global, transboundary (e.g. pesticides into watercourses)
- Diffuse impact (e.g. water pollution in rivers, the sea and on beaches)
- Cumulative effects (e.g. multiple sources of pollution)
- Long-term effects (e.g. health impact from radiation)

Human fatality, serious injury or ill health
- Human fatality
- Serious injury (e.g. loss of limb or loss of sight)
- Ill health (e.g. persistent respiratory problems)

Health of flora and fauna
- Animal health (e.g. endangered species killed or poisoned)
- Flora health (e.g. air pollution affecting crops and plants)

State of mind of the defendant
- Intentional (deliberate breach of the law) (e.g. collecting wildlife)
- Reckless (behaviour might lead to an offence) (e.g. pollutant run-off)
- Carelessness/lack of awareness (mitigates offence) (e.g. unaware)

Assessing the potential harm and risks taken
- Negligence (e.g. risk/potential harm to workers)
- Characteristics of pollutant (e.g. radioactivity and threat to health)

Relationship with regulatory authorities
- Advice from enforcing authority (e.g. complete disregard when an enforcing authority advises how to abate pollution)
- Warnings from enforcing authority (e.g. failure to take notice when warned of committing an offence)
- Warnings from workforce (e.g. workforce notifying the employer of unsafe work methods)
- Disregard for an abatement notice (e.g. polluter does nothing)
- Lack of cooperation (e.g. failure to turn up for interview)

Licensing/permit
- Breach of licence
- No licence
- Fraudulent papers

Economic gain for the defendant
- Profit (e.g. collecting money for waste and dumping it illegally)
- Cost saving (e.g. disposing of waste illegally to avoid disposal costs)
- Neglecting preventative methods (e.g. failure to use air filters)
- Avoiding licence fees (e.g. carrying out an act regardless)
- Tax and duties evasion (e.g. avoiding import and/or export duties)

Continued

Table 8.2 continued

Offence pattern
*   Re-offending (e.g. previous conviction for same offence)
*   Repeat offender (e.g. broken the law but not received formal sanction from the court)
*   Unrelated previous offences
*   Isolated incident

Abatement and reparation
*   Any necessary reparation, clean-up and restoration work

Mitigation
*   Isolated incident (e.g. good past record of the defendant?)
*   Awareness (e.g. genuinely and reasonably lacked awareness)
*   Guilty plea
*   Cooperation
*   Role in the offending activity (e.g. relatively minor)
*   Personal position (e.g. genuine hardship or adverse social circumstances of the defendant)
*   Tackling the problem (e.g. steps taken to remedy the problem)
*   Public contrition and remorse

Source: drawing from Magistrates' Association 2009

penalty types, characteristics that relate to the objective seriousness or gravity of the offence, and subjective characteristics that relate to the particular offender. Such a tool is bound to have a major impact on judicial practice, in helping shape the way judges and magistrates approach environmental sentencing. It provides a public account of sentencing practices as these are practically linked to the principles and purposes of sentencing, and it provides a useful indicator of the penalties that generally obtain in specific circumstances. In essence, the database provides a platform for judicial decision-making that will contribute to the treatment of environmental harms as 'real crimes' with proportionate penalties.

The information in Table 8.2 provides a guiding template for determining the seriousness of environmental offences and sentencing environmental offenders. Court databases likewise provide a 'living' record of how judges and magistrates are treating different environmental offences in their courts. These are important jurisprudential tools insofar as a perennial problem in regards to those cases that do get to court has been the seeming undervaluing of environmental crimes.

Bell and McGillivray (2008: 278) observe that:

> The definition of environmental crime matters because it helps to frame many of the key aspects of criminal liability for environmental harm. Whether an activity is viewed as a technical regulatory breach or a 'crime against the environment'; whether liability for environmental crime should be strict and if so what the justification is for doing so; the extent to which offenders should be viewed as truly criminal; the attitudes that should be

taken toward enforcing the law; and the sanctions which should be imposed for breach.

Is environmental harm or crime 'valued' sufficiently by the law? This question can be explored in several different ways. First, let us consider the question philosophically in terms of the moral dimensions of the law. Second, we can refer to actual court processes and outcomes. In either case, penalty regimes generally reflect prevailing attitudes and perceptions within the criminal justice system regarding the nature of the harm.

Environmental crime frequently embodies a certain ambiguity. This is because it is not only located in frameworks of risk (e.g. precautionary principle) or evaluated in terms of actual harms (e.g. polluter pays), but also judged in the context of cost–benefit analysis (e.g. licence to trade or to pollute or to kill or capture).

> Criminal law is normally reserved for the punishment of socially unacceptable behaviour. Harm to the environment is, in many situations, considered to be acceptable (for example in certain circumstances we are prepared to allow such pollution under license or authorization) because it is an inherent consequence of many industrial activities which provide significant benefits. This is the rationale for having a system of regulation which defines the framework for determining whether such benefits outweigh the harm caused. The criminal law is not suited to such a balancing process, and thus is mainly used to address clearly unacceptable behaviour or to reinforce the regulatory system.
>
> (Bell and McGillivray 2008: 281)

Philosophically, therefore, some types of harm are seen as less damaging than others, and thus to warrant different treatment from those perceived to be more serious. The notion of trade-off implicit within a cost–benefit approach immediately undermines the potential seriousness of the harm in question.

In law, this is generally framed in terms of how crimes come to be legally defined as a crime. On the one hand there is *malum in se*, a phrase used to refer to conduct assessed as inherently wrong by nature, independent of regulations governing the conduct (e.g. murder, rape). These acts are seen to be naturally evil as judged by the sense of a civilised community. In practical terms we can relate this concept to environmental issues by considering how mass suffering, injury and harm are frequently portrayed as 'accidental' rather than intentional (although they may involve lax safety procedures such as in the BP oil spill in the Gulf of Mexico), or simply a matter of chance (as in the case of natural disasters). Without a sense of human agency, there is no perceived real harm in itself. Liability and responsibility may be claimed, but the originating act is rarely considered an evil in its own right.

On the other hand, *malum prohibitum* refers to crimes that are criminal not because they are inherently bad, but because the act is prohibited by the law of the state. These are seen to be wrong because they breach regulation and are thus less serious per se. Here we can relate this to the fact that more often than not environmental protection agencies are mainly and primarily concerned with compliance activities – that is, how individuals, firms and corporations comply with the terms of their licences. This reinforces the general idea that environmental crimes are essentially less serious than others. It also ties into the notion that environmental protection is less about crimes against the environment and more about balancing economic and environmental interests.

In the light of these observations, it should not be surprising to find that most offences involving the environment are prosecuted in lower courts (or dealt with by civil and administrative penalties), and most penalties are on the lower rather than higher end of the scale. This applies to the way courts approach animal cruelty as well as to environmental offences relating to pollution and land clearance. Consider the application of animal law in Australia.

> Prosecutions for animal cruelty offending generally take place in District or Magistrates' Courts, and appellate decisions are rare. Sentencing notes are difficult to obtain, and records kept by prosecuting agencies often lack the detail needed for comparative purposes. While a comprehensive analysis of sentencing outcomes is not possible, a review of the available materials does tend to confirm perceptions that the penalty provisions are not currently being realised, and that sentence levels are unduly low.
>
> (Markham 2009: 293)

Similar trends are apparent across diverse jurisdictions. For example, over 90 per cent of all environmental crimes in the United Kingdom are dealt with in the magistrates' court, the most common sanction is fines, and these are at a low level (see Bell and McGillivray 2008). A comparison of European states in regard to environmental prosecution and sentencing found that the fine is the criminal penalty most commonly used in legal practice, and that the amounts imposed are apparently relatively low on average (Faure and Heine 2000). In the United States, there is the anomaly that at the same time that appellate courts have interpreted environmental guidelines so as to provide for increasingly severe sentences, the district courts have actually been imposing increasingly lenient sentences. Prison time is the exception not the norm. Moreover, it seems that low-culpability defendants may receive harsher sanctions than high-culpability defendants, bearing in mind the way appellate courts have ignored culpability considerations when interpreting ambiguous provisions under environmental sentencing law guidelines (O'Hear 2004).

On the other hand, even where there are severe penalties available, these may not be applied by the judiciary, especially if they are not familiar with environmental crime and its consequences (Hayman and Brack 2002; see also O'Hear 2004). The experience in the UK has been that the trivialisation of environmental offences in the courtroom serves to impede enforcement as a whole, and to diminish the threats posed by prosecution (de Prez 2000).

Specifically, the level of sentences given in courts, principally magistrates' courts, for environmental crimes has been seen to be too low for them to be effective either as punishment or as deterrent. The following observations capture the relevant issues:

> Many different reasons were cited for this phenomenon of low sentences. Some proffered the view that magistrates were unsympathetic to the idea that environmental crime was *real* crime. Others felt that they *were* sympathetic but lacked the proper guidance or the necessary experience. It was also suggested that the higher maxima involved in many environmental crimes dissuaded the practitioner from using the full scope of sentencing available by dint of their very rarity: a magistrate used to sentencing by fines of no more than [pounds sterling] 5,000 will baulk at going higher, even when permitted, in an area in which he [*sic*] feels he has little experience.
>
> (Environmental Audit Committee 2004: 11, emphasis in original)

In the light of this, guidance on sentencing options and outcomes, and the integration of court statistical records into the sentencing process, are more urgently required than ever. The work of ecological economics is also essential in this regard. This kind of analysis provides multiple criteria by which to assess the value of natural resources, wilderness, animals, fish and other species (see Orr 1991; Richardson and Loomis 2009). In the context of courts, both economic and non-market valuation are a vital part of deliberation over the nature of harm and potential damage claims against perpetrators (Duffield 1997).

The application of environmental sanctions can also be analysed sociologically. Here the concern is less with available legal remedies than with how such remedies are applied depending upon the perpetrators or victims involved. For example, research undertaken in the United States has shown that the penalties relating to hazardous waste sites in areas with large white populations are higher than in those with minority or Indigenous populations. Furthermore, there is less environmental enforcement of facilities in communities with higher minority and low-income populations (Pinderhughes 1996; Lynch *et al.* 2004; Konisky 2009). Criminal justice needs to be applied equitably and fairly if social justice is to be the outcome.

Conclusion

The prosecution and sentencing of environmental crime really only finds purchase within particular jurisdictions and national contexts. The problem, however, is that frequently the key actors involved in such crimes are global creatures, able to take advantage of different systems of regulation and legal compliance (Braithwaite and Drahos 2000). If a global company, for example, is bound by rules in one country but not in another, its behaviour is likely to differ in each setting and across jurisdictions (see, for example, Hughes 2004).

From an eco-criminological perspective the realities of globalisation as this pertains to crime and criminally engaged organisations have profound implications for intervention. Effective environmental law enforcement will require collaboration and knowledge-sharing between different nation states and environmental law enforcement agencies. The capacity of perpetrators to move across borders, and to use differences between jurisdictions to their advantage, has to be matched by the flexibility of law enforcement agencies in undertaking enforcement tasks. This requires collaboration and coordination as core attributes of such enforcement. The concept of 'networks' is important in this context.

A network approach to environmental law enforcement focuses on sets of relationships and the forging of informal and formal ties between relevant agencies and people (see Pink 2010). In regards to transnational environmental crime, the International Network of Environmental Compliance and Enforcement provides a case in point, as does the Interpol Environmental Crimes Committee. Regional and national networks of enforcement personnel and regulatory agencies are further examples of grounded collaboration involving diverse sets of players.

This networking is essential in several different ways. It allows for sharing of ideas and information about 'best practice'. It involves gaining perspective on environmental crimes that occur within specific local and regional contexts and those that are more global in scope. It fosters cross-agency cooperation and intelligence exchanges within specific national contexts (horizontal connections that bring together EPA, police, customs and other agency personnel), as well as internationally (vertical connections that bring together national representatives from different parts of the world, including United Nations personnel). In Australia, the combination of networks, whether internal or external, informal or formal, and involving law enforcers, non-law enforcers and environmental enforcers, has been perceived to have resulted in superior efficiencies in enforcement efforts (Pink 2010). Networking provides a practicable basis for intervention in areas that are by their nature complex and multifaceted.

In addition to the strengthening of environmental law enforcement networks, it may well be that an international environment court (or equivalent) with requisite United Nations support is required (but see Hinde 2003). This is especially so if we are to deal adequately with environmental matters such as, for example, those pertaining to the international spaces of our oceans (e.g. pollution, concentrations of plastic, illegal fishing, transference of toxic materials). Such a court could draw together transboundary expertise from the various environmental law enforcement networks to assess environmental crimes and harms that have international or global consequences.

The imposition of sanctions for environmental harms, particularly in an international context, raises important issues for national sovereignty. Williams (1996: 35), for example, asks the question:

> ... at what point does environmental victimization start to represent a threat to human survival sufficient to permit us to shift from the ethics of justice to those of security? ... cross-border victimization, such as pollution, may

sanction military actions against another nation. This would represent a shift from a principle of international justice as the guiding ethic – the autonomy of nation-states over their territory – to the ethics of national security. How long before we see the security forces of a wealthy nation 'take out', by force, an upstream/upwind polluting factory in a neighboring state, which has been the basis for environmental blackmail?

Dealing with environmental offenders involves grappling with conventional issues surrounding investigation, enforcement and sentencing while simultaneously considering what being a good global environmental citizen might actually entail. Major questions arise concerning who will wield the big stick, under what circumstances, and to whom they are accountable. These considerations entail matters of power and persuasion, of citizenship and deliberation. Looking over the horizon, the issues demand deep and extensive reflection on what is meant by 'the common good', how best to protect future generations, and what needs to be done to enhance ecological health and well-being.

9   Transnational activism

Introduction

Eco-global criminology is concerned with the ecological, the transnational and the harmful. This is expressed in its consideration of eco-justice issues as these pertain to transgressions against humans, ecosystems and animals, and ecological issues such as those relating to climate change, biodiversity and waste and pollution. Intrinsic to the framework of analysis offered by eco-global criminology is the idea of social change. Environmental harms are accumulating and threatening the basis of life itself. In these circumstances urgent action is needed on many fronts.

Transnational environmental crimes require an international response that extends to non-government actors as well as nation states. The transnational environmental activist occupies this important democratic space. At a formal governmental level, there is a major role for institutions such as the United Nations, and agencies such as Interpol, supported by various legislation, conventions, protocols and agreements at national and regional levels as well as those that are worldwide in scope and application. So, too, given the paucity of political will on many issues, especially that of global warming, it is essential that pressure be put on governments from outside the mainstream political arena and external to the often cosy relationship between government and corporations.

Transnational activism incorporates a huge number of organisations, groups and individuals, informed by many different missions and employing a vast array of strategies and tactics. The focus of activists varies greatly. 'Brown' issues tend to be defined in terms of urban life and pollution (e.g. air quality), 'green' issues mainly relate to wilderness areas and conservation matters (e.g. logging practices), and 'white' issues refer to science laboratories and the impact of new technologies (e.g. genetically modified organisms). Conceptualising environmental issues in this way helps demonstrate the link between environmental action (usually involving distinct types of community and environmental groups), and particular sites (such as urban centres, wilderness areas or sea coast regions). Groups are also demarcated by particular notions of justice, including those relating to environmental justice (e.g. specific human communities), ecological justice (e.g.

protection and conservation of particular ecosystems) and species justice (e.g. animal rights and welfare).

The environmental justice movement comprises a wide range of marginalised and disempowered people (the poor, people of colour, women) who are most affected by inequalities in environmental conditions. In the United States, it has included urban African American and Latino communities and Native American peoples residing on traditional lands (Low and Gleeson 1998: 107). The environmental justice discourse can be critical of some mainstream environmental groups because of their 'focus on the fate of "nature" rather than humans' (Harvey 1996: 386). Rhodes (2003: 11), for instance, has noted that the differential impact of environmental policy and practices across racial, ethnic, income and gender 'has not been a major concern of the environmental movement'. The criticism here is that mainstream environmentalism has concentrated on the ecological concerns of the white middle class rather than issues such as the disproportionate burden of toxic contamination on minority communities (Low and Gleeson 1998).

In some cases therefore the interests of specific groups and movements may be at cross purposes to others, although there is growing momentum towards shared political agendas, whether this is in relation to human rights and environmental protection or animal liberation and ecological justice (Clark 2009; Pezzullo and Sandler 2007). The trend towards cooperation and appreciation of the specific project of environmental justice activists or animal rights campaigners or conservationists is not only driven by strategic considerations of effectiveness and building popular alliances; it is also informed by a strong sense of issue overlap (e.g. GMOs and land degradation and loss of habitat for animals) and temporal urgency (i.e., species are dying out, now).

Eco-global criminology must have a forward-looking component if human, biosphere and non-human interests are to be protected into the future. This means interventions now to guarantee environmental well-being later. Differences in opinion over future consequences means that those who take action now (such as protesting against a large polluting pulp mill) for the sake of up-and-coming generations may well be criminalised in the present. But the history of law reform is built precisely upon such tensions. The uncertainties surrounding future impacts and consequences mean that debate will occur over when preventative measures need to be introduced as a precautionary measure. This is especially so in relation to global warming and the debates over what to do about climate change. The politics of ecological sustainability will inevitably collide with the interests of economic growth, since greater adherence to the precautionary principle will almost always lead to curtailment of existing profit-making enterprises.

Environmental activism thus deals with acts and omissions that are already criminalised and prohibited, such as illegal fishing or illegal dumping of toxic waste. But it also comes to grips with events that have yet to be designated officially as 'harmful' but that show evidence of exhibiting potentially negative consequences. It deals with different kinds of harms and risks, as these affect humans, local and global environments, and non-human animals.

Internationalism as a practical tool of activism

Of the four key pillars of social change – that include activism, state regulation, economic reformation and international governance – it is activism that is the most fundamental driver of environmental reform (Buttel 2003). Non-governmental organisations (NGOs) are active in many different ways, but activism is not reducible to NGOs since unplanned spontaneous activities, such as riots, can involve participants and events that are not expressly linked to any particular organisation. A range of activities can be identified, that include confrontational tactics and practices through to the more cooperative. Some of these are summarised in Table 9.1.

These activities are not mutually exclusive, although not all organisations or all activists engage in them or necessarily agree with them as specific tactics. In some cases activist practice may be illegal, an issue that is discussed again later in the chapter. There is no one practice that is effective on its own. Most successful campaigns and movements for social change involve a wide range of interventions and activists. What works depends upon the context, although specific organisations may disagree over overall strategic directions. For example, the Sea Shepherd Society campaign around whales was initiated by a former member of Greenpeace who believed that direct action was the central plank in this area of activist work.

The response to environmental harm takes a variety of organised and unorganised forms. The riot, for example, represents a spontaneous reaction to

Table 9.1 Continuum of activist engagement

Confrontational/radical	Conciliatory/conventional
Mass mobilisation and public demonstrations	Behind-the-scenes negotiation or cooperation
Protest actions	Petitions
Trespass and breaking in	Leafleting
Sit-ins and office takeovers	Website
Symbolic use of media	Information table or stall
Blocking roads	Lobbying of politicians
Eco-sabotage	Media advertising
Riots	Press releases

specific issues and the perceived lack of democratic voice on environmental matters. When the people are not engaged in decision-making, the streets become an important venue for democratic participation. Environmental (and animal rights) NGOs have a crucial role to play in monitoring illegal activity, challenging corporate agendas and fostering radical social change. They are also pivotal in monitoring and gathering data on environmental offences, sometimes at great personal risk to themselves.

Importantly, in terms of the present concern with transnational environmental crime, there has been a steady rise in the number of NGOs working across international borders in recent years (French 2000). Some of the more familiar international NGOs include Friends of the Earth, Greenpeace, International Fund for Animal Welfare, Humane Society International, Sierra Club, Environmental Investigations Agency and the World Wide Fund for Nature. The list is extensive, including, for example, BirdLife International, Pesticide Action Network, Climate Action Network, Biodiversity Action Network, and the International POPs Elimination Network. There are also various NGOs working specifically around issues such as forests (e.g. Amazon Watch, Rainforest Alliance), and waste (e.g. Basel Action Network, Silicon Valley Toxics Coalition).

Some organisations engage in militant and spectacular actions (e.g. Greenpeace anti-coal campaigns and Sea Shepherd anti-whaling campaigns). Others focus on specific issues and work closely with governments and international regulatory bodies to enact change. For example, the Antarctic and South Ocean Coalition (ASOC) is an NGO established in 1976 to coordinate the activities of over 250 conservation groups on matters such as Patagonian toothfish management. The Coalition works closely with governments in confronting issues associated with illegal, unreported and unregulated fishing. So, too, do groups such as the Environmental Investigations Agency and the Freeland Foundation for Human Rights and Wildlife, which engage in independent investigations of illegal environmental activities, gathering evidence that is eventually handed over to local police authorities and which is suitable for prosecutions in relevant jurisdictions and courts.

Groups such as the Animal Liberation Front (ALF) use a variety of tactics that raise awareness about systematic animal cruelty. Breaking the law (such as illegal entry into animal laboratories or battery hen farms) is considered legitimate if it means that public consciousness is heightened and immediate harms to animals diminished through such actions. Some groups resort to tactics that have been described as eco-terrorism. Earth First!, for instance, has advocated a form of 'strategic ecotage', that is, environmentally related sabotage, that has involved sabotaging the machines that destroy forests (e.g. monkey-wrenching).

The struggle over ideas and activities will intensify in the coming years as the effects of global warming, in particular, proliferate. The worldwide effect of many environmental events and trends (e.g. cutting down of rainforest in the Amazon) is being matched by the efforts of activists to utilise the world stage in pursuing social and ecological change. It is precisely the transnational nature of much campaigning that renders its strength and potential for success.

This is aptly illustrated in a case involving anti-logging activists in Tasmania, Australia.

The Gunns 20 Case

On 13 December 2004, Gunns Limited issued a writ in the Victorian Supreme Court against 20 environmental activists (see White 2005, 2010d). At the time, Gunns Limited was Australia's largest fully integrated hardwood forest products company. It owned 175,000 hectares of freehold land and managed in excess of 90,000 hectares of plantations. The company, at the time, employed over 1,200 people and had a turnover in excess of AUS$600 million. The timber company sued the group of environmentalists, protesters and Green MPs for AUS$6.3 million.

In this first version of the lawsuit, Gunns Limited claimed damages for financial loss allegedly suffered as a result of protest actions related mainly to the activities of the company in Tasmania. The writ claimed that the overall campaign against Gunns Limited constituted a conspiracy to injure Gunns (the company), through interference with Gunns' trade and business by unlawful means. The case finally reached settlement on 28 January 2010, by which time 16 of the original 20 defendants had either settled or been dropped from the suit. The final four defendants were not ordered to pay any costs or damages nor to give any undertakings (Swales 2010).

In a curious way, this writ provides interesting indicators of 'good practice' in activist movements – insofar as they publicly identify those parties and those activities that are most threatening to (and thus successful in challenging) corporate interests. As indicated in the original writ, Gunns was most concerned about four main areas of campaign activity:

* campaigns and actions that disrupt logging operations;
* corporate vilification campaigns relating to their 'clean' and 'green' image;
* campaigns against overseas customers of their products;
* corporate campaigns targeting shareholders, investors and banks.

It was the international nature of the activist campaign that particularly upset the company, and that had a direct impact on its actual and future operations. For example, the Wilderness Society, in conjunction with the Japan Tropical Forest Action Network (Tokyo) and Greenpeace Japan, was active in 2000 in targeting the Japanese corporate customers of Gunns. The campaign involved disseminating information about Gunns in major cities across Japan, and writing letters directly to the relevant Japanese companies about Gunns' environmental track record. The key demand was to force Gunns to immediately cease woodchipping of old-growth forests. The main message was that present types of timber production were environmentally disastrous and that Japanese corporate consumers and individual citizen consumers could play a role in preventing the destruction of such forests.

The internationalisation of the struggle over the forests was threatening to Gunns, and to Gunns' customers, on several different levels. Links were forged between different activist organisations in Australia and Japan, and between separate organisations with different mandates and approaches vis-à-vis environmental activism (i.e., Wilderness Society, Greenpeace). Japanese corporate consumers wished to protect their public claims that they believed in pursuing corporate activity that is in harmony with nature. However, local organisations in Japan that were associated with the Tasmanian activist groups ensured that Japanese citizens would most definitely hear about the issues. Meanwhile, the reputations of the Wilderness Society and of Greenpeace in relation to creating adverse publicity, engendering consumer boycotts and engaging in direct actions, and the international profile and consequences of such activities, were causing considerable angst among the Japanese corporate consumers. This is illustrated in a letter reproduced in the original writ (see Box 9.1).

The internationalisation of the struggle, with a specific focus on corporate and citizen consumer markets, proved to be a particularly effective activist strategy. This was borne out, for example, in correspondence from Nippon Paper Industries to the Premier of Tasmania, in which the General Manager pleaded with the Premier to meet the Wilderness Society and seek out a 'middle ground'. They wanted to have 'the focus moved back to Tasmania' and they wanted to move the 'argument back to Australia instead of Japan' (White 2010d). The political heat was being felt in Japan, and the companies wanted Australian political and economic leaders to deal with it since it was blowing up as a problem for everyone concerned.

A moral framework for transnational environmental activism

What is effective environmental activism depends very much upon the immediate political struggles and social contexts in question. However, what works in environmental activism should not be reduced to the formula that 'the local' equals 'good'. The effectiveness of environmental activism largely depends upon going beyond localism as such, to forge links and allies outside of the immediate locale of an event, disaster or situation.

The transition from simply responding to special instances of environmental injustice, to broader movements towards ecological citizenship, hinges upon that vital link between social inequality and environmental degradation. This link is evident in cases of structural exploitation of humans (and surrounding environments), as with the location of factories on the Mexican side of the US–Mexican border. It is also apparent in analysis of the disproportionate consequences of 'accidents' such as Chernobyl or Bhopal for poor and dispossessed peoples and for those workers who live and work in proximity to potentially dangerous sites. In other words, environmental harm is unevenly distributed in geographical and social terms, and this is evident when we see which population groups generally constitute the bulk of environmental victims (Cifuentes and Frumkin 2007; Pellow 2007; Faber 2009; White 2010a).

Box 9.1 Letter to Gunns from Nippon Paper

Mr John Gay
President
Gunns Limited

You have already been informed that The Wilderness Society and The Green Peace Japan sent the plea to our president, requesting us to stop purchasing wood chips from your company, because they say your company devastates Tasmanian old growth virgin forests.

Judging from what we have so far heard or been told, including the presentation given by both the groups on July 14th, we believe that their dissatisfaction or discontent with the RFA [Regional Forest Agreement] underlies this issue.

We understand that the argument in your letter dated on July 3rd to our president is just and rational. However, to be honest with you, we are very much embarrassed with the activities of such environment groups, because we are focusing on how to develop our business in a way that emphasizes sustainability (a harmonious balance with nature and business).

We know that you cannot accept their criticism against the law-abiding logging. What we would like to call on you to do is to mediate between the Australian Government and the Tasmanian government for a discussion with the Wilderness Society. Our objective is to ensure we purchase your wood chips in accordance with our stated corporate principles.

F. Manoshiro
Forestry Department
Nippon Paper Industries

Source: White 2005

Table 9.2 outlines a shift in consciousness and activities that can materially further the cause of transnational environmental activism. What is being described in this table is the movement from singular and narrowly defined interests and localities to more universalising and global concerns that acknowledge the intrinsic commonalities across borders and a shared moral universe amongst political activists.

Such concerns are also evident in broad political and legal discussions of environmental rights. These rights are often seen as an extension of human or social rights, because the goal is one of enhancing the quality of human life (e.g. access to clean air, water, space, and a sustainable supply of natural resources

Table 9.2 From environmental justice to ecological citizenship

---

Environmental justice

➤ emphasis on harm as experienced in the here and now (e.g. death and disability caused by toxic dumping in local area)

➤ human-centred conceptions of harm and justice (e.g. social inequality and questions of social equity)

➤ differing demands amongst those most affected are constructed around human self-interests (e.g. compensation, rights)

➤ specific locality (i.e. territory) and particular issues (e.g. event) provide for a local conceptualisation of the key problem that warrants action

Ecological citizenship

➤ recognition of global nature of specific phenomenon (e.g. disposal of toxic waste in Third World involves transnational forces)

➤ acknowledgement of global effects of localised practices and victimisations (e.g. logging and climate change, radiation poisoning and wind currents)

➤ emphasis on pursuit of social and ecological justice (i.e., humans, biospheres, non-human animals)

➤ acknowledgement that NIMBY (including carbon emission trading schemes) puts the problem into someone else's backyard

---

Source: White 2010e

valued in relation to human health and amenity). This is reflected, for example, in the 1972 Stockholm Declaration on the Human Environment (see Thornton and Tromans 1999). This document encapsulates two key obligations: first, intergenerational responsibility – such that present generations do not act in ways which jeopardise the existence of future generations (intergenerational equity); and second, environmental justice in the here and now – such that access to and use of specific natural resources in defined geographical areas, and the impacts of particular social practices and environmental hazards, are 'shared out' on an equal rather than discriminatory basis (social equity).

A more expansive definition of rights alludes to the inclusion of the non-human into the moral equation (White 2007). For example, ecological notions of rights and justice see humans as but one component of complex ecosystems that should be preserved for their own sake, as supported by the notion of the rights of the environment (Smith 1998). What necessarily follow from this particular perspective are notions of interconnectedness and human obligations to the non-human world around us. All living things are bound together, and environmental matters are intrinsically global and transboundary in nature. Ecological justice demands that the way humans interact with their environment be evaluated in relation to potential harms and risks to specific creatures and specific locales as well as the biosphere generally. There is a strong link between the idea of ecological justice and the notion of ecological citizenship.

Ecological citizenship incorporates the key concerns of environmental justice, ecological justice and species justice. The notion of 'universal human interests' is useful here in contradistinction to sectoral human interests and narrowly defined notions of the 'national interest'. In the course of ostensibly protecting or promoting the 'national interest', for instance, the state frequently engages in conduct that violates human rights and degrades and destroys environments and species. These environmental harms are justified by the state on the basis that the net result will be for the benefit of the majority, even though the main beneficiaries tend to be transnational corporations and local business firms. The result is the systemic and intensive violation of human rights and the undermining of overall environmental well-being; something that is particularly evident in free trade zones and geographical areas covered by multilateral free trade agreements (see Cifuentes and Frumkin 2007).

Conversely, there are basic ecological interests that need to take priority over specific sectoral interests if humans are, as a species, to survive. However, while everybody on the planet has a common interest in the survival of the human race, the specific commercial interests of companies and transnational corporations mean that they are reluctant to implement or enact strategies and policies that further common human interests. The state continues to play a prominent role in protecting the interests of the elite and ruling classes, both at a domestic country level and through transnational consortiums and international agreements governing commercial activities. The abject failure of the Copenhagen talks to actually do something about carbon emissions and to address climate change issues in a substantive fashion is a striking example of the fusion of state and corporate interests to the detriment of the majority.

Having said this, what people on the ground do does matter when it comes to the role of the state in respect of environmental issues. It is 'people power' that gives shape to and helps construct certain issues as significant or important enough to warrant some kind of state response (see Hannigan 2006). The mobilisation of opinion is likewise crucial to determination of what is or is not considered a 'crime', and how the state will respond to a specific phenomenon. The precise nature and visibility of an environmental issue is in itself linked to specific group interests and consciousness of harm. Some issues tend to resonate more with members of the public, politicians and the media than others; other issues generally only emerge if an accident or disaster brings them to the fore.

From an activist perspective, global ecological citizenship provides a general philosophical viewpoint from which to gauge the performance of a state in relation to environmental matters. Processual accounts can be useful in evaluating the overall human and ecological rights performance of a state over time. For instance, Ward and Green (2000) describe a process whereby states may be involved in either a 'virtuous' spiral or a 'vicious' spiral in relation to gross violations of human rights. Each spiral makes reference to the dynamic ways in which norms about the institutionalisation of human rights are reinforced or abandoned, depending upon the particular political context. The virtuous spiral, for example, may involve a process whereby 'human rights violations are labelled as deviant by domestic and later by transnational civil society in a mutually reinforcing process and, as a result, human rights norms are gradually adopted as criteria of the state's legitimacy. Human rights violations become illegitimate, in the process, because they are successfully labelled as state crimes' (Ward and Green 2000: 86). Such an analytical approach provides insight into how and why particular nation states change their practices over time, either away from human rights violations or towards more intense ones.

A similar processual analysis can be made in regards to state crimes relating to the environment. Towards this end, a framework of ecological citizenship provides an ideological and symbolic platform from which to challenge narrowly defined 'national interests' and specific state interventions that degrade and destroy environments. Ecological citizenship positions the actor as an international citizen, a status that allows them to transcend narrow state interests (as defined by local elites) yet still make claims on the state according to notions of universal human interests (as reflected in the Universal Declaration of Human Rights, for example). From the point of view of ecological citizenship, state laws and actions (and omissions) should be tempered by the acknowledgement that human interests are intimately bound up with the well-being of the planet as a whole. Human intervention, of any kind, needs to be considered in the light of this. Hence, the importance of the precautionary principle in gauging potential and real impacts arising from human activity, and the role of activists in using this to pressure states to do the right thing.

Environmental activism, crime and criminalisation

Nation states differ in how they respond to environmental issues. For instance, the precautionary principle has been generally integrated into the regulatory and legal frameworks of the European Union, but has been less popular in the United States. Moreover, internationally the concept is contested and has 'become a chess piece in the struggles over genetically modified foods, for example' (Leiss and Hrudey 2005: 9). Policy differences are apparent in other areas as well, as with the assessment of pesticide hazards in the United States, Britain and the European Union (see Irwin 2001).

How different nation states act, react or do not act in relation to environmental issues helps to shape local, regional and transnational activist campaigns. It also provides impetus for the adoption of different kinds of strategies and tactics. Depending upon the issue, and the activist, the interplay between state and society sometimes leads to extremism and the conscious stretching of the boundaries of existing law. This occurs in a moral climate in which certain justifications are claimed in support of particular actions.

> If, between states and between state and citizen, the need to ensure human security 'must prevail' over justice norms as reflected in international or domestic law, and we accept the inference that military force may then

legitimately be used against the entity posing the threat to human security, do we then accept that the principle extends to violence by community activists against the threat posed by the lead smelter down the road?

(Williams 1996: 36)

However, assuming the moral high ground is not without its political and social costs. As discussed below, it is frequently accompanied by sustained efforts on the part of states to criminalise people and those activities that threaten the legal status quo and the established political and economic order.

Here a distinction can be made between environmental crime (e.g. illegal logging) and crimes associated with the environment (e.g. anti-logging protests). The criminalisation of environmental activism is neither new nor unusual. It applies to particular social movements, to individual activists and to particular social groups. It has been noted, for example, that 'Indian people who have challenged multinational corporate giants and the government through political activism in an effort to halt environmentally destructive projects on their lands have been criminalized and arrested to silence their claims' (Robyn 2002: 198). This story is common in many different places around the globe among many different communities (Robin 2010; Duffy 2010).

Crime associated with the environment includes what has been described as eco-terrorism or ecotage, acts that are sometimes committed by environmental activists involved in specific campaigns (e.g. tree spiking, damaging earthmoving equipment), and which are in themselves legally defined as criminal (Martin 1990; Amster 2006). These are crimes committed on behalf of, or in defence of, the environment, rather than crimes against the environment. There is nevertheless an important connection between these two sorts of activity (damage to the environment, and criminality related to protests over environmentally harmful activities). Moreover, each type of 'crime' calls forth major arguments over definition and what are deemed to be appropriate social responses.

Human rights violations

The persecution of environmental activists takes a number of different forms and involves different actors. Often it is environmental victims who are the targets for legal action and government redefinitions of victimhood, and who bear the brunt of the economic penalties meted out by the very same corporations which have harmed their communities (see Chapter 7). But it is not only environmental victims who are treated in this way.

The struggles over forests, over whales, over GMO crops and many other ecological issues vary greatly in terms of immediacy and intensity. In some countries, as recent events in Peru have shown, many lives have been lost as a consequence of riots on the part of protestors and repressive action on the part of the state (Boekhout van Solinge 2010). Here and elsewhere, these kinds of deaths have been linked to kidnappings (on both sides), to the sabotage of work sites, to the hostile engagement of military and police services against protestors, activists and communities, and to the use of hired thugs to remove and bulldoze people's homes and villages (Robin 2010; Clark 2009).

While the resistance of environmental activists has occasionally led to deadly outcomes, this is not a simple two-sided, balanced violence equation. Such incidents continue to be the exception rather than the rule. The overwhelming evidence is that power is skewed on the side of the nation state and corporations, which are jointly determined to push certain economic and social agendas. In this case, and on this side of the equation, the violation of human rights is becoming too frequent to be ignored.

Attention to the violation of human rights is also very much tied to certain governmental regimes, and to particular parts of the world. As Clark (2009: 132) observes:

> ... it can be argued that environmental degradation is more likely to occur in countries where there are human rights abuses. In these countries, citizens are not able to stand up to either the large multinational corporation, with its vested interest, or the government, which may be more concerned with economic development. Conversely, it can be argued that human rights development will often result in an improved environment since human rights allows for the participation of local communities. As a result, both environmental and human rights organizations are declaring that these two issues are linked.

A typical list of the countries implicated in human rights abuses includes Brazil, Ecuador, Guatemala, Honduras, Mexico, Myanmar (Burma), Cambodia, China, Congo, Kenya, Nigeria and the list keeps going on (Clark 2009). Types of abuses include unlawful arrest, intimidation, threats, detention, beatings, rape, threatened rape of family members, fabrication of evidence, burning of homes, the redesignation of traditional lands as 'militarised areas', torture, murder and disappearances. Organisations such as Human Rights Watch and Amnesty International, as well as local and regional environmental, community and human rights organisations, play a crucial role in documenting such abuses whenever and wherever they occur.

Undoubtedly environmental injustice also takes place in so-called First World countries – witness the rise and growth of the environmental justice movement in the United States. This is so regardless of the fact that legal conventions and a modicum of press freedom provide for at least some ostensible limits to the harms able to be perpetrated. Systematic analysis of US laws and law enforcement around environmental concerns demonstrates, however, the pervasive nature of the loopholes, and the continuation of harms over a period of many years (Collins 2010). While it is easy for those in the West to point to Third World countries and to decry poor political systems and the perils of poverty, much more attention is simultaneously required in their own backyard. Repression is not unique to developing countries, as the next topic indicates.

Eco-terrorism

Another inhibiting factor when it comes to taking action over environmental issues relates to the alleged link between environmental activism and 'terrorism'. Consider for example the following list of direct actions taken by some environmental activists and activist groups (Brisman 2008: 754):

> firebombing, defacing, or slashing the tires of SUVs; vandalizing business walls and windows with glass-etching cream and spray-paint; damaging construction equipment used for housing developments or mega-stores; burning buildings (such as laboratories, horse corrals, and unoccupied housing developments); tree-spiking (placing spikes in trees to fend off loggers' chainsaws); 'net-ripping' (which, similar to tree-spiking, involves dumping into the ocean tons of steel I-beams welded together to form large spikes that destroy bottom-trawling nets); blocking access to forest land that would otherwise be logged; disrupting hunts or otherwise preventing recreational hunters from hunting; sabotaging research or facilities using animal-testing techniques; and liberating or removing animals from fur farms or laboratories and industries that conduct animal-based research.

Many of these activities are harmful, dangerous and serious in their consequences. Many are also illegal or criminal. Yet all are defended and justified on the basis of fighting for the general interest or some higher good.

This raises the issue of how far can or should one be allowed to go in order to defend environmental interests (as variously defined)? The rationale for such actions is generally along the lines of breaking the law for the sake of the greater good (i.e. environmental/animal protection). Indeed, social change has long been based upon such principles that argue that if existing laws and practices are unjust or unfair, then justice itself demands they be challenged. Such was the case with the suffragette movements of the late nineteenth and early twentieth centuries, the civil rights struggles of the 1960s and 1970s and, today, in the social movements around environmental issues and animal rights.

The state is implicated in the use of such tactics insofar as avenues for deliberative democracy are diminished (by outlawing public assembly in certain places) or when sectoral interests (e.g. the large timber company) are allowed to predominate even in the face of widespread negative public opinion. Frustration about the lack of state action on the one hand (such as preventing the pollution of a river) or particular kinds of state action that facilitate ecological harm on the other (such as granting licences for the clear-felling of old growth forests), combined with a democratic deficit when it comes to decision-making, provides fertile ground for the employment of new activist strategies and tactics, not all of which are, strictly speaking, legal.

Further ambiguity on these issues stems from two quarters. On the one hand, as scientific evidence firms up certain harms (for example, global warming), then public support is likely to grow in favour of actions that appear to address these (for example, attempts to stop the cutting down of old-growth forests). Political support from mainstream parties will also be reflected in such trends, and indeed a general greening of politics is now taking place worldwide. Thus, what was once seen as the preserve of extremists is currently being transformed into the concerns of the mainstream, albeit generally excluding more extreme forms of direct action.

On the other hand, different jurisdictions view and respond to acts of environmental 'resistance' in different ways. For example, in the US the recent tendency has been to brand damage-causing acts of protest as forms of ecotage or environmental terrorism, and to prosecute and sanction offenders heavily (Rovics 2007; Brisman 2008). By contrast, consider a recent court case in England involving six Greenpeace activists (McCarthy 2008). The six had been charged with criminal damage after being involved in scaling and defacing a chimney at a plant at Kingsnorth, in a location earmarked for the development of a new generation of coal-fired plants. At the conclusion of the eight-day trial, the jury decided that the activists had been justified in causing damage to the coal-fired power station due to the larger threat of global warming. The jurors thus accepted the defence arguments that the six defendants had 'lawful excuse' (under the Criminal Damage Act 1971) to damage the property at the power station to prevent even greater damage caused by climate change.

Mass public opinion is affected by a range of cultural and material factors, including propaganda campaigns (from both sides) and corporate green washing (see Beder 1997). Specific kinds of anti-environmentalist attacks will also influence legal decision-making and legislative change in this area. A polarisation of views can be one consequence of this. In the United States, for example, there are two opposing understandings of environmental activism as this pertains to civil disobedience and the employment of direct-action tactics. These are encapsulated in the following phrases:

- *The threat of eco-terrorism* refers to extremism in the animal rights and environmental movements, and which typically involves causing damage to the operations of companies or terrorising executives and employees of companies. A key emphasis is on the notion of environmental extremism as terrorist activity (ADL Law Enforcement Agency Resource Network 2009).
- *The green scare* refers to a systematic movement, similar to the Red Scare of the 1950s, to discredit and penalise environmental and animal activists through application of new laws and punitive prosecutions in ways that involve heavy-handed government interventions and crackdowns, accompanied by sustained scaremongering fostered by corporate and media interests, around the theme of terrorism (Potter 2008).

The social construction of environmental activism is a collective process involving many different players and interests. The justification for legal and illegal actions around environmental and animal issues relates to perceptions that many currently legal activities in fact constitute a crime against nature (whether this be a forest or in relation to animals). Conversely, some of the types of actions to protest against these alleged crimes are themselves subject to considerable criticism on the basis of their present illegality (and, indeed, the harm they bring to others).

Whether construed as eco-terrorism or justified resistance, it is clear that the more extremist acts demand some sort of ethical parameters that can constrain both the acts themselves and the circumstances in which they may be undertaken (see Vanderheiden 2005). This is a crucial point, otherwise the potential to do good – on both sides – is undermined by ideological blindness, personal vindictiveness and wilful denial of consequence.

Climate change and transnational activism

National security agendas are increasingly reflected in the interplay between how crime and sovereignty are socially constructed, and how the relationship between local, national, regional and global interests is construed within diverse social and political formations (e.g. United States, European Union, Association of South East Asian Nations, African Union). The nation state remains an essential platform for concerted action to deal with the causes and consequences of environmental harm, as well as mitigating the worst outcomes of such harm. But the global nature of some problems – such as climate change – means that inevitably our collective survival will require planetary cooperation and worldwide action. For a critical eco-global criminology, this demands both an appreciation of the limitations of existing state/corporate strategies, and creative thinking to take intervention in new directions.

For example, insofar as one of the key proposed solutions to global warming is carbon emission trading, and the sequestration of carbon emissions (in the form of carbon emission storage, as well as in protection of the world's tropical and other old-growth forests), the introduction of a wide range of regulatory sanctions is probable. To be effective, new laws will need to be backed up by new forms of policing and enforcement, and the use of compliance strategies that are flexible, global and multipronged (including, for example, restorative-justice-based methods of restitution and conflict resolution). Collaborative policing efforts across national boundaries, and the further development of international institutions of justice (such as an international environment court), imply new areas of expertise, exchange of ideas and personnel, and strategic emphasis (see Chapter 8). The focus and direction of all this regulatory activity is of utmost importance, as is its entrenchment within the fabric of global democratic deliberations. The politics of climate change will have a part in shaping the legal and criminal justice institutions of the future, as will the growing number of environmental harms that will ultimately demand some kind of international criminal justice response.

Critical analysis of key areas such as food and energy alerts us to the ways in which sectional interests (that is, particular transnational corporations such as those pertaining to agribusiness and the nuclear industry, and particular hegemonic nation states such as the US and China) are vying for control over and exploitation of resources vital to human existence (see Chapter 3 and Chapter 4). Concepts such as human rights, ecological citizenship and the global commons can be developed in ways that assert the primacy of 'climate justice' over these kinds of narrow sectional interests. The causes and the effects of climate change can be analysed in terms of global distributions of social power, and the winners and losers in the global warming stakes. Current mitigation and adaptation strategies are in this respect profoundly unjust.

At its broadest level, the way in which laws and regulatory instruments work or do not work is fundamentally shaped by systemic imperatives and philosophical vision. For instance, Boyd (2003) contrasts a model of regulation based upon an effort to mitigate the environmental impacts of an energy- and resource-intensive industrial economy with that based upon ecological principles that are oriented to decreasing the consumption of energy and natural resources. However complex the laws and regulations in the first scenario, they cannot succeed in achieving sustainability because the system as a whole is inherently geared to growth in energy and resource consumption (see White 2002). In the latter case, the emphasis is on restructuring the economy to incorporate ecological thresholds, and thus to reduce environmental harm, including global warming, over time.

The development of counter-hegemonic strategies that challenge the logic and the specific institutional expressions of global capitalism are crucial in the struggle against global warming. This may mean working in and against mainstream political institutions at all levels of intervention. For example, the United Nations Environment Programme, Interpol and other transnational organisations are important forums for information gathering and potential imposition of sanctions. Application of the precautionary principle as informed by agencies such as the Intergovernmental Panel on Climate Change will possibly be of benefit in struggles around regions that are especially vulnerable to certain kinds of practices (such as deforestation). However, the precautionary principle itself can point in two opposing directions at the same time – climate change (we need to take these measures now to forestall further global warming) *and* pollution (we need to take these measures now to forestall future ecological disasters) – that will complicate and politicise debates over mitigation and adaptation strategies. This is precisely the nature of paradoxical harm (as discussed in Chapter 3). The legitimacy and ideological power of specific state agencies (including those of the United Nations) will partly depend upon whose interests are most threatened or advantaged by agency work.

There is thus a simultaneous need for strong action within civil society to progress a more radical social change agenda. Social movements at local, regional and global levels will have to engage in concerted political interventions around climate change issues. Criminologists among others must insist upon the protection of democratic spaces within which popular struggles can occur. Campaigns are needed on many different fronts, from exposure of corruption (especially in environmentally and developmentally vulnerable states) through to use of public interest litigation and class actions (especially in environmentally and developmentally advantaged states). The law can be used on behalf of activists, and as a weapon against activists (White 2008a). This dual character makes the law a site for contestation that will be ongoing. Who gets criminalised, and for what, will be perennial matters of concern for activists and social movements. Eco-terrorism and the 'green scare' are likely to feature in state interventions; but so too is greater reliance by nation states upon global social movements in forging alternative responses to climate change.

The 'national interest' can be used to justify the most brutal of policies (witness current interventions on asylum seekers) and to weave together cross-class alliances at a nation state level (that pit the interests of the people of the North against those of the South, for example). Might makes right, when resources are scarce, and this fact alone will make it difficult for those working for social and ecological justice. To convince and mobilise people means convincing them, concretely, that the chance for survival is only guaranteed through global and socially inclusive processes. To act otherwise is to seal the fate of humanity as the planet heats up. This means addressing the core contradiction of capitalism, and the instruments and institutions of power that sustain this contradiction.

In relation to the conflicts that lie ahead, another paradoxical harm that needs to be acknowledged is the mode by which governments assert a particular kind of social order. Consider for example the ecological costs of securing the climate future, at least from a US point of view: '... the Pentagon is the single largest consumer of oil in the world. There are only 35 countries, in fact, that consume more oil than the Pentagon' (Baer and Singer 2009: 38). From greenhouse gas emissions to environmental degradation, the operational demands of the military are enormous. The US military, for example, has a heavy reliance upon energy-inefficient equipment and vehicles. It also extensively uses depleted uranium in weapons and armour (see White 2008b). The social processes of war are themselves implicated in climate change: '... global warming and war are thus mutually reinforcing, with war and war production fuelling global warming and global warming pushing countries to war' (Baer and Singer 2009: 39). Responding to this kind of climate-related challenge as well as other paradoxical harms will require conceptualisations of harm that acknowledge inequality for the evil it is, and that provide leverage for major shifts in legal and criminological thinking.

Conclusion

Transnational environmental activists have been integral to exposing many of the harms identified in the course of this book and instigating public action around them. Eco-global criminology likewise argues that ultimately we need to go beyond parochial and conventional criminological viewpoints and those perspectives that frame harm in terms of national or regional interests. Our concern has to be for the planet as a whole, rather than being bound by a narrow prescriptive patriotism based on nation. The global nature of these problems means that inevitably our collective survival will require planetary cooperation and worldwide action. For eco-global criminology, this is best undertaken under the guidance of an eco-justice framework, rather than protection of existing privilege or 'might makes right' strategies. For the latter only lead to further violation of rights, and the downward spiral to our mutual destruction.

The nature and content of environmental activism are simultaneously context-bound (culturally and socially within certain national boundaries), related to different forms of consciousness (for example, localism versus consciousness of global ecological citizenship) and determined by specific kinds of social experience (as victim, as activist, as bystander, as citizen). Debate will inevitably occur in regards to the adoption of what are deemed to be suitable or appropriate tactics of dissent. Those with less to lose may be more inclined to push the boundaries of legality when it comes to social protest. Given the present environmental circumstances of the planet – which point to all of us being losers in the end – our collective future rests squarely on how far and how quickly these boundaries are pushed. This, too, is of major concern to eco-global criminology.

References

Aas, K. (2007) *Globalization & Crime*. Los Angeles: Sage.

ADL Law Enforcement Agency Resource Network (2009) 'Ecoterrorism: Extremism in the Animal Rights and Environmentalist Movements', http://www.adl.org/learn/ext_us/Ecoterrorism_print.asp (accessed 6 April 2009).

Akella, A. and Cannon, J. (2004) *Strengthening the Weakest Links: Strategies for Improving the Enforcement of Environmental Laws Globally*. Washington, DC: Center for Conservation and Government.

Amster, R. (2006) 'Perspectives on Ecoterrorism: Catalysts, Conflations, and Casualties', *Contemporary Justice Review*, 9(3): 287–301.

Ascione, F. (2001) 'Animal Abuse and Youth Violence'. *Juvenile Justice Bulletin*. Washington, DC: Office of Juvenile Justice and Delinquency Prevention, US Department of Justice.

Australian Council of Recyclers (2007) 'Ecological Disaster Forecast Unless Fluorescent Tubes Recycled', Media Release, 27 March 2007.

Australian Federal Police (2008) AFP Website (accessed 1 April 2008).

Baer, H. and Singer, M. (2009) *Global Warming and the Political Economy of Health: Emerging Crises and Systemic Solutions*. Walnut Creek, CA: Left Coast Press.

Bakan, J. (2004) *The Corporation: The Pathological Pursuit of Profit and Power*. London: Constable.

Banerjee, D. and Bell, M. (2007) 'Ecogender: Locating Gender in Environmental Social Science', *Society and Natural Resources*, 20: 3–19.

Basel Action Network/Silicon Valley Toxics Coalition (2002) *Exporting Harm: The High-Tech Trashing of Asia*. Seattle and San Jose: BAN/SVTC.

Bayley, D. (1999) 'Policing: the World Stage', in R. Mawby (ed.) *Policing Across the World: Issues for the Twenty-First Century*. London: UCL Press.

Beck, U. (1996) 'World Risk Society as Cosmopolitan Society? Ecological Questions in a Framework of Manufactured Uncertainties', *Theory, Culture, Society*, 13(4): 1–32.

Beder, S. (1997) *Global Spin: The Corporate Assault on Environmentalism*. Melbourne: Scribe Publications.

Beder, S. (2006) *Suiting Themselves: How Corporations Drive the Global Agenda*. London: Earthscan.

Beirne, P. (2004) 'From Animal Abuse to Interhuman Violence? A Critical Review of the Progression Thesis', *Society & Animals*, 12(1): 39–65.

Beirne, P. (2007) 'Animal Rights, Animal Abuse and Green Criminology', in P. Beirne and N. South (eds) *Issues in Green Criminology: Confronting Harms Against Environments, Humanity and Other Animals*. Devon: Willan Publishing.

Beirne, P. (2009) *Confronting Animal Abuse: Law, Criminology, and Human–Animal Relationships*. New York: Rowman & Littlefield Publishers.

Beirne, P. and South, N. (2007) (eds) *Issues in Green Criminology: Confronting Harms Against Environments, Humanity and Other Animals*. Devon: Willan Publishing.

Bell, S. and McGillivray, D. (2008) *Environmental Law* (7th edition). London: Oxford University Press.

Bello, W. (2008) 'How to Manufacture a Global Food Crisis: Lessons from the World Bank, IMF, and WTO', Transnational Institute, 16 May 2008, http://www.tni.org/detail_page.phtml?&&act_id=18285 (accessed 3 June 2008).

BioSecurity New Zealand (2006) 'Climate Change and Biosecurity', Biosecurity Summit 2006. Wellington: BioSecurity New Zealand.

Blindell, J. (2006) *21st Century policing – The Role of Police in the Detection, Investigation and Prosecution of Environmental Crime*, ACPR Issues No. 2. Adelaide: Australasian Centre for Policing Research.

Block, A. (2002) 'Environmental Crime and Pollution: Wasteful Reflections', *Social Justice*, 29(1–2): 61–81.

Boekhout van Solinge, T. (2008a) 'Crime, Conflicts and Ecology in Africa', in R. Sullund (ed.) *Global Harms: Ecological Crime and Speciesism*. New York: Nova Science Publishers.

Boekhout van Solinge, T. (2008b) 'The Land of the Orangutan and the Bird of Paradise under Threat', in R. Sullund (ed.) *Global Harms: Ecological Crime and Speciesism*. New York: Nova Science Publishers.

Boekhout van Solinge, T. (2010) 'Equatorial Deforestation as a Harmful Practice and a Criminological Issue', in R. White (ed.) *Global Environmental Harm: Criminological Perspectives*. Devon: Willan Publishing.

Boyd, D. (2003) *Unnatural Law: Rethinking Canadian Environmental Law and Policy*. Vancouver: UBC Press.

Braithwaite, J. and Drahos, P. (2000) *Global Business Regulation*. Cambridge: Cambridge University Press.

Brickey, K. (2008) *Environmental Crime: Law, Policy, Prosecution*. New York: Aspen Publishers.

Bridgland, F. (2006) 'Europe's New Dumping Ground: Fred Bridgland reports on how the West's toxic waste is poisoning Africa', *Sunday Herald*, 1 October 2006 (accessed 2 October 2006).

Brisman, A. (2008) 'Crime–Environment Relationships and Environmental Justice', *Seattle Journal for Social Justice*, 6(2): 727–817.

Brook, D. (1998) 'Environmental Genocide: Native Americans and Toxic Waste', *American Journal of Economics and Sociology*, 57(1): 105–13.

Bruno, K., Karliner, J. and Brotsky, C. (1999) *Greenhouse Gangsters vs. Climate Justice*. San Francisco: Transnational Resource and Action Centre.

Bulkeley, H. and Newell, P. (2010) *Governing Climate Change*. London: Routledge.

Bullard, R. (1994) *Unequal Protection: Environmental Justice and Communities of Color*. San Francisco: Sierra Club Books.

Burns, R., Lynch, M. and Stretesky, P. (2008) *Environmental Law, Crime, and Justice*. New York: LFB Scholarly Publishing LLC.

Buttel, F. (2003) 'Environmental Sociology and the Explanation of Environmental Reform', *Organization and Environment*, 16(3): 306–44.

Carson, R. (1962) *Silent Spring*. Boston: Houghton and Mifflin.

Castles, S. (2002) *Environmental Change and Forced Migration: Making Sense of the Debate. New issues in refugee research*, Working paper no. 70. Geneva: Evaluation and Policy Analysis Unit, United Nations High Commissioner for Refugees.

Caughley, J., Bomford, M. and McNee, A. (1996) 'Use of Wildlife by Indigenous Australians: Issues and Concepts', in M. Bomford and J. Caughley (eds) *Sustainable Use of Wildlife by Aboriginal Peoples and Torres Strait Islanders*. Canberra: Bureau of Resource Sciences, Australian Government Publishing Service.

Chunn, D., Boyd, S. and Menzies, R. (2002) '"We All Live in Bhopal": Criminology Discovers Environmental Crime', in S. Boyd, D. Chunn and R. Menzies (eds) *Toxic Criminology: Environment, Law and the State in Canada*. Halifax: Fernwood Publishing.

Cifuentes, E. and Frumkin, H. (2007) 'Environmental Injustice: Case Studies from the South', *Environmental Research Letters*, 2: 1–9.

Clapp, J. (2001) *Toxic Exports: The Transfer of Hazardous Wastes from Rich to Poor Countries*. Ithaca and London: Cornell University Press.

Clapp, J. (2002) 'Seeping Through the Regulatory Cracks', SAIS Review, XXII(1): 141–55.

Clark, R. (2009) 'Environmental Disputes and Human Rights Violations: a Role for Criminologists', *Contemporary Justice Review*, 12(2): 129–46.

Clarke, E. (2009) 'The Truth about … Nuclear Waste', ClimateChangeCorp.com (accessed 21 January 2010).

Cohen, S. (2001) *States of Denial: Knowing About Atrocities and Suffering*. Cambridge: Polity Press.

Cole, M. and Elliott, R. (2003) 'Determining the Trade-Environment Composition Effect: the Role of Capital, Labor and Environmental Regulations', *Journal of Environmental Economics and Management*, 46: 363–83.

Collins, C. (2010) *Toxic Loopholes: Failures and Future Prospects for Environmental Law*. Cambridge: Cambridge University Press.

Commission for Environmental Cooperation (2001) *Special Report on Enforcement Activities: Report prepared by the North American Working Group on Enforcement and Compliance Cooperation*. Montreal: CEC.

Connell, R. (2007) *Southern Theory: The Global Dynamics of Knowledge in Social Science*. Sydney: Allen & Unwin.

Conservation International (2007) 'New Zealand: Human Impacts'. (http://www.biodiversityhotspots.org/xp/Hotspots/new_zealand/Pages/impacts.aspx) (accessed 1 April 2008).

Cornforth, M. (1976) *Dialectical Materialism: An Introduction – Volume 2: Historical Materialism*. London: Lawrence and Wishart.

Croall, H. (2007) 'Food Crime', in P. Beirne and N. South (eds) *Issues in Green Criminology: Confronting Harms against Environments, Humanity and Other Animals*. Devon: Willan Publishing.

Cullinan, C. (2003) *Wild Law: A Manifesto for Earth Justice*. London: Green Books in association with The Gaia Foundation.

Dadds, M., Turner, C. and McAloon, J. (2002) 'Developmental Links between Cruelty to Animals and Human Violence', *Australian and New Zealand Journal of Criminology*, 35(3): 363–82.

Davison, A. (2004) 'Sustainable Technology: Beyond Fix and Fixation', in R. White (ed.) *Controversies in Environmental Sociology*. Melbourne: Cambridge University Press.

Department of the Environment, Water, Heritage and the Arts, Australia (2010) 'Fact Sheet – Fluorescent lamps, mercury and end-of-life management'. Canberra: Department of the Environment, Water, Heritage and the Arts.

DeSombre, E. (2006) *Global Environmental Institutions*. London: Routledge.

de Prez, P. (2000) 'Excuses, Excuses: the Ritual Trivialization of Environmental Prosecutions', *Journal of Environmental Law*, 12(1): 65–77.

Dodson, L., Piatelli, D. and Schmalzbauer, L. (2007) 'Researching Inequality Through Interpretive Collaborations: Shifting Power and the Unspoken Contract', *Qualitative Inquiry*, 13(6): 821–43.

Dorn, N., Van Daele, S. and Vander Becken, T. (2007) 'Reducing Vulnerabilities to Crime of the European Waste Management Industry: the Research Base and the Prospects for Policy', *European Journal of Crime, Criminal Law and Criminal Justice*: 23–36.

Duffield, J. (1997) 'Nonmarket Valuation and the Courts: The Case of the Exxon Valdez', *Contemporary Economic Policy*, 15(4): 98–110.

Duffy, R. (2010) *Nature Crime: How We're Getting Conservation Wrong*. New Haven: Yale University Press.

Du Rees, H. (2001) 'Can Criminal Law Protect the Environment?', *Journal of Scandinavian Studies in Criminology and Crime Prevention*, 2: 109–26.

Elliot, L. (ed.) (2007) *Transnational Environmental Crime in the Asia-Pacific: A Workshop Report*. Canberra: Australian National University.

Engdahl, F. (2007) *Seeds of Destruction: The Hidden Agenda of Genetic Manipulation*. Montreal: Global Research.

Engel, S. and Martin, B. (2006) 'Union Carbide and James Hardie: Lessons in Politics and Power', *Global Society*, 20(4): 475–90.

Environmental Audit Committee (2004) *Environmental Crime and the Courts*. London: House of Commons.

Equipment Energy Efficiency Committee (2009) *Regulatory Impact Statement for Decision: Proposed MEPS (Mini-Energy Performance Standard) for incandescent lamps, compact fluorescent lamps and voltage converters*. Canberra: Department of the Environment, Water, Heritage and the Arts.

European Union (2008) Directive 1008/98/EC of the European Parliament and of the Council of 19 November 2008 on waste and repealing certain Directives. *Official Journal of the European Union*, 22 November 2008, L 312/3–30.

Faber, D. (2009) 'Capitalising on Environmental Crime: A Case Study of the USA Polluter-Industrial Complex in the Age of Globalization', in K. Kangapunta and I. Marshall (eds) *Eco-Crime and Justice: Essays on Environmental Crime*. Turin, Italy: United Nations Interregional Crime Research Institute (UNICRI).

Fattah, E. (2010) 'The Evolution of a Young, Promising Discipline: Sixty Years of Victimology, a Retrospective and Prospective Look', in S. Shoham, P. Knepper and M. Kett (eds) *International Handbook of Victimology*. Boca Raton, FL: CRC Press.

Faure, M. and Heine, G. (2000) *Criminal Enforcement of Environmental Law in the European Union*. Copenhagen: Danish Environmental Protection Agency.

Field, R. (1998) 'Risk and Justice: Capitalist Production and the Environment', in D. Faber (ed.) *The Struggle for Ecological Democracy: Environmental Justice Movements in the US*. New York: Guilford Press.

Findlay, M., Odgers, S. and Yeo, S. (1994) *Australian Criminal Justice*. Melbourne: Oxford University Press.

Forni, O. (2010) 'Mapping Environmental Crimes', *Freedom From Fear Magazine*, March. Turin: United Nations Interregional Crime and Justice Research Institute.

Fortney, D. (2003) 'Thinking Outside the "Black Box": Tailored Enforcement in Environmental Criminal Law', *Texas Law Review*, 81(6): 1609–30.

Foster, J. (2002) *Ecology Against Capitalism*. New York: Monthly Review Press.

Franklin, A. (2006) *Animal Nation: The True Story of Animals and Australia*. Sydney: University of New South Wales Press.

French, H. (2000) *Vanishing Borders: Protecting the Planet in the Age of Globalization*. New York: W.W. Norton and Company.

Friedrichs, D. (2007) 'Transnational Crime and Global Criminology: Definitional, Typological, and Contextual Conundrums', *Social Justice*, 34(2): 4–18.

Fyfe, N. and Reeves, A. (2009) 'The Thin Green Line? Police Perceptions of the Challenges of Policing Wildlife Crime in Scotland', in R. Mawby and R. Yarwood (eds) *Policing, Rurality and Governance*. Aldershot: Ashgate.

Gibbs, C., Gore, M., McGarrell, E. and Rivers III, L. (2010a) 'Introducing Conservation Criminology: Towards Interdisciplinary Scholarship on Environmental Crimes and Risks', *British Journal of Criminology*, 50: 124–44.

Gibbs, C., McGarrell, E. and Axelrod, M. (2010b) 'Transnational White-Collar Crime and Risk: Lessons from the Global Trade in Electronic Waste', *Criminology and Public Policy*, 9(3): 543–60.

Glasbeek, H. (2004) *Wealth By Stealth: Corporate Crime, Corporate Law, and the Perversion of Democracy*. Toronto: Between the Lines.

Gorz, A. (1989) *Critique of Economic Reason*. London: Verso.

Grafton, Q., Adamowicz, W., Dupont, D., Nelson, H., Hill, R. and Renzetti, S. (2004) *The Economics of the Environment and Natural Resources*. London: Blackwell.

Green, P. and Ward, T. (2000) 'State Crime, Human Rights, and the Limits of Criminology', *Social Justice*, 27(1): 101–15.

Green, P. and Ward, T. (2004) *State Crime: Governments, Violence and Corruption*. London: Pluto Press.

Green, P., Ward, T. and McConnachie, K. (2007) 'Logging and Legality: Environmental Crime, Civil Society, and the State', *Social Justice*, 34(2): 94–110.

Gros, J-G. (2008) 'Trouble in Paradise: Crime and Collapsed States in the Age of Globalization', in N. Larsen and R. Smandych (eds) *Global Criminology and Criminal Justice: Current Issues and Perspectives*. Peterborough, Ontario: Broadview Press.

Gunningham, N., Norberry, J. and McKillop, S. (eds) (1995) *Environmental Crime, Conference Proceedings*. Canberra: Australian Institute of Criminology.

Hackett, S. and Uprichard, E. (2007) *Animal Abuse and Child Maltreatment: A Review of the Literature and Findings from a UK Study*. London: National Society for the Prevention of Cruelty to Children (NSPCC).

Hagedorn, J. (2007) 'Introduction: Globalization, Gangs, and Traditional Criminology', in J. Hagedorn (ed.) *Gangs in the Global City: Alternatives to Traditional Criminology*. Urbana and Chicago: University of Illinois Press.

Halsey, M. (2005) *Deleuze and Environmental Damage: The Violence of the Text*. London: Ashgate.

Halstead, B. (1992) *Traffic in Flora and Fauna. Trends and Issues in Crime and Criminal Justice, No.41*. Canberra: Australian Institute of Criminology.

Hannigan, J. (1995) *Environmental Sociology: A Social Constructionist Perspective*. London: Routledge.

Hannigan, J. (2006) *Environmental Sociology* (2nd edn). London: Routledge.

Harvey, D. (1996) *Justice, Nature and the Geography of Difference*. Oxford: Blackwell.

Hayman, G. and Brack, D. (2002) *International Environmental Crime: The Nature and Control of Environmental Black Markets*. London: Sustainable Development Programme, Royal Institute of International Affairs.

Heckenberg, D. (2010) 'The Global Transference of Toxic Harms', in R. White (ed.) *Global Environmental Harm: Criminological Perspectives*. Devon: Willan Publishing.

Herbig, J. (2010) 'The Illegal Reptile Trade as a Form of Conservation Crime: a South African Criminological Investigation', in R. White (ed.) *Global Environmental Harm: Criminological Perspectives*. Devon: Willan Publishing.

Herbig, F. and Joubert, S. (2006) 'Criminological Semantics: Conservation Criminology – Vision or Vagary?', *Acta Criminologica*, 19(3): 88–103.

Hinde, S. (2003) 'The International Environmental Court: Its Broad Jurisdiction as a Possible Fatal Flaw', 32 *Hofstra Law Review*.

Hughes, S.D. (2004) 'The Current Status of Environmental Performance Reporting', *National Environmental Law Review*, No. 4: 41–58.

Iafrica.com (15 May 2007) 'West Should Pay for "Ruining" Africa' (accessed 17 May 2007).

Interpol Pollution Crime Working Group (2007) 'Arguments for Prosecutors of Environmental Crimes', *Advocacy Memorandum*, 5 June.

Interpol (2009) *Electronic Waste and Organised Crime: Assessing the Links. Phase II Report for the Interpol Pollution Crime Working Group*. Lyon: Interpol.

Irwin, A. (2001) *Sociology and the Environment: A Critical Introduction to Society, Nature and Knowledge*. Cambridge: Polity Press in association with Blackwell Publishers Ltd.

Julian, R. (2004) 'Inequality, Social Differences and Environmental Resources', in R. White (ed.) *Controversies in Environmental Sociology*. Melbourne: Cambridge University Press.

Khagram, S. (2004) *Dams and Development: Transnational Struggles for Water and Power*. Ithaca, NY: Cornell University Press.

Kirsch, S. (2006) *Reverse Anthropology: Indigenous Analysis of Social and Environmental Relations in New Guinea*. Stanford University Press.

Ko, W. and Kwon, E. (2009) 'Implications of the New National Energy Basic Plan for Nuclear Waste Management in Korea', *Energy Policy*, 37: 3484–88.

Konisky, D. (2009) 'The Limited Effects of Federal Environmental Justice Policy on State Enforcement', *Policy Studies Journal*, 37(3): 475–96.

Lack, M. (2007) *Catching On? Trade-related Measures as a Fisheries Management Tool*. Cambridge: TRAFFIC International.

Lambrecht, B. (2006) 'Exported E-waste Pollutes Africa', www.stltoday.com (accessed 19 December 2006).

Langton, M. (1998) *Burning Questions: Emerging Environmental Issues for Indigenous Peoples in Northern Australia*. Darwin: Centre for Indigenous Natural and Cultural Resource Management.

Larsen, N. and Smandych, R. (eds) (2008) *Global Criminology and Criminal Justice: Current Issues and Perspectives*. Peterborough, Ontario: Broadview Press.

Lawrence, K. (2009) 'The Thermodynamics of Unequal Exchange: Energy Use, CO_2 Emissions, and GDP in the World-System, 1975–2005', *International Journal of Comparative Sociology*, 50(3–4): 335–59.

Leiss, W. and Hrudey, S. (2005) 'On Proof and Probability: Introduction to "Law and Risk"', in Law Commission of Canada (eds) *Law and Risk*. Vancouver: UBC Press.

Lemieux, A. and Clarke, R. (2009) 'The International Ban on Ivory Sales and its Effects on Elephant Poaching in Africa', *British Journal of Criminology*, 49(4): 451–71.

Low, N. and Gleeson, B. (1998) *Justice, Society and Nature: An Exploration of Political Ecology*. London: Routledge.

Lugten, G. (2005) 'Big Fish To Fry – International Law and Deterrence of the Toothfish Pirates', *Current Issues in Criminal Justice*, 16(3): 307–21.

Lynch, M. (1990) 'The Greening of Criminology: A Perspective on the 1990s', *The Critical Criminologist*, 2(3): 1–4 and 11–12.

Lynch, M. and Stretesky, P. (2001) 'Toxic Crimes: Examining Corporate Victimization of the General Public Employing Medical and Epidemiological Evidence', *Critical Criminology*, 10: 153–72.

Lynch, M. and Stretesky, P. (2010) 'Global Warming, Global Crime: A Green Criminological Perspective', in R. White (ed.) *Global Environmental Harm: Criminological Perspectives*. Devon: Willan Publishing.

Lynch, M., Stretesky, P. and Burns, R. (2004) 'Determinants of Environmental Law Violation Fines Against Petroleum Refineries: Race, Ethnicity, Income, and Aggregation Effects', *Society and Natural Resources*, 17(4): 343–57.

Lynch, M., Stretesky, P. and Hammond, P. (2000) 'Media Coverage of Chemical Crimes, Hillsborough County, Florida, 1987–97', *British Journal of Criminology*, 40: 112–26.

Lynch, M., Stretesky, P. and McGurrin, D. (2002) 'Toxic Crimes and Environmental Justice: Examining the Hidden Dangers of Hazardous Waste', in G. Potter (ed.) *Controversies in White-Collar Crime*. Cincinnati: Anderson Publishing.

Madsen, F. (2009) *Transnational Organized Crime*. London: Routledge.

Magistrates' Association (UK) (2009) *Costing the Earth: Guidance for Sentencers*. London: Magistrates' Association.

Markham, A. (2009) 'Animal Cruelty Sentencing in Australia and New Zealand', in P. Sankoff and S. White (eds) *Animal Law in Australasia: A New Dialogue*. Sydney: The Federation Press.

Marsden, B (2003) 'Cholera and the Age of the Water Barons'. Centre for Public Integrity (www.icij.org) (accessed 1 July 2004).

Marshall, I. (2008) 'The Criminological Enterprise in Europe and the United States: A Contextual Exploration', in N. Larsen and R. Smandych (eds) *Global Criminology and Criminal Justice: Current Issues and Perspectives*. Peterborough, Ontario: Broadview Press.

Martin, M. (1990) 'Ecosabotage and Civil Disobedience', *Environmental Ethics*, 12: 291–310.

McAdam, J. and Saul, B. (2008) 'An Insecure Climate for Human Security? Climate-Induced Displacement and International Law', in A. Edwards and C. Fertsman (eds) *Human Security and Non-Citizens: Law, Policy and International Affairs*. Cambridge: Cambridge University Press.

McCarthy, M. (2008) 'Cleared: Jury Decides that Threat of Global Warming Justifies Breaking the Law', *The Independent*, 11 September 2008 (http://www.independent.co.uk/environment/climate-change/cleared-jury-decides-that ...) (accessed 10 October 2008).

McGrath, M. (2008) 'Extinction Risk "Underestimated"', BBC News, 3 July 2008 (accessed 11 January 2010).

McMullan, J. and Perrier, D. (2002) 'Lobster Poaching and the Ironies of Law Enforcement', *Law and Society Review*, 36(4): 679–720.

Meyers, G., McLeod, G. and Anbarci, M. (2006) 'An International Waste Convention: Measures for Achieving Sustainable Development', *Waste Management and Research*, 24(6): 505–13.

Mgbeoji, I. (2006) *Global Biopiracy: Patents, Plants, and Indigenous Knowledge*. Vancouver: UBC Press.

Mitchell, D. (2008) 'A Note on Rising Food Prices', draft World Bank paper, circulated online by *The Guardian* newspaper (guardian.co.uk/environment) (accessed 11 July 2008).

Mossville Environmental Action Now, Inc., Wilma Subra and Advocates for Environmental Human Rights (2007) *Industrial Sources of Dioxin Poisoning in Mossville, Louisiana: A Report Based on the Government's Own Data*. Mossville Environmental Action Now, Inc.

Munro, L. (2004) 'Animals, "Nature" and Human Interests', in R. White (ed.) *Controversies in Environmental Sociology*. Melbourne: Cambridge University Press.

Murphy, B. and Morrison, R. (2007) *Introduction to Environmental Forensics*. Amsterdam: Elsevier.

Natali, L. (2010) 'The Big Grey Elephants in the Backyard of Huelva, Spain', in R. White (ed.) *Global Environmental Harm: Criminological Perspectives*. Devon: Willan Publishing.

NatureCape (2010) 'Threats to Biodiversity', www.capenature.co.za/biodiversity. htm?sm[p1][category]=602 (accessed 6 May 2010).

New Zealand Ministry for the Environment/Manatū Mō Te Taiao (2007) *Environment New Zealand 2007: Summary*. Wellington: Ministry for the Environment.

O'Brien, M. (2008) 'Criminal Degradations of Consumer Culture', in R. Sollund (ed.) *Global Harms: Ecological Crime and Speciesism*. New York: Nova Science Publishers.

O'Hear, M. (2004) 'Sentencing the Green-Collar Offender: Punishment, Culpability, and Environmental Crime', *Journal of Criminal Law and Criminology*, 95(1): 133–276.

Organisation for Economic Cooperation and Development (2007) 'Conclusions and Recommendations', OECD Environmental Performance Review of New Zealand. Paris: OECD.

Orr, D. (1991) 'The Economics of Conservation', *Conservation Biology*, 5(4): 439–41.

O'Sullivan, S. (2009) 'Australasian Animal Protection Laws and the Challenge of Equal Consideration', in P. Sankoff and S. White (eds) *Animal Law in Australasia*. Sydney: The Federation Press.

Peacock, M. (2009) *Killer Company: James Hardie Exposed*. Sydney: ABC Books.

Pellow, D. (2007) *Resisting Global Toxics: Transnational Movements for Environmental Justice*. Cambridge: The MIT Press.

Pepper, D. (1993) *Eco-Socialism: From Deep Ecology to Social Justice*. New York: Routledge.

Pezzullo, P. and Sandler, R. (2007) 'Introduction: Revisiting the Environmental Justice Challenge to Environmentalism', in R. Sandler and P. Pezzullo (eds) *Environmental Justice and Environmentalism: The Social Justice Challenge to the Environmental Movement*. Cambridge, Massachusetts: The MIT Press.

Pickard, W. (2010) 'Finessing the Fuel: Revisiting the Challenge of Radioactive Waste Disposal', *Energy Policy*, 38: 709–14.

Pickering, S. (2005) *Refugees and State Crime*. Sydney: Federation Press.

Pickering, S. and McCulloch, J. (2007) 'Introduction: Beyond Transnational Crime', Special Issue of *Social Justice*, 34(2): 1–3.

Picou, J., Formichella, C., Marshall, B. and Arata, C. (2009) 'Chapter 9: Community Impacts of the Exxon Valdez Oil Spill: A Synthesis and Elaboration of Social Science Research', in S. Braund and J. Kruse (eds) *Synthesis: Three Decades of Research on Socioeconomic Effects related to Offshore Petroleum Development in Coastal Alaska*. Anchorage, Alaska: United States Department of the Interior.

Pimental, D., Marklein, A., Toth, M., Karpoff, M., Paul, G., McCormack, R., Kyriazis, J. and Krueger, T. (2009) 'Food Versus Biofuels: Environmental and Economic Costs', *Human Ecology*, 37(1): 1–12.

Pinderhughes, R. (1996) 'The Impact of Race on Environmental Quality: An Empirical and Theoretical Discussion', *Sociological Perspectives*, 39(2): 231–48.

Pink, G. (2010) 'Governmental Co-ordination to Enforce Environmental Laws: the Experiences of an Australian Environmental Regulator'. Canberra: Compliance and Enforcement Branch, Department of the Environment, Water, Heritage and the Arts.

Pollen, M. (2007) 'Unhappy Meals', *The New York Times Magazine*, 28 January: 38–47, 65–70.

Potter, W. (2008) 'What is the "Green Scare"?' (http://www.greenisthenewred.com/blog/green-scare/) (accessed 6 April 2009).

Preston, B. (2007) 'Principled Sentencing for Environmental Offences – Part 2: Sentencing considerations and options', 31 *Criminal Law Journal*, 142.

Preston, B. and Donnelly, H. (2008a) *Achieving Consistency and Transparency in Sentencing for Environmental Offences*. Monograph 32, June 2008. Sydney: Judicial Commission of New South Wales.

Preston, B. and Donnelly, H. (2008b) 'The Establishment of an Environmental Crime Sentencing Database in New South Wales', 32 *Criminal Law Journal*, 214.

Putt, J. and Anderson, K. (2007) *A National Study of Crime in the Australian Fishing Industry*, Research and Public Policy Series, No.76. Canberra: Australian Institute of Criminology.

Pyper, W. (2005) 'On the Trail of Sexual Chemistry', *ECOS*, 123, January–March: 26–28.

Ramroth, L. (2008) *Comparison of Life-Cycle Analyses of Compact Fluorescent and Incandescent Lamps Based on Rated Life of Compact Fluorescent Lamp*. Rocky Mountain Institute.

Refugee Studies Centre (2008) *Forced Migration Review: Climate change and displacement, Issue 31*. University of Oxford: Refugee Studies Centre.

Reliable Plant (2007) 'New Study Favors Tree Over Corn as Biofuel Source' (online). Available at: http://www.reliableplant.com/article.asp?articleid=10046 (accessed 25 February 2008).

Rhodes, E. (2003) *Environmental Justice in America*. Bloomington, IN: Indiana University Press.

Richardson, L. and Loomis, J. (2009) 'The Total Economic Value of Threatened, Endangered and Rare Species: An Updated Meta-Analysis', *Ecological Economics*, 68(5): 1535–48.

Rist, L., Ser Huay Lee, J. and Pin Koh, L. (2009), 'Biofuels: Social Benefits', Letters, *Science*, Vol. 326: 1344.

Roberts, G. (2008) 'The Bad Oil on Ethanol: Biofuels are Losing Favour but Some Governments are Still Backing Them', *The Weekend Australian*, 31 May– 1 June p. 20, Inquirer.

Robin, M-M. (2010) *The World According to Monsanto: Pollution, Corruption and the Control of Our Food Supply*. New York: The New Press.

Robinson, B. (2003) *Review of the Enforcement and Prosecution Guidelines of the Department of Environmental Protection of Western Australia*. Perth: Communication Edge.

Robyn, L. (2002) 'Indigenous Knowledge and Technology', *American Indian Quarterly*, 26(2): 198–220.

Rock, P. (2007) 'Theoretical Perspectives on Victimisation', in S. Walklate (ed.) *Handbook of Victims and Victimology*. Devon: Willan Publishing.

Rovics, D. (2007) 'Pivotal Moment in the Greem Scare', *Capitalism Nature Socialism*, 18(3): 8–16.

Ruggierro, V. (1996) *Organized and Corporate Crime in Europe: Offers That Can't Be Refused*. Aldershot: Dartmouth.

Rush, S. (2002) 'Aboriginal Resistance to the Abuse of Their National Resources: The Struggles for Trees and Water', in S. Boyd, D. Chunn and R. Menzies (eds) *Toxic Criminology: Environment, Law and the State in Canada*. Halifax: Fernwood Publishing.

Saha, R. and Mohai, P. (2005) 'Historical Context and Hazardous Waste Facility Siting: Understanding Temporal Patterns in Michigan', *Social Problems*, 52(4): 618–48.

Sandler, R. and Pezzullo, P. (eds) (2007) *Environmental Justice and Environmentalism: The Social Justice Challenge to the Environmental Movement*. Cambridge, MA: The MIT Press.

Sankoff, P. and White, S. (eds) (2009) *Animal Law in Australasia: A New Dialogue*. Sydney: The Federation Press.

Sarangi, S. (1996) 'The Movement in Bhopal and Its Lessons', *Social Justice*, 23(4): 100–108.

Saro-Wiwa, K. (1995) *A Month and a Day: A Detention Diary*. London: Penguin.

Schmidt, C. (2004) 'Environmental Crimes: Profiting at the Earth's Expense', *Environmental Health Perspectives*, 112(2): A96–A103.

Schneider, J. (2008) 'Reducing the Illicit Trade in Endangered Wildlife: The Market Reduction Approach', *Journal of Contemporary Criminal Justice*, 24(3): 274–95.

Scholsberg, D. (2004) 'Reconceiving Environmental Justice: Global Movements and Political Theories', *Environmental Politics*, 13(3): 517–40.

Scholsberg, D. (2007) *Defining Environmental Justice: Theories, Movements, and Nature*. Oxford: Oxford University Press.

Scoop Independent News (2008) 'Professor Slams Environmental Performance Report' (http://www.scoop.co.nz/stories/SC082/S00062.htm) (accessed 28 March 2008).

Scott, D. (2005). 'When Precaution Points Two Ways: Confronting "West Nile Fever"', *Canadian Journal of Law and Society*, 20(2): 27–65.

Secretariat of the Convention on Biological Diversity (2010) *Global Biodiversity Outlook 3*. Montreal: SCBD.

Setiono, B. (2007) 'Fighting Illegal Logging and Forest-Related Financial Crimes: The Anti-Money Laundering Approach', in L. Elliot (ed.) *Transnational Environmental Crime in the Asia-Pacific: A Workshop Report*. Canberra: Australian National University.

Sharman, K. (2009) 'Farm Animals and Welfare Law: An Unhappy Union', in P. Sankoff and S. White (eds) *Animal Law in Australasia*. Sydney: Federation Press.

Shelley, T. and Crow, M. (2009) 'The Nature and Extent of Conservation Policing: Law Enforcement Generalists or Conservation Specialists?', *American Journal of Criminal Justice*, 34(1): 9–27.

Shiva, V. (2000) *Stolen Harvest: The Hijacking of the Global Food Supply*. Cambridge, MA: South End Press.

Shiva, V. (2002) *Water Wars: Privatization, Pollution, and Profit*. Cambridge, MA: South End Press.

Shiva, V. (2008) *Soil Not Oil: Environmental Justice in an Age of Climate Crisis*. Brooklyn: South End Press.

Singh, M. (1996) 'Environmental Security and Displaced People in Southern Africa', *Social Justice*, 23(4): 125–33.

Situ, Y. and Emmons, D. (2000) *Environmental Crime: The Criminal Justice System's Role in Protecting the Environment*. Thousand Oaks: Sage.

Smandych, R. and Kueneman, R. (2010) 'The Canadian-Alberta Tar Sands: a Case Study of State–Corporate Environmental Crime', in R. White (ed.) *Global Environmental Harm: Criminological Perspectives*. Devon: Willan Publishing.

Smandych, R. and Larsen, N. (2008). 'Introduction: Foundations for a Global Criminology and Criminal Justice', in N. Larsen and R. Smandych (eds) *Global Criminology and Criminal Justice: Current Issues and Perspectives*. Peterborough, Ontario: Broadview Press.

Smith, D. and Vivekananda, J. (2007) *A Climate of Conflict: The Links Between Climate Change, Peace and War*. London: International Alert.

Smith, J. (2003) *Seeds of Deception: Exposing Industry and Government Lies About the Safety of the Genetically Engineered Foods You're Eating*. Fairfield, Iowa: Yes! Books.

Smith, M. (1998) *Ecologism: Towards Ecological Citizenship*. Minneapolis: University of Minnesota Press.

Solana, J. and Ferrero-Waldner, B. (2008) *Climate Change and International Security*, Paper from the High Representative and the European Commission to the European Council. Brussels: European Union.

Sollund, R. (2008) 'Causes for Speciesism: Difference, Distance and Denial', in Sollund, R. (ed.) *Global Harms: Ecological Crime and Speciesism*. New York: Nova Science Publishers.

Stanley, E. (2008) *Torture, Truth and Justice: The Case of Timor-Leste*. London: Routledge.

Steele, J. (2001) 'Participation and Deliberation in Environmental Law: Exploring a Problem-solving Approach', *Oxford Journal of Legal Studies*, 21(3): 415–42.

Stevens, S. (1996) 'Reflections on Environmental Justice: Children as Victims and Actors', *Social Justice*, 23(4): 62–86.

Stretesky, P. and Hogan, M. (1998) 'Environmental Justice: An Analysis of Superfund Sites in Florida', *Social Problems*, 45(2): 268–87.

Stretesky, P. and Lynch, M. (2009) 'A Cross-National Study of the Association Between Per Capita Carbon Dioxide Emissions and Exports to the United States', *Social Science Research*, 38: 239–50.

Sutherland, W. J. *et al.* (2009) 'A Horizon Scan of Global Conservation Issues for 2010', *Trends in Ecology and Evolution*, 25(1): 1–7.

Suzuki, D. with McConnell, A. and Mason, A. (2007) *The Sacred Balance: Rediscovering Our Place In Nature*. Sydney: Allen & Unwin.

Svard, P-A (2008) 'Protecting the Animals? An Abolitionist Critique of Animal Welfarism and Green Ideology', in R. Sullund (ed.) *Global Harms: Ecological Crime and Speciesism*. New York: Nova Science Publishers.

Swales, P. (2010) '"Gunns 20" Reaches a Final Settlement', *Alternative Law Journal*, 35(1): 39.

Tailby, R. and Gant, F. (2002) 'The Illegal Market in Australian Abalone', *Trends and Issues in Crime and Criminal Justice*, No. 225. Canberra: Australian Institute of Criminology.

Thornton, J. and Tromans, S. (1999) 'Human Rights and Environmental Wrongs: Incorporating the European Convention on Human Rights: Some Thoughts on the Consequences for UK Environmental Law', *Journal of Environmental Law*, 11(1): 35–57.

Tilman, D., Socolow, R., Foley, J., Hill, J., Larson, E., Lynd, L., Pacala, S., Reilly, J., Searchinger, T., Somerville, C. and Williams, R. (2009) 'Beneficial Biofuels – the Food, Energy, and Environment Trilemma', *Science*, Vol. 325: 270–71.

Tomkins, K. (2005) 'Police, Law Enforcement and the Environment', *Current Issues in Criminal Justice*, 16(3): 294–306.

United Nations Development Programme (2010) *Biodiversity Conservation and Sustainable Land Management*. Website information, UNDP (accessed 11 January 2010).

United Nations Environment Programme (2006) *Call for Global Action on E-waste*. New York: UNEP.

United Nations Environment Programme (2007) *Global Environment Outlook*. New York: UNEP.

Van Daele, S., Vander Becken, T. and Dorn, N. (2007) 'Waste Management and Crime: Regulatory, Business and Product Vulnerabilities', *Environmental Policy and Law*, 37(1): 34–8.

Vanderheiden, S. (2005) 'Eco-Terrorism or Justified Resistance? Radical Environmentalism and the "War on Terror"', *Politics and Society*, 33(3): 425–47.

Van Dijk, J. (2008) *The World of Crime: Breaking the Silence on Problems of Security, Justice, and Development across the World*. Los Angeles: Sage.

Van Geet, M., De Craen, M., Mallants, D., Wemaere, I., Wouters, L. and Cool, W. (2009) 'How to Treat Climate Evolution in the Assessment of the Long-term Safety of Disposal Facilities for Radioactive Waste: Examples from Belgium', *Climate of the Past Discussions*, 5: 463–94.

Victoria Government (2009) *Securing Our Natural Future: A White Paper for Land and Biodiversity at a Time of Climate Change*. Melbourne: Victoria.

Waldman, L. (2007) 'When Social Movements Bypass the Poor: Asbestos Pollution, International Litigation and Griqua Cultural Identity', *Journal of Southern African Studies*, 33(3): 577–600.

Walker, C. (2006) 'Environmental Racism in Australia', *Chain Reaction* No. 96, Autumn 2006 (Friends of the Earth Australia national magazine: http://www.foe.org.au/mainfiles/cr.htm) (accessed 10 July 2010).

Walters, R. (2004) 'Criminology and Genetically Modified Food', *British Journal of Criminology*, 44(1): 151–67.

Walters, R. (2005) 'Crime, Bio-Agriculture and the Exploitation of Hunger', *British Journal of Criminology*, 46(1): 26–45.

Warchol, G., Zupan, L. and Clarke, W. (2003) 'Transnational Criminality: An Analysis of the Illegal Wildlife Market in Southern Africa', *International Criminal Justice Review*, 13(1): 1–26.

Ward, T. and Green, P. (2000) 'Legitimacy, Civil Society, And State Crime', *Social Justice*, 27(4): 76–93.

Wellsmith, M. (2010) 'The Applicability of Crime Prevention to Problems of Environmental Harm: a Consideration of Illicit Trade in Endangered Species', in R. White (ed.)

Global Environmental Harm: Criminological Perspectives. Devon: Willan Publishing.

White, R. (2002) 'Environmental Harm and the Political Economy of Consumption', *Social Justice*, 29(1 and 2): 82–102.

White, R. (2005) 'Stifling Environmental Dissent: On SLAPPS and Gunns', *Alternative Law Journal*, 30(6): 268–73.

White, R. (2007) 'Green Criminology and the Pursuit of Social and Ecological Justice', in P. Beirne and N. South (eds) *Issues in Green Criminology: Confronting Harms against Environments, Humanity and Other Animals*. Devon: Willan Publishing.

White, R. (2008a) *Crimes Against Nature: Environmental Criminology and Ecological Justice*. Devon: Willan Publishing.

White, R. (2008b) 'Depleted Uranium, State Crime and the Politics of Knowing', *Theoretical Criminology*, 12(1): 31–54.

White, R. (ed.) (2009a) *Environmental Crime: A Reader*. Devon: Willan Publishing.

White, R. (2009b) 'Climate Change and Social Conflict: Toward an Eco-Global Research Agenda', in K. Kangaspunta and I. Marshall (eds) *Eco-Crime and Justice: Essays on Environmental Crime*. Turin, Italy: United Nations Interregional Crime Research Institute (UNICRI).

White, R. (2009c) 'Toxic Cities: Globalising the Problem of Waste', *Social Justice*, 35(3): 107–19.

White, R. (ed.) (2010a) *Global Environmental Harm: Criminological Perspectives*. Devon: Willan Publishing.

White, R. (2010b) 'Transnational Environmental Crime and Eco-Global Criminology', in S. Shoham, P. Knepper and M. Kett (eds) *International Handbook of Criminology*. New York: Taylor and Francis.

White, R. (2010c) 'Prosecution and Sentencing in Relation to Environmental Crime: Recent Socio-Legal Developments', *Crime, Law and Social Change*, 53(4): 365–81.

White, R. (2010d) 'The Right to Dissent: the Gunns 20 Legal Case', in F. Gale (ed.) *Pulp Friction*. Launceston: Pencil Pine Press.

White, R. (2010e) 'Environmental Victims and Resistance to State Crime Through Transnational Activism', *Social Justice*, 36(3).

White, R. (2011) 'Gangs and Transnationalisation', in B. Goldson (ed.) *Youth in Crisis? Gangs, Territoriality and Violence*. Devon: Willan Publishing.

White, R. and Habibis, D. (2005) *Crime and Society*. Melbourne: Oxford University Press.

White, R. and Perrone, S. (2010) *Crime, Criminality and Criminal Justice*. Melbourne: Oxford University Press.

White, S. (2009) 'Animals in the Wild: Animal Welfare and the Law', in P. Sankoff and S. White (eds) *Animal Law in Australasia: A New Dialogue*. Sydney: The Federation Press.

Williams, C. (1996) 'An Environmental Victimology', *Social Justice*, 23(4): 16–40.

Wilson, R. and Tomkins, K. (2007) 'The Australian Approach to Combating Illegal Foreign Fishing', in L. Elliot (ed.) *Transnational Environmental Crime in the Asia-Pacific: A Workshop Report*. Canberra: Australian National University.

Wright Mills, C. (1959) *The Sociological Imagination*. New York: Oxford University Press.

Wynne, B. (1996) 'May the Sheep Safely Graze? A Reflexive View of the Expert/lay Knowledge Divide', in S. Lash, B. Szerszynski and B. Wynne (eds) *Risk, Environment and Modernity: Toward a New Ecology*. London: Sage.

Zhang, M., Takeda, M., Nakajima, H., Sasada, M., Tsukimura, K. and Watanabe, Y. (2009) 'Nuclear Energy and the Management of High-Level Radioactive Waste in Japan', *Journal of Hydrologic Engineering*, 14(11): 1208–13.

Index

Added to a page number 'f' denotes a figure and 't' denotes a table.

abalone poaching 10, 125
abolitionism 107
accidental suffering 135
accidents 104
accountability 92–3, 98–101, 103, 131
acid rain 13, 110
activism *see* environmental activism;
    mobilisation
'acts of God' 116
actus reus 100
adaptation 37, 49, 115
affirmation 122
affluence 17, 92
Africa 10, 13, 42, 56, 72, 75, 76, 80, 113
Agreement of the Conservation of Polar Bears
    (1973) 54t
agribusiness 43, 45, 46, 58, 155
agricultural chemicals 47
agricultural exploitation 56
agricultural subsidies 42
agriculture 27, 57–9, 91
    see also food production; large-scale
        agriculture
air pollution 25, 27, 74t, 110
Alberta tar sands 12, 81, 101–2
algae bloom 60
alternative sentencing 131–2
Amazon 13
Amnesty International 151
Amoco 96
Amsterdam Port Services (APS) 97t
animal abuse 52, 69, 106, 107–8
animal law 107, 136
Animal Liberation Front (ALF) 143
animal rights 23, 34, 107
animal rights activists 20
animal welfare 67–8, 107, 124
animals
    biodiversity 63–9
    categories 65t
    production 65–6
species reduction 56
    as victims 106–8
    see also wildlife
answerability 93
Antarctic and South Ocean Coalition (ASOC)
    143
anthropogenic causes 33
anti-logging activists 144–5, 146
aquaculture 66
Arctic 9, 33, 40, 69
Argentina 63
armed gangs 44
asbestos 116, 121
Asia 42t, 75, 113
assessment, of victimisation 118–19, 120
assisted colonisation 64–5
at-risk populations 110
Australia 10, 56, 110, 112, 113
    alternative sentencing 131–2
    animal law 136
    animal production 65–6
    animal welfare 67–8
    compact fluorescent lamps 81
    criminal justice agencies 125–6
    electricity production 82
    grain trade 42t
    idea of 'country' 11–12
    impact of cane toad introduction 65
    lack of information sharing in fisheries
        127–8
    Pacific Solution 43–4
    victims' narrative accounts 121
    see also Tasmania
Australian Council of Recyclers 81
Australian Federal Police 125–6
Austria 13t
average risk 120

Band-Aid solutions 113–14
banned substances 22, 26, 34
Banton, Bernie 121
Basel Convention on the Transboundary
    Movement of Hazardous Wastes and their
    Disposal (1989) 4, 74t, 83, 84, 87

Bayer 96
Belgium 13t
best practice 138
Bhopal 98, 117, 145
BHP 111, 116
biodiverse fields 59
biodiversity 52–70
    agricultural practices and reduction of 46
    animals 63–9
    criminological interest 52–3
    defined 52
    eco-global criminology 25–6, 56
    ecological perspective 22
    environmental offences 28t
    implications of climate change 14
    international instruments 53–5
    key ecological message 53
    loss of 52
    particular threats to 57
    plants 56–63
biofuel 91
biofuel production 40–1, 59–61
biopiracy 30, 43
bioprospecting 56–7
birds 54t
blackmarketeering 44
blame 77, 88
Bolivia 94
Bonn Convention (1979) 54t
bourgeois 85
bovine growth hormone 64
BP 96, 98, 135
Brazil 13, 56, 60, 61, 62, 127
bribery 56, 64
British Colombia 12
brown issues 14, 124, 140
Burma 13
butterflies, assisted colonisation 64
butterfly effect 1, 10–11

Canada 37, 64, 110, 125, 129
    see also Alberta; Arctic; British Colombia;
        Nova Scotia
cane toad 65
capacity building 127
capitalism 25, 45, 73, 92–3, 102
carbon capture 80–1
carbon colonialism 50, 114
carbon commodification 114
carbon credit schemes 114
carbon disposal 80–1
carbon emission(s)
    Band-Aid solutions 113–14
    and energy demands 48–50
    public debate about 49
    storage 45, 49, 154
    trading 14, 44, 49, 50, 154
carbon offsetting 50
carbon sinks 114
Caribbean 64, 75, 76
Cartagena Protocol on Biosafety (2000) 54t

cash-buyer nexus 41
causal chains 18, 33, 34t
causation 101
chemical industries 75
Chernobyl 121, 145
Chevron 96
child soldiers 44
children, vulnerability to environmental harm
    110, 117
China 13, 17, 155
chlorofluorocarbons 130t
CITES *see* Convention on International Trade
    in Endangered Species of Wild Fauna and
    Flora
civil penalties 131
classist culture 77
clean energy 91
climate change 36–51
    accountability 92–3
    criminology 38–45
    disagreement about causes 37
    eco-global criminology 24–5, 38, 40, 51
    ecological perspective 22
    environmental offences 28t, 44t
    governmental action 45
    impact/implications 9, 13–14, 25, 39–41,
        51, 57
    international instruments 37–8
    lack of action 36
    as a multi-level problem 17
    paradoxical harms 45–50
    public debate 37
    public policy 45
    state-corporate collusion 101
    transnational activism 154–6
    understandings and responses 37, 64
    vulnerability to 39–40, 114
    waste production 79–82
    see also air pollution; global warming;
        ozone depletion
climate injustice 114
climate justice 155
climate-induced migration 43–5
climate-induced subsistence activities 113
climate-related disasters 25, 80
CMS Convention (1979) 54t
coastal areas, protection from sea-level rise 115
collaboration 30, 127, 138
collective knowledge 99
collective practice 91
collusion, state-corporate 101–3
colonialism 29, 40, 90, 113, 114
coloured peoples, and climate change 51
commodification 26, 43, 73, 75–6, 92, 114
community discourses 119t
compact fluorescent light bulbs 45, 81–2
comparative criminology 15
comparative transnational research 16–17
competition 40, 67, 73, 91
complexity, establishing causation 101
composition effect 78

computers, old 27, 72
conciliatory tactics 142t
conflict timber 56
confrontational tactics 142t
conservation 113, 117, 124
conservation criminology 56
conservation dependent species 66t
conservation police 124–5
consumer demand, and harmful production 49
consumption 18, 37, 41, 73, 78–9
contested definitions 15
control 26, 155
controlling mind 99
Convention on Biological Diversity (1992) 54t
Convention on the Conservation of Antarctic
    Marine Living Resources (1980) 54t
Convention on the Conservation of Migratory
    Species (1979) 54t
Convention on Fishing and Living Resources
    of the High Seas (1958) 54t
Convention on International Trade in
    Endangered Species of Wildlife Fauna and
    Flora (1971) 4, 53–5
Convention on Long-Range Transboundary Air
    Pollution (1979) 74t
Convention on the Prevention of Marine
    Pollution by Dumping of Wastes and Other
    Matter (1972) 4, 74t
Convention on Wetlands of International
    Importance Especially as Waterfowl Habitat
    (1971) 54t
conventional criminology 21–2
corn (maize) 60, 62, 120
corporate behaviours, toxic crimes 83
corporate colonisation of nature 8
corporate form 95
corporate liability 99, 100
corporate misconduct 49–50
corporate officers, designated responsible 99,
    100
corporate reporting 95
corporate veil 95
corporatisation 57, 65–6
corrupt officials 56, 63
cost-benefit analyses 110, 135
cost-benefit-trade off, doing business 100
costs of waste, externalising 77–8
counter-hegemonic strategies 155
country, idea of 11–12
court databases 134
crime(s)
    definitions 4–5, 135–6
    global perspective on 16
    tied to climate-related events 44
    see also environmental crime(s)
criminal justice agencies 123–8
criminal justice responses 123–37
    environmental law enforcement 123–8
    measuring the value of environmental harm
        132–7
    penalties and remedies 128–32

criminal law 5, 99, 135
criminal syndicates 71, 83
criminalisation 20, 25, 44, 117, 149–56
criminology
    alternative data sources 121
    climate change 38–45
    mainstream 20, 29, 56
    see also eco-global criminology;
        international criminology
critical criminology 7, 20
critical thinking 19
critically endangered species 66t
crop diversity 59
cropland 57
crops *see* genetically modified crops
cross-agency cooperation 138
cross-disciplinary/cultural considerations 30
cultural ignorance 117
cumulative penalties 131
customs services 124
cyclones 114

dairy farming 47
data collection 31–2
data sources, alternative 121
deaths, disaster-related 115
deforestation 52, 56, 60, 63
delegation of responsibility 99
denial 122
Denmark 13t
depleted uranium 85, 156
desertification 13, 38t
designated responsible officers 99, 100
destruction (ecological) 20, 73
differential victimisation 110, 116
dioxins 111–12
direct discrimination 100
directors, personal liability 99–100
dirty industries 45
disaster-related deaths 115
disasters 25, 80, 114, 115, 116
discourse diversity 119t
discrimination 100
displacement 43, 112
dispossession 113
distribution 18
domestic animals 64–7
droughts 13, 38t, 114
Du Pont 96
dumping *see* illegal dumping; local dumping

e-waste 4, 10, 27, 72, 75, 76, 94
Earth First 143
Eastern Europe 42t
eco-criminology 22–3
eco-global criminology 19–35
    activism 157
    analysis of major oil companies 98
    biodiversity 25–6, 56
    challenge of climate-induced migration
        43

climate change 24–5, 38, 40, 51
  conceptual categories 1–2
  environmental harm 1, 20–4, 33–5
  explanation of social disorder 43
  interest in criminal justice responses 123
  perpetrator-offender distinction 103
  researching the global in 28–33
  state crimes 101
  waste and pollution 26–7
eco-terrorism 143, 150, 152–4, 156
ecocide 101
ecological citizenship 7, 23, 147t, 148, 149,
    155
ecological consciousness 17
ecological footprint 91
ecological justice 6, 20, 23, 24, 33, 34t, 107,
    140, 147, 148
ecological rights 23, 34, 147
ecological rights activists 20
ecological sustainability 34, 35, 45
ecological welfare 20
ecological well-being 34
economic domestic animals 65t
economic restructuring 42, 102
economic vulnerability 102
economic wild animals 65t
ecotage 143, 153
egalitarian concerns 34
electronic industry 76
  see also e-waste
elephant poaching 10
elites/elitism 29, 41, 148
Emission Trading Scheme (EU) 50
endangered 66t
energy demands, carbon emissions 48–50
enforceability 93
environment rights 20, 23, 105
environmental activism 141–2
  continuum of activities 142t
  victims 115–17, 118t
  see also transnational environmental
    activism
environmental activists 102
environmental casualties 115
environmental crime(s) 3, 4–6
  ambiguity 135
  definition and liability 134–5
  sentencing database 132–4
  see also transnational environmental crime
environmental criminology *see* green
  criminology
environmental degradation 14, 46, 89, 102, 151
environmental genocide 101
environmental harm(s)
  conceptualising 20–4
  cost-benefit-trade off, doing business 100
  defining as 'consequence of' 101
  eco-global criminology 1, 20–4, 33–5
  horizon scanning 33, 34t
  mapping 4, 10, 11f
  measuring the value of 132–7

national interest 148
oil companies responsible for 98
species decline 68t
transboundary nature of 4
transfer of hazardous waste 72
vulnerability of children 110, 117
waste removal and externalising 76–9
see also paradoxical harms; seriousness
    of harm; transference of harm;
    transnational environmental harm
environmental injustice 51, 151
Environmental Investigations Agency 143
environmental justice 23, 33, 34t, 105, 107,
    111, 140, 147t, 148
environmental justice movements 105, 116,
    141, 151
environmental law 95, 124, 156
environmental law enforcement 123–8, 129
  need for collaboration and knowledge
    sharing 138
  network approach 138
  trivialisation of offences as an impediment
    to 136
environmental offenders 103–4, 113
environmental protection 3–4, 102
environmental quality 111
environmental racism 71, 100, 112
environmental reform 17
environmental regulation
  circumvention 84–5
  discourses 119t
  influences on 155
  international systems 25
environmental suffering 115, 135
environmental victimisation
  assessment 118–19, 120
  cost-benefit analysis 110
  defined 109
  likelihood of 110
  types 116–17
  universal 39
  vulnerability to 51, 111–15
environmental victims
  human 105–6
    accounts and stories 121
    defining 109–11, 115
    mobilisation/activism 115–17, 118t
    politics of knowing and knowledge
      117–22
    treatment of 108–9
  non-human 106–8
epistemological issues 28–9
Estonia 97
Europe 13t, 42t, 76, 102
European Union 9, 43, 50, 61, 149
evidence
  medical and epidemiological 71
  scientific 117–18, 152
  of victimization 119
exchange values 73
expansion 92

experience, localised 120–1
expertise, to undertake research 29–30
exploitation 20, 24, 30, 41t, 102–3, 155
    agricultural 56
    of knowledge 30
    species extinction 55
    see also overexploitation
exposure, safe levels 120
extinct 66t
extinct in the wild 66t
extinction 55, 57, 69
extraction *see* mining; resource extraction
extreme weather 40
extremism, environmental 153
Exxon Mobil 96
Exxon Valdez oil spill 98

farming *see* agriculture
federal law enforcement 125
feminist theory 107
fertilisers 47, 48, 60, 96
Finland 13t
fiscal crises 102
fish species 57, 63
fisheries 66, 67, 124, 127–8
fishing *see* illegal fishing; overfishing
floods 51, 114
flora and fauna *see* plants; wildlife
Florida 125
Fly Region 116
focus, need for 16
food
    competition for 67
    conflict over 40–1, 41–3
    price rises and shortages 60, 61
    production 26, 46–8, 57, 58
    riots 43, 44
forest sector industries 129
forestry commissions 124
forests 20, 114, 143
    see also deforestation; logging; tropical
        forests
fortress mentality 43
France 80
Frankenstein effect 63
Fraser River Action Plan 129
fraud 50
free trade 96
Freeland Foundation for Human Rights and
    Wildlife 143
futures orientation, horizon scanning 33, 34t

garbage imperialism 76
gender, and victimisation 51, 110
genetic contamination 62
genetic modification 25, 58
genetic modification technologies
    applied to animals 63
    food production and biodiversity reduction
        58
    species homogenisation 26

genetically modified crops
    illegal sowing 62
    key players 96
    lucrative market for 63
    pressure to adopt 58
    rapid increase in 62
    rejection by Zambian government 120
genetically modified organisms 61
    criminological research 52
    global political economy 26
    greater reliance on 46, 58
    invasion of endemic crops 62
    loss of biodiversity 14
    patent protection 43
genetically modified seeds
    corruption and spread of 63
    illegal smuggling 62
    producers of 96
genocide 15, 101
genotypes, GMOs and destruction of 62
geographical regions, crimes related to 10
Germany 13t
global capitalism 102
global context 13–14
global criminology 15, 16
    see also eco-global criminology
global ecological health 22
global financial crisis 87, 102
global mapping, harmful practices 4, 10, 11f
global perspective, on crime 16
global political economy 8–10, 18, 26
global transnational research 16
global warming 9, 20, 36, 110
    big business response to 93–4
    combating environmental harm 128
    complexity of problem 45–6
    consequences 40
    environmental offences linked to 44
    human activity 37
    social conflict linked to 39, 41t
    tar oil sand production 102
    war 156
    waste storage strategies 80
globalisation 7, 26, 29, 76, 92, 138
government subsidies 101
grain 40–1, 42
green credentials 49
green criminology 19, 105
    animal rights discourse 107–8
    basic premise of 18, 21
    environmental harm 23–4
    see also eco-global criminology
green issues 124, 140
Green Police 124
green scare 153, 156
greenhouse gas emissions 38t, 46–8
Greenpeace 143, 144, 145
greenwashing 49–50, 93, 153
growth states 17
Gulf of Mexico 60, 98, 135
Gunns 20 Case 144–5, 146

harms
    perpetrated by states and corporations 6
    see also environmental harm(s); social
        harms
hazardous chemicals 74t
hazardous waste 9, 10, 72, 74t, 77, 84
health departments 124
heatwaves 37
hegemonic knowledge/values 120
hegemonic nation states 41, 45, 155
hegemony, in criminology 29
hemp growing 20
herbicides 60, 96
hidden costs 110
high-level waste 79, 80
historical approach 16, 17
holistic understandings, of harm 34
horizon scanning 32–3, 34t, 51
hormone injections 63
human activity, and climate change 37
human agency 106
human health and wellbeing 27, 112
human interests 45, 107
human intervention 64, 149
human needs/services, and species value
    68–9
human rights 6, 7, 23, 34, 155
human rights violations 148–9, 150–1
Human Rights Watch 151
human trafficking 44
human-animal interaction/relationship 69, 107
human-made disasters 114, 116
humans, as perpetrators 89–90

illegal dumping 14, 44, 71, 97
illegal fishing 10, 11, 24, 34, 44, 52, 69
illegal logging 56, 69
illegal smuggling 15, 26, 62
illegal trade, plants and wildlife 26, 55, 66–7,
    69, 95
illegal, unreported and unregulated (IUU)
    fishing 67, 96, 143
illegal waste management 84–5
imperialism 40, 90
incentives, biofuel production 61
India 17, 98, 112, 117
indigenous knowledge 113, 120
indigenous people
    colonialism and dispossession 113
    idea of 'country' 11–12
    objection to terminator seed technology
        61–2
    relationship with nature 89
    scapegoating 102–3
    victimisation 110, 112, 115
indigenous technologies 120
indirect discrimination 100
individual-level responsibility 89–90
Indonesia 13, 56, 60, 61, 63, 80, 127
industrialisation 17, 20, 58, 90
inequality 51, 71, 111

information gathering 126, 143, 155
information sharing 126, 127–8, 138
insect blights 12
intensive food production 48, 59
intentional discrimination 100
intentional harm 68t
interconnectedness 1
intergenerational equity 33, 34t, 147
intergenerational responsibility 147
Intergovernmental Panel on Climate Change
    155
intermediate level waste 79
international agreements 3, 4
    climate change 37–8
    protection of biodiversity 53–5
    waste and pollution 74t
International Convention for the Prevention of
    Pollution from Ships (1973) 74t
International Convention for the Protection of
    Birds (1950) 54t
International Convention for the Protection of
    New Varieties of Plants (1961) 54t
International Convention for the Regulation of
    Whaling (1946) 54t
international cooperation 22
international criminology 15–16
international environment court 138
International Forestry Research 114
international law 5, 15, 130
International Monetary Fund (IMF) 42, 60
international NGOs 143
international trade 53
International Tropical Timber Agreement
    (1994) 4, 38t
International Union for the Conservation of
    Nature 66
Internet resources 121
Interpol 155
interpretive focus groups 30–1
introduced wild animals 65t
Inuit populations 9
invasive species 65
investigation 118, 127, 128
iodine deficiency 115
Israel 124
Italy 13, 13t
Ivory Coast 96, 97

James Hardie Corporation 122
Japan 14, 76, 80, 145
Japan Tropical Forest Action Network 144
justice conceptions, of harm 34–5
justice orientation, horizon scanning 33, 34t
justice perspective, green criminology 23
justified resistance 153, 154

knowing and knowledge, politics of 117–22
knowledge mining 30
Kyoto Protocol to the United Nations
    Framework Convention on Climate Change
    (1998) 4, 38t

land, compulsory takeover 63
land acquisitions 112–13
land clearance 56, 60
Land and Environment Court of New South
    Wales 132–5
land use 46–7, 57, 124
large-scale agriculture 46, 58, 60
Latin America 10, 12–13, 42t, 76, 94, 114
    see also Amazon; Argentina; Brazil; Peru
law *see* animal law; criminal law;
    environmental law; international law
law reform 95, 131, 141
lay discourses 119t
leachate 82
lead 27, 76
'least concern' species 66t
legal definitions, crime 3, 5, 33–4, 135–6
legal discourses 119t
legal-illegal divide 20, 21, 22, 24, 27, 35, 56,
    82–5
legality 69
legislative change 131
leniency 136
liability 77, 99–100, 101, 131, 134–5
Liberia 56
lionfish 64
litigation discourses 119t
lobster poaching 10, 11
local context 11–12
local dumping 83
localised knowledge/experience 120–1
logging, illegal 56, 69
    see also anti-logging activists
looting 44
luxury emissions 113

Mafia 13
magistrates courts (UK) 136, 137
mainstream criminology 20, 29, 56
maize (corn) 60, 62, 120
Malaysia 13
malum prohibitum 135–6
malum in se 135
marginalised people, research involving 30–1
Marine Life Conservation 54t
marine pollution 74t
marine resources 54t
market reduction approach, wildlife crime 96t
massification 92
media discourses 119t
mens rea 99, 100, 131
mercury 9, 27, 76, 81, 82
methane 47
methodology, horizon spanning 33
methyl-mercury 82
Mexico 62, 127
microbes 69
microchip waste 72, 75
Middle East 42t
migration, climate-induced 43–5
migratory species 54t

militant actions 143
militarism 90
mining 111
mitigation 37, 49
mobile phones 27
mobilisation 101, 115–17, 148, 156
monoculture 59, 60
monopolisation 96
Monsanto 60, 63, 64, 96, 98
Montreal Protocol on Substances that Deplete
    the Ozone Layer (1987) 4, 74t
moral responsibility 89
Mossville, Louisiana 111–12
Multilateral Environmental Agreements 5

nation states
    eco-terrorism 152
    environmental action 3
    environmental law 124
    hegemonic 41, 45, 155
    human rights violations 148–9, 151
    protection of elite and ruling classes 148
    see also growth states; state crimes; state
        security; state-corporate collusion
national context 12
national interest 3, 148, 156
national parks authorities 124
national sovereignty 138
native species 65t
natural climate change 37
natural disasters 80, 114, 115, 116
nature 8, 86, 89
'near threatened' species 66t
neglect 100
neo-liberalism 42, 45, 78
Netherlands 13t, 115, 125
network analysis, wildlife crime 96
network approach, law enforcement 138
New Zealand 12, 42, 46–7, 58
Nigeria 27, 31, 97
Nippon Paper Industries 145, 146
nitrogen fertilisers 47, 60
nitrous oxide 47
nominated accountability 131
non-economic animals 65t
non-governmental organisations (NGOs) 71–2,
    117, 142, 143
non-hazardous waste 84
non-human oppression 107
non-human victims 106–8
non-intentional harm 68t, 69
non-toxic disasters 114t
North-South divide 40, 51, 91, 113–14
'not in my backyard' syndrome 14, 79
Nova Scotia 11
nuclear energy 45
nuclear power 79, 80, 91
nuclear waste 80

occupation discourses 119t
oceans, rubbish-filled 14

oil corporations 96–8
oil production, tar sands 12, 81, 101–2
oil spills 98, 135
Ok Tedi River 111
ontological being 11–12
openness 30
organised crime 9, 13, 15, 71, 83
Ottawa Citizen 64
outsider/insider 30
overexploitation 57
overfishing 14
overpopulation 91
ownership 26, 113
ozone depleting substances 74t, 130
ozone depletion 24, 74t, 110

Pacific Solution 43
Pakistan 51
palm oil 60
Papua New Guinea 111, 116
paradoxical harms 45–50, 59, 60, 156
Paraguay 62
park rangers 124
parochialism 29
pastoral industry 46–7, 48
patents/patenting 30, 43, 96
paternalism 29
PCBs (polychlorinated biphenyl) 63
penalties and remedies 128–32, 137, 138–9
    see also sentencing
penalty infringement notices (PINs) 131
people power 148
peripheral societies, knowledge from 120
perpetrators 88–104
    responsibility 89–95
    state-corporate collusion 101–3
    studying 95–101
persistent organic pollutants (POPs) 9, 63, 74t,
    75
personal liability 99–100
Peru 13, 56, 61, 150
pesticides 12, 74t, 105, 110
pests, wild animals as 65t
petty bourgeois 85
Philippines 42, 127
piracy 14
place, need for a sense of 16
plants
    biodiversity 56–63
    illegal taking/trade 22, 26, 66–7
    international agreement on 53–5
    species reduction 56
    transfer of 14
Poland 62
polar bears 33, 54t, 69
police/services 124–5
policing discourses 119t
policy, horizon spanning 33
political choices, risk assessments 78
political culture 73
political mobilisation 101

politics of knowing and knowledge 117–22
pollution
    conventional perspective 22
    cross-border 13, 39
    eco-global criminology 26–7
    ecological perspective 23
    endangerment of animals 63
    environmental offences 28t
    factors effecting extent of 78
    land use 46
    persistent, Mossville, Louisiana 111–12
    see also air pollution; waste
POPS *see* persistent organic pollutants
population, as responsible 91–2
population growth 92
poverty 39, 112
power interests 21, 31, 36, 59, 92, 93
power relationships 115
pre-emptive action, migration 43–4
precautionary principle 33, 34t, 81, 135, 149,
    155
Prince, Anne 81
prison time 136
privatisation 92
Probo Koala 97
processual accounts 148
production 18
    animals 65–6
    chlorofluorocarbons (1950–97) 130t
    and destruction 73
    food 26, 46–8, 57, 58
    need for change in mode of 37
    waste associated with 73
    see also biofuel production; waste
        production
profit-making 21, 45, 64, 76, 83–4
profitability 26, 73, 86, 94
progression thesis 106
progressive values 51
property animals as 106, 107
prosecution 98–9, 118, 131, 136, 137
protective factors, climate change 39
public opinion 153

racist culture 77
radioactive waste 14, 44, 79–81
Ramsar Convention (1971) 54t
record keeping 32
recycling 27, 75, 77, 82, 84–5
Reducing Emissions from Deforestation and
    Forest Degradation (REDD) 63
regional context 12–13
regulation
    animal welfare 67–8, 69
    of fisheries 124
    see also environmental regulation; species,
        regulation
relabellling waste 84–5
religious beliefs 116
remediation 101
remedies *see* penalties and remedies

renewable energy technologies 91
report-back purposes, data collection 32
resilience 63
resistance
    justified 153, 154
    to data collection 31
resources(s)
    colonisation 113
    depletion 8, 9, 20, 40
    exploitation 20, 24, 30, 41t, 102–3, 155
    extraction 112
    social conflict linked to 9, 39, 40, 41t
    structure and allocation 102
responsibility 33, 37, 88, 89–95, 98–101, 147
responsible corporate officers 99, 100
restorative justice 131
rights *see* animal rights; environment rights;
    human rights
rights theory 107
risk assessment 78, 120
risk factors, climate change 39–40
risks
    environmental victimisation 110
    horizon scanning 33, 34t
Rotterdam Convention on the Prior Informed
    Consent Procedures for Certain Hazardous
    Chemicals and Pesticides in International
    Trade (1998) 74t
Roundup 60
Royal Commission on Genetic Modification
    (New Zealand) 58
Royal Society for the Prevention of Cruelty to
    Animals 124
Russia 13, 37, 80

'safe levels', of exposure 120
satellites 14
savannahs 63
scale, need for consideration of 16, 35
scale of remediation 101
scapegoating 102
science-based risk levels 120
scientific discourses 119t
scientific evidence 117–18, 152
scientific uncertainty 77
Sea Shepherd Society 142, 143
sea-level rise, protection from 115
self-interest 45
sensitivity, in research 30, 35
sentencing
    alternative 131–2
    consistency in 132
    database 132–4
    guidance on 137
    levels 137
    severity of 136
    see also penalties and remedies
seriousness of harm 5
seriousness of offence 132, 133–4t
severity of sentencing 136
Seymour, Frances 114

shareholders 95
Shell 96
Sierra Leone 56
situated knowledge 35
smog 27
social conflict 9, 27, 39–41, 56
social constructionism 68, 119, 122, 153
social harms 61, 72, 102
social inequality 51
social interests 21, 45, 118
social movements 12, 155
social situations, awareness of 35
socialisation of harms 77–8
socially expendable victims 115
Somalia 14
South Africa 57, 116, 117
South America 113
South Asia 76
South Korea 80
South-East Asia 10, 13, 72, 76
Southern Ocean 10, 14
southern theory 28–9
soybean cultivation 62
species
    decline 8, 68t
    extinction 55, 57, 69
    Frankenstein effect 63
    GMO invasion of endemic 62
    homogenisation 26
    justice 23, 33, 34t, 107, 148
    reduction 56
    regulation 25
    survival status 66t
spent reactor fuel 79
stakeholders, assessment of victimisation
    118–19
state crimes 6, 122
state security 43–4
state-corporate collusion 101–3
stigmatisation, ordinary victims 115–16
Stockholm Convention on Persistent Organic
    Pollutants 74t
Stockholm Declaration on the Human
    Environment (1972) 147
strategic ecotage 143
strategic lawsuits against public participation
    (SLAPPs) 31
strategic thinking 40, 51
strict liability 100, 131
structural adjustment 42
studying up 121
subcontracting, waste disposal 84
subsidies *see* agricultural subsidies; government
    subsidies
subsistence activities, climate-induced 113
Sudan 15
suffering 115, 135
summer fires 80
superspecies 63
supranational criminology 16
survival emissions 113

survival status, species 66t
sustainability 69
sustainable agriculture 91
Syngenta 96
system-level structures/pressures 23–4, 88
systemic herbicides 60

tar sands (Alberta) 12, 81, 101–2
Tasmania 68, 105, 125, 144–5
technology, as responsible 90–1
terminator seed technology 61–2
Texaco 96
Thailand 13
theory, horizon spanning 33
threat, wild animals as 65t
threat of eco-terrorism 153
toothfish, illegal fishing 10, 143
toxic crimes 83
toxic disasters 114t
toxic waste 44, 71, 75, 96, 97
    see also dioxins; lead; mercury; persistent
        organic pollutants
trade liberalisation 42, 78
traditional relationships 12
trafficking 44
Trafigura 97, 98
transference of harm 14, 18, 33, 34t, 39, 41t
transference of waste 75
transformation of nature 8
transformation of use values 73
transgenes, instability of 62
transnational context 14
transnational corporations 41, 45
    harms perpetrated by 6
    judging perpetrators 100
    likelihood of prosecution 99
    need for criminological analysis 40
    oil production 96–8
    as responsible 93–5
    sectional interests 154–5
    waste disposal 76
    see also state-corporate collusion
transnational crime 6–7, 16
transnational criminology 15
transnational environmental activism 140–57
    crime and criminalisation 149–56
    internationalism as a practical tool for
        142–5
    moral framework for 145–9
transnational environmental crime 1–18
    analysis see eco-global criminology
    biodiversity 70t
    climate change 44t
    contextualising 10–14
    defining 3–7
    ecological and social dimensions 28t
    involving plants 61–3
    perpetrators see perpetrators
    pollution/waste 86t
    responses see criminal justice responses
    seriousness of offence 132, 133–4t

studying 15–17
trivialisation 136
types 7–10
victims see environmental victims
transnational environmental harm 3, 4
    international recognition as crime 15
    systemic causal chains 18
transnational organised crime 15
trivialisation of offences 136
tropical forests 12–13, 38t
tumour disease, Tasmania 105

Uganda 114
underground waste depositories 14, 80, 81
Union Carbide 98
United Kingdom
    accumulation of radioactive waste 79
    criminal justice 136, 137
    localised knowledge/experience 120–1
    personal liability of directors 99–100
    wildlife officers 125
United Nations Convention to Combat
    Desertification in Those Countries
    Experiencing Serious Drought and/or
    Desertification (1994) 38t
United Nations Declaration of Basic Principles
    of Justice for Victims of Crime and Abuses
    of Power 108–9
United Nations Environment Programme
    (UNEP) 22, 24, 32, 61, 155
United Nations Framework Convention on
    Climate Change (1992) 4, 38t
United States 96, 110, 113, 149
    biofuel production 60, 61
    carbon emission and energy demand 49
    conservation police 125
    environmental justice movement 141, 151
    felony convictions 99
    grain trade 42t
    impact of lionfish expansion 64
    military 156
    nuclear waste storage 80
    resource exploitation 155
    response to activism 153
    transfer of waste 76
    varying definitions of animals 68
    see also Florida; Mossville, Louisiana
universal human interests 45, 148
universal knowledge/values 120
universal victimisation 39
uranium 79, 85, 156
use-values, transformation of 73
utilitarian theory 107

value(s)
    capitalism and 73
    of environmental harm, measuring 132–7
    non-human animals 67–9, 106
    progressive 51
    universal 120
    of waste 76

value system, transnational 44
vicarious liability 99
vicious spiral, human rights violations 148
victims *see* environmental victims
Vienna Convention for the Protection of the
    Ozone Layer 4, 74t
virtuous spiral, human rights violations 148–9
vulnerability
    of children 110, 117
    economic 102
    to climate change 39–40, 114
    to victimisation 110, 111–15
vulnerable species 66t

war, and climate change 156
waste 71–87
    categories 72–3
    eco-global criminology 26–7
    environmental offences 28t
    and pollution 72–6
    transferring 76–7
waste corporations, major 94t
waste depositories 14, 80, 81
waste disposal
    commodification 75
    discussions of 71–2
    ecological perspective 23
    externalising harm 76–9
    general crimes related to 8
    involvement of Mafia 13
    legal-illegal divide 27, 82–5
    opportunities from crime 9
    research 71

specific crimes related to 9
transnational corporations 76
Waste Framework Directive (EU) 9
waste production
    associated with growth 73
    climate change 79–82
    externalising harm at point of 78–9
    research 71
waste removal companies 75, 76, 85–6
water corporations, major 94t
water quality 47
weapons, transferring waste in 85
Western Europe 42
wetlands 54t, 63
whales 54t
wild animals
    biodiversity 64–7
    protection 53–5
Wilderness Society 144, 145, 146
wildlife
    illegal taking/trade in 14, 22, 26, 55, 66–7,
        69, 95, 96t
    officers 125
    reserves 113
women, and victimisation 51, 110
World Bank 42
World Trade Organisation 96
worldwide processes, global crimes
    9–10

Yucca Flat 79

Zambia 120